Party Ideology

Party Ideology in Britain

Edited by

Leonard Tivey

and

Anthony Wright

ROUTLEDGE
London and New York

First published 1989
by Routledge
11 New Fetter Lane, London EC4P 4EE
29 West 35th Street, New York, NY 10001

© 1989 Leonard Tivey and Anthony Wright

Phototypeset in 10pt Times by
Mews Photosetting, Beckenham, Kent
Printed and bound in Great Britain by
Mackays of Chatham PLC, Chatham, Kent

British Library Cataloguing in Publication Data

Party ideology in Britain edited by
Leonard Tivey and Anthony Wright.
  1. Great Britain. Political parties
I. Tivey, Leonard, *1926–* II. Wright,
Anthony, *1948–*
324.241
  ISBN 0-415-02307-6
  ISBN 0-415-02308-4 (Pb)

Library of Congress Cataloging-in-Publication Data

Party ideology in Britain / edited by Leonard Tivey and Anthony
  Wright.
      p. cm.
    Bibliography: p.
    Includes index.
    ISBN 0-415-02307-6. — ISBN 0-415-02308-4 (pbk.)
    1. Political parties — Great Britain. 2. Right and left (Political
science) I. Tivey, Leonard James, 1926–   II. Wright, Anthony,
1948– .
JN1121.P38 1989
324.2'3'0941–dc19
                                            89-31074
                                              CIP

To our Two Ms

Contents

Notes on the Contributors

Robert Behrens is Senior Lecturer in Social Policy at the Civil Service College, Sunningdale on secondment from Coventry Polytechnic. He is the author of *The Conservative Party from Heath to Thatcher* (1980), has written on race relations, and is currently working on a study of Disraelian conservatism.

John Callaghan is Senior Lecturer in Politics at Wolverhampton Polytechnic. He is the author of *The Far Left in British Politics* (1987) and of a forthcoming study of British socialism since the 1880s.

Nicholas Deakin is Professor of Social Policy at the University of Birmingham. He has written widely on race and urban issues, and his most recent book is *The Politics of Welfare* (1987).

Martin Durham is Lecturer in Politics at Wolverhampton Polytechnic. He has published a number of articles on modern right-wing politics, and is currently working on a study of the Thatcher government and the 'pro-family' lobby.

Edward Johnson is Senior Lecturer in the Department of Government and Economics at Birmingham Polytechnic. His research interests are in the role of the United Nations in British foreign policy since 1945, and he is currently studying the approach of the Attlee government to the United Nations.

Leonard Tivey is Head of the Department of Political Science and International Studies at the University of Birmingham. He has published *The Politics of the Firm* (1978), *The Nation-State* (ed. 1981), and *Interpretations of British Politics* (1988).

Anthony Wright is Senior Lecturer in Political Studies in the School of Continuing Studies at the University of Birmingham. His books include *G.D.H. Cole and Socialist Democracy* (1979), *Socialism: Theories and Practices* (1986), and *R.H. Tawney* (1987).

Preface

This book is offered as an introduction to the study of British politics by a particular route. There are many accounts of British political parties, but nearly all of them neglect their ideas. There are increasing numbers of works on political ideology in Britain, often relating their material to traditional currents of thought. What we have tried to do is to bridge the gap, by putting ideology into its partisan forms, the better to illuminate the parties, their conflicts and their ideas. We have also wanted to relate these ideas to policies and practice in the post–1945 years, in order to avoid any impression that these matters can be understood by themselves, as it were, without contact with the reality that is always testing them and tripping them up.

If the relative neglect of ideology in British political studies in the past is now being replaced by a revival of interest, the reason is not hard to find. The 1980s has seen a marked increase in overt ideological conflict. Ideas clearly matter. Historians may eventually find the ideological underpinnings of consensus as interesting as those of more desperate and discordant times. But in the contemporary situation there can be little doubt of the need for students and general readers alike to understand the ideas, to grasp what is at stake, and to get them straight.

So that has been our aim in putting this book together. We have been much helped by continuing political discussion with friends and colleagues, the fortitude of our contributors in the face of our various demands, the secretarial services of Marjorie Davies, Frances Landreth, Grace Palmer and Anne Hollows, and the two people to whom it is dedicated. We thank them all.

Leonard Tivey

Anthony Wright

Chapter one

Introduction: Left, Right, and Centre

Leonard Tivey

There is no royal road to the understanding of politics. Since the subject matter is by definition concerned with controversy and conflict, it is hard to be sure where the heart of the matter lies — and hence where the best approach might be found. 'Just go into the wood and start chopping down the trees' is one possibility. In practice students of politics have been led along several paths. For many years in Britain they were encouraged to study 'The Constitution', itself a flexible and ill-defined topic. They were also invited to learn about the component institutions — Cabinet, Parliament, parties, pressure groups, the administration. In recent decades it has been considered that the actual behaviour of people should be observed — not mere formal arrangements, but what politicians, administrators, and voters really do.

Developments on these lines have vastly enriched the fare offered to present-day students. Nevertheless, this book attempts to add something more. What is British politics *about*? It is vital to understand the logic of party conflict, the power of various interest groups, the factors which influence voting. No serious understanding can be achieved without such knowledge. Yet there is surely a need also to clothe the skeleton with a little flesh. What are the politicians disputing? What is the content of public debate? What do people say and believe about politics? What do political parties stand for? Hence we offer an introduction to the politics of ideas. Some sort of ideological map is needed. It may help students to orient themselves. More important, it should add depth and meaning to their understanding of institutions and of behaviour. There is, of course, some writing to this purpose already (Birch 1964; Beer 1965; Greenleaf 1983) of the highest quality. Nevertheless, there is scope for more, and in particular a place where recent party ideologies are made plain. A scrutiny of the student texts of the last twenty or thirty years — even those concerned specifically with political parties (McKenzie 1955; Lees and Kimber 1972; Ball 1981), reveals a striking absence of material about ideas; only Stephen Ingle gives them much attention (Ingle 1987). Since there has been in the last twenty years a revival of

1

ideological controversy, the gap has become all the more obvious. Current controversy often sounds like a cacophony: a guide is needed to help students distinguish major themes.

Ideologies are taken in this book to be clusters of ideas. They are not just lists or collections of different ideas; an ideology has internal links and connections. The ideas on various matters fit together somehow. Ideologies, moreover, are not just policies. They are more general, perhaps more fundamental. They have important functions in any political arena. They provide a system of reasoning within which policies can be fashioned, and at the same time they link political action with wider notions about human life (Drucker 1974).

Left and Right

Before examining these functional problems further, it is necessary to say something about classification. This book unashamedly treats ideas, and ideologies, as if they were clearly associated with organizations — with British political parties. The reason for doing so is expository. The intention is to introduce readers to British politics through its ideas, and parties are salient features of politics, already visible to all comers. So party ideas are a way to begin.

Parties and political attitudes are frequently described by the terms 'left' and 'right'. These terms originated in the National Assembly in the French Revolution in 1790, when the radicals sat on the left of the President of the Assembly and conservatives on the right. Although not much used in Britain in the nineteenth century, they have since become the habitual designations of political parties and opinions all over the world. They offer a simple scale on which these things can be placed. There is no way in which writers in this book can avoid using them, since they have become deeply embedded in political discourse. Yet there are hazards in their deployment.

First, they are far too simple to be entirely true. Not only is it the case that substantial sections of opinion lie between the two wings, in a political 'centre', but in fact many people hold a collection of political views which cannot be fitted neatly into any point on the scale. Often individuals hold contradictory views — indeed it is exceptional for anyone to be so clear about these matters that no tensions and complications are present. Even if there is no logical incompatibility, there is usually in a person's outlook a mix of attitudes which cannot be fitted into a simple scale.

It is not merely, however, a case of individual opinions. It can be strongly argued that the left-right scale is seriously misleading even at the conceptual level. In his magisterial study, Greenleaf suggested that 'individualist' and 'collectivist' traditions could be found in all three mainstream parties (Greenleaf 1975,1983). Sam Brittan agreed that the contrast between left and right was 'a bogus dilemma' (Brittan 1968).

One view is that the left can be defined as the partisans of change, from revolution to mild reform; and consequently the right is by definition opposed to any such alterations — it supports the existing system. A similar contrast regards the left as 'progressive' and the right as essentially 'traditional'. The difficulty with this type of definition is that it precludes the possibility of left-wing values being dominant in government or becoming securely established long term — for success of any one set of left-wingers would merely result in their opponents being defined as a new 'progressive' cause trying to change things. Thus after a period of success the left becomes defensive, and hence conservative, while the right desires change, and turns radical.

Another principle would see the right as concerned with authority and order, and the left valuing freedom and emancipation of all sorts. However, there are many freedoms, some of them traditional and others new. Some people want 'freedom' to organize political power; but once in power they intend to curtail other freedoms. There is no secure usage to be found in this area.

The rise of socialism in the nineteenth century led to another dichotomy in which the left is socialist and the right is anti-socialist or capitalist. This makes the terminology hard to apply to countries where the socialist/capitalist clash is not an issue, or to periods of history when this conflict was not alive. Some authoritarian governments run many state-controlled services or industries. Where do they stand?

Again, the right may appear as the party of whoever or whatever is considered orthodox or 'normal' in a particular society, while the left embraces all the outsiders — whether ethnic or linguistic or religious minorities, or poor people, or underprivileged sections of society. This, however, seems to mistake a recruiting ground for the beliefs which emerge from such conditions.

The difficulties which became apparent led to proposals for revised classifications (Brittan 1968). One way out is to suggest that there is a *political* left and right and an *economic* left and right (Finer 1987). Political orientation concerns progress and liberty, or authority and tradition; economic orientations concern state intervention, welfare, the free market, and like matters. A double classification implies the possibility of (at best) a set of four categories. Instead of the simple linear scale which the left-right distinction produces, it has been suggested that a circular or two-dimensional diagram would be more appropriate. A horizontal axis would show (say) the capitalist-socialist gradation, but a vertical axis would reflect authoritarian/libertarian values. Thus authoritarian capitalist regimes and authoritarian centralized socialist systems would be shown to be similar in some respects, and in that matter very different from both libertarian free enterprise and decentralized socialist ideals. Another view is that the two concepts of left and right are inadequate in that they leave major distinct ideas in the centre, which implies mere lack of clarity and conviction. There should be, therefore, at least a triangular model of some sort.

However, the complications of these variants give rise to doubts about the whole critique. They could be complicated much further. Other dimensions, relating to religious differences or to attitudes to use of violence might be added. If they were, then an advanced system of classification might be constructed. But such a system would lack the prime virtue of the original left/right scheme — its simplicity. It would not provide an easy reference model which could pass into common usage.

So there are grounds for keeping the left, right (and centre) terminology in spite of its obvious defects. There is no widely-known alternative language. The most persuasive, and perhaps the most fundamental, political value of all underlies its operation — the difference between those who take a relatively optimistic view of the possibility of human improvement, and those who are pessimistic about human nature and hence feel the need to conserve and retain such order as exists. Moreover, in spite of the logical contradictions of the model, it is easy to find similar faults in the application of more complex schemes. The left tends to recognize its fellows, in other countries, for example; and whatever the right is, it is not the left. On the whole, in Britain (and in many other places but not all) parties have tended to line up along this axis. *Organized* politics, that is to say, recognizes this scheme. For this book, which relates ideas to parties, this constitutes a significant reason for using it.

Levels and Loyalties

There does remain a difficulty, however. It is one which leads to a major question in the exposition of political ideologies. Among the creators, developers, and adherents of any ideology, however defined, there will be some profound philosophers, some able analysts, some keen followers, and numbers of others who merely share its attitudes and understandings. Others will give it confused and inconsistent support; others will be temporarily or loosely attached to some of its facets. In expounding ideas, which of these levels is to be given prominence?

The left/right model is long established, is used in many countries, and is constantly used by scholars, politicians and journalists. Nevertheless, there is reason to suppose that in Britain it is not well understood by ordinary people, or by the electorate. Interviewers find that when questioning randomly selected individuals, many of them are puzzled by questions using these terms, and certainly they cannot readily place politicians or particular policies on this scale, even though such ratings would be second nature to political activists of all colours (Benney, *et al.* 1956; Butler and Stokes 1969, 1974).

If this piece of common political analysis is not understood throughout society, then it is very likely that other things are not understood either. It was, indeed, a commonplace of post-war electoral and opinion research, that many people held 'contradictory' views, that they opposed values and policies promoted by parties to which they had strong loyalties. Or as Richard Rose put it:

> Whatever the party leaders say, as a rule voters show interparty consensus. Across a range of different issues, a majority or plurality of Labour and Conversative voters have agreed with each other seven out of ten times.
>
> (Rose 1984)

Perhaps ideology should be regarded, therefore, as an elite phenomenon.

The question must be put, therefore. Does ideology matter? It matters, of course, to ideologues. It matters, that is to say, to those who believe in the ideals and share the visions of the world which ideologies provide. Leaders and members of political parties are obviously (though not necessarily) likely to be such people. No doubt they are much concerned with policies and tactics. Nevertheless, it is the current of ideas, perhaps perceived as a traditional way of thinking, or as an abstract set of principles, which supports and sustains the other activities, and which serves as a justification or at least a rationalization of the practicalities. For the activist, therefore, ideology fulfils a moral purpose. Even at this level distinctions may be made. Henry Drucker has explained the difference between 'doctrine' (socialist principles) and 'ethos' (sentiments and traditions) in the Labour Party. Such a distinction can obviously be made in other parties (Drucker 1979).

Nevertheless, it still can be argued that such beliefs, of any sort, do not influence events very much.

The case against ideology in practice is behavioural. It asserts that what rulers do — governments and bureaucrats — is determined very largely by circumstances. In part the circumstances are political — Is the party in power popular? Is an election imminent? — but they are also economic, social and strategic. So, faced by these constraints, the room for manoeuvre is very small. All governments do much the same: there is very rarely any alternative. Party considerations might make some difference, but that is because the pressures rather than the values are different. The anguish of idealists in office is a common phenomenon — they complain of their colleagues, of civil servants, of hostile interests. But, say the realists, that is the way of the world: the ideologues have misunderstood the nature of political life. In Britain, in the post-war period, this lack of ideological direction was aggravated by the problems of decline. Saving the nation was more urgent than making moral progress.

There is another view to consider. Marxists say that ideology — the dominant ideas in society — may appear to contain contrast and argument. In practice, however, the ideas that influence rulers are those that sustain them in their power. In other words, the ideas of consequence are those of the ruling class. These notions are spread to the rest of society so that there will be less challenge to that rule. Ideology, extending beyond politics itself into a cultural hegemony, is therefore an instrument of oppression. It serves to limit the consciousness of the large majority of people of their true situation. Conflict also is a surface phenomenon, a show which gives the illusion of choice.

Our answers to these various charges are twofold. First, the view that ideas make little difference takes too short and narrow a perspective. It does not see the wood for the trees. It proves too much. It is hardly plausible to suggest that no ideas carry change: it is difficult to understand history without such a background. So similarity of action is occasional and temporary: over longer periods ideological development and ideological contrasts are plain to see. This is not to assert a causal sequence. We do not insist that the ideas caused the events. But at least the ideas are part of the events: they happened, as much as the wars and crises. To neglect them is to ignore major relevant factors. And, furthermore, it is *party* ideas that structure the debate.

Second, to treat all ideas as expressions of economic interest is self-defeating. It is, of course, possible that this is true. It is indeed clear that from time to time cultural hegemony prevails in societies — the political consensus of 1945–75 was such a condition. Nevertheless, these *are* the political ideas of society — they are the forms through which social cause and effect must pass. And the 'cultural hegemony' view is itself such an idea — a useful critical weapon for expression of a political interest. There is no superior point of vantage from which illusion and reality can be discerned. The best way is to travel the landscape, and such a journey is what we offer, in a preliminary way, in this book.

The Long Development

The main purpose of the journey will be to witness the contemporary scene. Yet this does require a brief historical sketch by way of preparation.

In the Middle Ages political ideas were developed within the framework of the Christian religion. The period was the age of faith, and no other concepts presented themselves. Nevertheless, two notions could be discerned — one described by Walter Ullman as an ascending theory, in which legitimate power rose from the community, and the other a descending theory, in which it was delegated from God (Ullman 1965). In many respects ideas from these times seem remote, but these alternatives still reverberate.

In the early modern period, during the reigns of the Tudor monarchs in England, political controversy was dominated by the question of Church/State relations. The Reformation had divided Christendom, and in England, as in the rest of Europe, any stability was problematic. The national Church of England devised by the Tudors eventually prevailed, but the question of whether England should be a Catholic or Protestant country was not finally determined until the end of the seventeenth century. The emerging political structures included a more powerful Parliament, but open political conflict was not possible since it was believed to indicate subversion and to endanger the regime. In these circumstances the crucial ideological development of the period was the consolidation of English nationalism. The unity of England dates, of course, from the years before the Norman Conquest, but until the end of the Middle Ages there had been a persistent dream of uniting the lands claimed in France with the English domains of the monarchs. The Tudor quarrels with the papacy and the Elizabethan settlement all emphasized the English national identity; and the same cause was triumphantly endorsed by the national poet, William Shakespeare, in his historical dramas.

For the emergence of the more familiar ideological streams attention has to be paid to later periods. Religion did not disappear from political controversy in Britain until the beginning of the twentieth century, and perhaps not even then (Cowling 1980, 1985). In the politics of Ireland, and particularly of Northern Ireland (and hence of the United Kingdom), the fierce conflicts of the seventeenth century still rage. But from the eighteenth century onwards new ideas came forward, and from this time the main ideological thrusts in British politics (as elsewhere) concern economic and social arrangements. Perhaps such matters were always of underlying importance. From the time of industrial revolution, however, they came into the open. They shape the major (but not the only) lines of dispute and cleavage and form the subject matter of hostile creeds.

The Civil War of 1642–51 and its aftermath provided a new creative stage in ideological development, and it is possible to assert that the great divisions of British politics — even those of the twentieth century — can be traced back to this epoch. The Royalists asserted a doctrine of monarchical authority, the right of the king to rule above and beyond the other institutions of the realm. This right was divine in origin, and dependent on legitimate descent in the royal dynasty. Such rule was under

God, and God alone; wise and prudent monarchs took advice and preserved the laws and customs of their subjects, but they were not dependent on them. Such dependence would be a perversion of the natural God-ordained system, and hence was impious. This was not the only way to defend monarchical rule. Students of political theory will know that Thomas Hobbes developed a secular doctrine which argued that a single sovereign was the only way to ensure social peace and order. Nevertheless, for most Royalists the connection between religion and monarchy was the crucial principle.

The parliamentarians mostly relied on a view of English history which asserted that various rights, duties, and laws were inherent parts of the existing order. The kings had usurped this traditional system by neglecting Parliament, particularly in tax-raising, and so justified rebellion against him. The Civil War and their own success led them along other paths, including the establishment of a republican Commonwealth (1653–8). In practice this was a military dictatorship. The experience might have led to the formulation of new constitutionalist ideas: but at the time Cromwell and the others with effective power did not perceive what they might be.

The other effect of the war was the emergence of more radical ideas, particularly in the parliamentary army. Once the need to acknowledge divine right was removed, then other submerged notions could appear. At Putney in 1647, at celebrated debates, many officers urged a system of government in which even the poorest would have a part, presumably a vote. The parliamentary leaders were opposed to such a development; and indeed after experience of the severities of Puritan rule it is likely that any wide franchise would have shown majority sympathy with the Royalists. The radical elements also brought into the open — briefly — schemes of economic change. The Diggers at St George's Hill in Surrey established in 1649 a communal agricultural system. The Levellers, advocates of a householder or even manhood suffrage, were led by Gerrard Winstanley who developed a theory of equal property, with land cultivated both individually and co-operatively (Hill 1973). Thus were political and economic reforms linked. None of these doctrines prospered at the time, and they disappeared from overt politics for 200 years. But they show perhaps significant, if suppressed, traditions, ancestors of some twentieth-century socialist ideas. Moreover, the parliamentary ideological divisions provide some evidence for the view that there are three (not two) long ideological traditions to be traced through English history (Woolrych 1987).

A better-known set of partisan ideas can trace origins to the late seventeenth and eighteenth centuries. These are associated with the Whigs and the Tories. Neither of these terms describes an organized party in the sense now familiar. Nevertheless, there were distinct attitudes to be discerned and sometimes strong and acrimonious debates in which great principles were asserted to be at stake.

The terms first came into use in 1680 in debates about the Exclusion Bill, which was designed to exclude the Duke of York (the brother of King Charles II) from the throne, on grounds of his Roman Catholic religion. Both were originally abusive epithets used by opponents. The issue was still that of legitimate rule — did Parliament have the right, by law, to determine the line of succession? The Bill failed, but the terms survived; and, of course, later events in 1688 and 1714 determined the Protestant succession, and established a period of Whig ascendancy.

In these years some Whigs developed a broader philosophy and eventually within them 'strong Whig' or 'radical' elements appeared. They certainly thought of themselves as firm advocates of liberty. In the main they saw this as a counter to despotism, at home or abroad. The liberties at stake were believed to be the traditional liberties of the English, and included freedom of expression and, to an extent, of political activity. They insisted on 'constitutional' government as against arbitrary rule: in practice this resulted in an oligarchy of landowners, but parliamentary and judicial autonomy were not illusory.

Tory principles in the eighteenth century were held by some aristocrats but were more common among the gentry (small landowners and farmers) and the parsons of the Church of England. What they derived from their predecessors was a belief in authority. This may have been most significant in localities, for they were often the real powers in small towns and country districts. Similarly, they liked local power as distinct from London government, and they stood by traditional and customary laws. Eventually they were regarded as the 'country' party, the main protectors of the agricultural interest (Hill 1976).

The eighteenth century was in general a period of political stability but of economic change. The advocates of agricultural improvement, by new methods, became also advocates of a new landowning system, of consolidated holdings or enclosures in which these methods, given adequate capital, could be deployed. Moreover, there was a change in economic philosophy at the end of the eighteenth and beginning of the nineteenth century. The beliefs of seventeenth- and eighteenth-century traders had been mostly 'mercantilist' — they saw the positive value of trade, internal and international, firmly enough. Since the object, however, was for the nation to profit by it, then restrictive devices which limited foreign shippers or restricted imports, were likely to be of advantage. There was no clear set of mercantilist practices, but the idea of governmental protection was commonly held (Coleman 1969). Intellectually the turning point was undoubtedly the publication of Adam Smith's *Wealth of Nations* in 1776.

Whether as a result of reading this great work or not, many political activists began to turn to the new ideas of economic liberalism. International trade should be free of tariffs or other restrictions; internal economic activity should be free of governmental control, local or national. The ideological impact of these principles is still with us. They have been elaborated and refined, they have been attacked and challenged, but here there is the arrival of one main type of twentieth-century ideology.

In Britain this doctrine was not particularly Whig or Tory: at first it was more radical than either. In political life it was accompanied by two other influences. One of these was the philosophy of utilitarianism, fostered by Jeremy Bentham and James Mill. The other was the impact in Britain of the Revolution of 1789 in France.

Utilitarianism — the view that policy should be judged by whether or not it tended to promote the greatest happiness of the greatest number — had immense long-run influence through the nineteenth century. Its force was twofold — it was reformist, and it paid little respect to traditional ways or customary practices. Anything might be transformed. It also embraced individualism in a political sense, and hence the democratic principle — the way to ensure that policies favoured the 'greatest number' was to give each person a vote, so as to equalize impact on government. Allied with economic liberalism (though it was not necessarily the same) it encouraged the break-up of existing arrangements in all parts of society (Taylor 1972; Thomas 1979).

The French Revolution brought inspiration and reaction to Britain. The preceding American War of Independence had encouraged the notion that people should somehow determine their own government. The events in France, however, had a very different impact. The ideas were those of natural rights — the 'rights of man' — universal and unqualified, and not based on custom and experience of particular countries; and of the sovereignty of the people, taken to mean the unrestricted power of the masses. These doctrines spread to radicals in England, and for a time there was a popular revolutionary movement. The reaction was, however, more lasting. Edmund Burke, a Whig, was moved in his *Reflections on the Revolution in France* (1791) to expound, eloquently, the doctrines of cautious change, of reliance on traditional practices for guidance, and of scepticism about rationalist attempts to change society by large-scale reforms, which became part of the foundations of Conservative ideas in Britain until the 1980s. Tory respect for authority was henceforward buttressed by Conservative (and Whiggish) hostility to grand ideas and theories, since these were likely to mislead people into over-ambitious disruptions — and which had led France to rule by terror, and to the military dictatorship of Napoleon.

The Nineteenth-Century Alignment

The nineteenth century saw the establishment of firm lines of conflict in British politics. There were cross currents and there were new ideas emerging, but by the end of the century a well-organized two-party system had established itself. What ideas supported the great components of this system?

The Liberal Party as such was created in the 1860s from the remnants of the Whigs, the Radicals and those who had followed Robert Peel out of the old Tory Party. One of these, W.E. Gladstone, was the obvious leader of the new party. It derived its principles from all its predecessors, but it saw itself as the vehicle of progress in society, and therefore open to new ideas and determined to promote change. Much of its voting strength was derived from the members of Nonconformist churches, an echo of its Puritan ancestors.

Its economic outlook remained constant in one respect: it was the party of free trade. Its Peelite as well as its radical inheritance ensured this continuity. In domestic affairs, however, its practice reflected changing ideas. Many of its adherents advocated the *laissez-faire* which (supposedly) derived from Adam Smith. There was, however, much argument about its application; and in practice the Liberal became more of a modernizing party than one of strict non-intervention. They helped to create the company registration and limited liability legislation which enabled large firms to supersede individual businesses as the normal form of enterprise. They helped to found the reformed civil service, eventually to grow into a mammoth bureaucracy. They established a nationwide system of state education.

What arguments led to this revised orientation? Liberals still proclaimed individual liberty as their overriding political objective. But just as John Stuart Mill had found that some forms of happiness were of higher quality than others, then the promotion of liberties might be no simple quantitative matter. Better educated people, healthier people, people free from excessive demoralizing toil would want and appreciate liberties not at first apparent to them. So legislative compulsion might be, in some circumstances, an appropriate means of raising people to freedoms on this level. Liberty might be maximized by some well-contrived laws.

In international affairs the Liberals saw themselves as a peace-seeking party, avoiding foreign entanglements if possible, but sympathetic to movements of 'liberation' and unity in Europe. In the matter of the Empire , however, they were divided. Some thought the Empire a burden and a distraction. But many thought this a narrow-minded, inward-looking attitude — the Empire provided an opportunity for the spread of commerce, of raising the standards of many peoples, and not least, for the diffusion of liberal principles. The question of independence for colonies did not arise; it was assumed that the withdrawal of the British connection would merely open the way to conquest by some other European imperial power.

The Liberals were, of course, the party of constitutional reform, and the radical wing of the party was instrumental in pressing the movement towards a wider franchise, and eventually a democratic system. In practice they had no monopoly of such changes: nevertheless in terms of ideology there was no doubt that the ideal of popular sovereignty was largely Liberal property.

The Conservative tradition re-emerged in the second half of the century. After the party split following Peel's repeal of the Corn Laws in 1845, there were two decades of weakness. They were in danger of becoming a party of mere resistance to change, suspicious of the trend of new developments. The events of the 1860s and 1870s, instigated by Benjamin Disraeli, led to a new vigour, so that the party has become dominant in English politics since then, and has been in government for three-quarters of the years.

It did not abandon its dislike of abstract theory, but it fostered a practice of response to change, rather than resistance. Social and economic change should not be imposed by government — indeed, in some versions this was regarded as undemocratic — but Conservatives could govern in societies in which such changes took place of their own accord. Indeed, conservatism became primarily an ideology of government — rule by a flexible, non-doctrinaire elite, guiding the nation and avoiding disastrous extremes.

The nation became a key Conservative concept: Disraeli complained that there were two nations, the rich and the poor, instead of the 'one nation' of Burke's rhetoric (Disraeli 1845). There could not be equality — a foolish illusion — but there would be a bond of responsibility between the classes. It was the first duty of rulers, at all levels, to seek the well-being and liberty of their subjects. The nation meant more, however. Its power and influence should be promoted in the world. So by the end of the century most Conservatives had become imperialists.

However, a new voice was also emerging by the end of the century. Socialism can trace a long ancestry. In Britain the followers of Robert Owen and the Christian Socialists gave it a mid-century presence. In the 1880s, however, the works of Karl Marx were translated into English, and a new and immensely more formidable intellectual challenge was born. Socialism became a matter of class conflict, a historical process whereby the majority working class would eventually supersede the ruling bourgeoisie in power. Some British Labour leaders and intellectuals were attracted to this view. It was rivalled in Britain, however, by supporters of socialist ideals on ethical grounds, and by a moderate gradualist approach. The twentieth century heard much more of these ideas.

The Twentieth-Century Realignment

The first half of the twentieth century saw a considerable transformation of the ideological structure of British politics. One issue slipped out of major controversy at the beginning: religion. In the debates over the expansion of education in 1902, it was proposed to provide financial support for Church of England schools. Many nonconformists objected bitterly, sometimes to the point of conscientious refusal to pay local rates. But this was the last battle. Religion has not departed from politics as a source of inspiration and of underlying values, but it scarcely ever breaks the surface as an open issue. The contrast with earlier centuries is very great indeed.

The Irish issue, and the 'unionist' principle which Conservatives and their allies upheld, had little significance between 1921 and the 1970s. The imperial cause was still important at the beginning, but faded in the inter-war period, and after the independence of India and Pakistan in 1947, the shrinkage of Empire caused very little controversy. In a sense relations with the European Community took the place of the Empire as a cross-cutting issue in partisan terms.

The first thing to emphasize, therefore, is the way in which — in mid-century at any rate — economic issues dominated ideological controversy. It has already been noted that this had become increasingly the case from the end of the eighteenth century. But in the twentieth century ideologies couched in explicit economic and social terms became the central, dominant, and pervasive creeds. They were scarcely less divisive than the religious passions of the seventeenth century.

It was the rise of socialism, in various forms, that deepened this political chasm. Socialism claimed to be not an alternative set of policies but another system altogether. Its most fervent advocates argued that a revolution would be necessary to bring it about. As it seeped into mainstream politics, of course, less dramatic transformations became commonly proposed: but the ultimate change in view was claimed to be of a fundamental nature. The values were fraternal and egalitarian. Fraternity meant working and living in harmony and co-operation, not in conflict and competition. Equality meant the reduction of wide disparities of well-being. Further advances in freedom, prosperity and peace were to be approached from these directions. The means, in Britain, were almost always some form of collective action, usually by the state, but possibly by local or group action.

The means to these ideals were highly controversial. Some saw the tactics of the class struggle as essential — strikes, industrial aggression, a militant consciousness. Others suspected the centralizing tendencies of state action, and preferred community or voluntary schemes. But the strategy, and the ideology which upheld it in Britain, was that of the

13

Fabian Society. Socialism would be brought about gradually, by constitutional (that is electoral and parliamentary) means, and would develop the existing state institutions in relevant directions — by public ownership of industry, by social services, and by redistributive taxation. Socialism might amount to a new economic system, but it was *within* the political system.

In practical politics the Labour Party and its ideas replaced the Liberals as a major party in the 1920s. It would be wrong, however, to suppose that there was any eclipse of Liberal ideology. There was continued division between exponents of *laissez-faire* and those who were prepared to limit and to supplement it. On the whole the 'new' liberalism was successful. In 1928 a Liberal study group published *Britain's Industrial Future* ('the yellow book'). It recommended a programme of public works, to be financed by borrowing, to reduce unemployment. It thus approved a role for the state beyond that of regulation and piecemeal intervention.

Conservatives too, moved their ideas. The party itself gathered into its ranks, step by step, most members of the business community — big businessmen, as well as small, entrepreneurs, managers, farmers. This involved adaptation of ideas. Tariff protection attracted many Conservatives, and was finally achieved in the 1930s. It became the main body of resistance to socialism in its egalitarian forms, but it was prepared to accept collective action in many directions, in support of industry and gradually in social welfare. It was increasingly to distance itself from the principles of *laissez-faire* and non-intervention, which it pointed out had never been Tory dogmas.

Since 1945

The period since 1945 is treated in the essays that follow, and need not be explained in full here. Readers will be aware of the main political events (Childs 1979, 1986; Sked and Cook 1986). In 1945 the Labour Party secured large majorities in the Commons, and a government led by Clement Attlee ruled for six years. From this time, therefore, a move towards social democratic ideals was in train — more public ownership, more social welfare, and control and direction in other directions, conducted in a general spirit of 'fair shares'. Similar ideologies were in vogue in other countries; nevertheless, at the world level the period also saw the establishment of the 'cold war' between 'the west' and the communist bloc in Eastern Europe as the main feature of power politics, and hence of ideological cleavage.

The 1950s provided a period of consolidation in Britain. Conservative rule ended the social experiments, in favour of moderate change emphasizing economic well-being, while the Labour Party in opposition tried to find an outlook that made its ideals seem urgent to a complacent electorate. By the 1960s the decline of British imperial connections and world role led to a new 'European' message which at one time had ideological ambitions. The economic problem was both international — how to keep up with rivals — and domestic, how to raise the economic basis for welfare and general prosperity.

The post-war period also saw the high tide of the two-party system. In fact, though the Conservative and Labour Parties were unchallengeable at the parliamentary level until the 1970s, they were both ideologically much influenced by new Liberal policy directions. Hence there was a period of relative consensus — not to be taken as anything like full agreement on policies, or in ultimate moral perspective — but in which practical possibilities, electoral pressures, and international problems encouraged the cultivation of common ground.

This degree of consensus fell apart in the 1970s in Britain as elsewhere. To a large extent the dissensus was focused on economic policy, but it reflected revaluations in priorities that went beyond mere practicalities. Thus arrived a new opening for ideological debate. These changes were not confined to Britain, but the supposition that the British had been ideologically innocent made them more noticeable there. This book provides readers with one sort of introduction to the developments.

A British Ideology?

The historical review in previous pages, and the chapters which follows, all indicate differences and divergencies in ideas — between periods, between parties, and between schools of thought. Nevertheless, it is important to stress that these differences occurred within a certain range. Some political beliefs, in spite of the rhetoric and the conflict, were held in common.

One of these was nationalism, the acceptance of a common culture and identity. It was no simple matter. Nationalism gradually became a world-wide creed in the nineteenth and twentieth centuries, so it now seems normal and universal. The national emotion which is relevant to this book is 'British'; and it relates predominantly to Great Britain. The long attempt to create a 'United Kingdom' patriotism collapsed in the nineteenth century; and the surviving loyalty of the Ulster Protestant majority is witness to a departed aspiration. Within the British national concept, however, there are also other nationalisms — Scottish, Welsh, and English. For the Scots and Welsh this involves a dual patriotism which has proved too much for some; hence there are 'nationalist' parties in those countries, not, for reasons of space, discussed in this book. For the English the main problem lies in remembering that they are not the only British people.

It is a frequent failing to underrate the importance of British nationalism. Few would expect to understand the United States without grasping the essentials of the 'American way of life', or France without appreciating the glory of its passionate indivisibility. The rise of sub-state nationalisms in the United Kingdom overshadowed in political analysis the concept of the whole nation. Yet surely in the years of imperial power, in the dangerous years of war, in relations within the European Community, and in attitudes to economic decline, the significance of British unity and self-esteem is clear enough. The point about modern nationalism is that it is an assumed value, often taken for granted. Nevertheless, the British outlook includes it in full measure.

One result of the supposed continuity of British history is to give a complacent sense of establishment, of completeness. The British nation, it is supposed, does not need to be built — unlike those in America, Australia, or new African countries. It already exists. So the arrival of numerous immigrants in the 1950s created special problems. British racism is in part the product of British imperialism and of British nationalism. In the post-war period the impact of racial problems caused not merely difficult policy manoeuvres, but a good deal of ideological confusion, to say the least.

In classifications of the ideological basis of various countries, Britain is usually listed as a 'liberal democracy'. Though the implications of the two words are capable of infinite exploration, the term fits well enough for most purposes. There was a long and hesistant evolution to political democracy (in the sense of universal franchise), but somewhere around the First World War it became the regular practice to assert that Britain had achieved democracy, and indeed the system was worth a war to defend it. Since then no mainstream party has challenged this status. Indeed, the position of democracy as an *existing* system means that its prestige protects existing constitutional arrangements.

It is also the case that civil liberties have high political prestige. The foundations of respect vary: Conservatives rely on long British traditions and the common law, while others appeal to more abstract principles of human rights. Claims of high standards in these matters go back at least to the eighteenth century, and though practice falls short of the more boastful rhetoric, there is certainly a deep feeling in all mainstream ideologies that limits on freedom of expression, for example, should be exceptional and, if possible, temporary. So this form of liberalism can be taken to be part of a British ideology.

Perhaps there is more to it. English, and indeed British, political unity was achieved relatively early. Since the seventeenth century there have been no civil wars or violent revolutions, except in Ireland. There have been some near things, but in the end continuity has been preserved. Nor has there been defeat in major war or foreign occupation. There has, hence, grown a belief, a self-image of the British as a relatively peaceful, law-abiding and politically restrained people. The creeds they espouse are not, it is suggested, extreme or indeed well-developed versions of the philosophies in question. This pragmatism was sometimes put forward as the British contribution to world politics.

There is surely something to be said for this view in the twentieth century. If it is accepted that the Labour Party was largely Fabian in spirit, that the Liberals were converts to 'new liberalism', and that the Conservatives were cautious adaptors to social change, then common attitudes can be discovered. Moreover, though consitutional reform never disappeared from the political agenda, it took a subordinate place after the Irish settlement of 1921. So there is also a case for a sort of 'procedural' political ideology that was specifically British: constitutional, gradual and tolerant.

On the other hand, there is danger of complacent illusion. Other countries have liberal democratic systems, also fashioned by historical circumstances. The reputation for peaceful change always excepts relations with Ireland. Other countries — including the United States — have low-ideological parties. Perhaps the overarching ideology of the British is merely a collection of habits, themselves imposed by social and political circumstances, and liable to fragment when the circumstances change.

Indeed in the 1980s it seems possible that the creation of ideologies largely internal to one country is becoming more and more difficult. Perhaps this decade is witnessing the end of genuine British conservatism (destroyed by the 'new right') and of British socialism in its ethical and pragmatic forms. Perhaps in the future only world ideologies will exist, in local translations. Nor is it clear that translation involves adaption to internal national circumstances: for world events have an immense impact. The lines of British politics were turned by the anti-Fascist crusades of the 1930s and 1940s, and by cold-war attitudes after 1944. Perhaps British politics are even now being refashioned for the rising generation, not by Margaret Thatcher, but by Mikhail Gorbachev.

Structure

The form of our book is straightforward. The expositions which follow are largely concerned with ideas which have been formulated and expressed: they do not delve deeply into the realms of the inarticulate. It is the *operative* ideals that concern us (Lindsay 1943). Later chapters all concentrate on post-1945 beliefs. Three authors expound the broad ideologies associated with major parties — with the currents of ideas in and around these parties. The four following chapters deal with the ideological background to policy. The actual policies will be explained in varying detail — but it is the underlying concepts that are our business. There is, of course, some overlap between these four accounts and the party ideas of the earlier chapters. It is important, however, to note that the sway of ideas, the movement of opinions, was not (and is not) confined merely within partisan boundaries. These chapters make clear wider developments. The themes are linked in a concluding chapter.

Nevertheless, in an introductory volume much has to be left out. Our material is that of the mainstream. Many other lesser currents (from nationalism to greenery) flow, some vigorously. We do not do them justice. Our excuse is that there is already enough for the student to make a good start.

Further Reading

Even more than in other aspects of the study of politics, readers need to distinguish between the works of the ideologists themselves — which are of course essential — and studies which at least attempt to examine and explain ideas from outside.

A useful introduction is Henry Drucker's *The Political Uses of Ideology* (Macmillan, 1974). The notions of left and right are criticized by Sam Brittan in *Left or Right — the bogus dilemma* (Secker & Warburg, 1968).

The ideas of the seventeenth century are well displayed in the book edited by David Wootton, *Divine Right and Democracy* (Penguin Classics, 1986), a vivid anthology of seventeenth-century political writing. B.W. Hill explains in *The Growth of Parliamentary Politics 1689–1742* (Allen & Unwin, 1976) what Whig and Tory meant at that time. An excellent introduction to nineteenth-century ideas is Robert Pearson and Geraint Williams, *Political Thought and Public Policy in the Nineteenth Century* (Longman, 1974), and it contains a good bibliography.

The best single volume on these matters is Greenleaf's *The Ideological Heritage*, volume 2 of his four-volume *British Political Tradition* (Methuen, 1983). There is also a short article by him in *Parliamentary Affairs*, volume 28 (1975) on 'The character of modern British politics'. The classic volume by Beer, *Modern British Politics* (Faber, 1965, 1982), is essential for understanding the underlying assumptions of political creeds. Birch, *Representative and Responsible Government* (Allen & Unwin, 1964) discusses the evolution of ideas about the proper form of government for Britain.

An older volume edited by Morris Ginsberg, *Law and Opinion in England in the Twentieth Century* (Stevens, 1959) contains articles by W.L. Burn, R.B. McCallum and G.D.H. Cole on the ideas of the three parties, as well as other useful material. See also Sir Ivor Jennings, *Party Politics*, volume 3, *The Stuff of Politics* (Cambridge University

Press, 1962) and Alan Beattie (ed.) *English Party Politics* (two volumes) (Weidenfeld, 1970) — readings, with an excellent introduction.

Bibliography (published in London unless otherwise stated)

Ball, A.R. (1981) *British Political Parties*, Macmillan.
Beer, S.H. (1965, 1982) *Modern British Politics*, Faber.
Benney, M., Gray, A.P., and Pear, R.H. (1956) *How People Vote*, Routledge, ch. 9.
Birch, A.H. (1964) *Representative and Responsible Government*, Allen & Unwin.
Brittan, S. (1968) *Left or Right — the bogus dilemma*, Secker & Warburg.
Butler, D. and Stokes, D. (1969, 1974) *Political Change in Britain*, Macmillan.
Calvocoressi, P. (1978) *The British Experience 1945–75*, Harmondsworth: Penguin Books.
Childs, D. (1979, 1986) *Britain since 1945*, Benn, Methuen.
Coleman, D.C. (ed.) (1969) *Revisions in Mercantilism*, Methuen.
Cowling, M. (1980, 1985) *Religion and Public Doctrine within England* (two vols) Cambridge University Press.
Disraeli, B. (1845) *Sybil, or the two nations*, reprinted Oxford University Press (1981).
Drucker, H.M. (1974) *The Political Uses of Ideology*, Macmillan.
Drucker, H.M. (1979) *Doctrine and Ethos in the Labour Party*, Allen & Unwin.
Finer, S.E. (1987) 'Left and Right', in *Encyclopaedia of Political Institutions*, Oxford: Blackwell.
Greenleaf, W.H. (1975) 'The character of modern British politics', *Parliamentary Affairs*, 28 (4).
Greenleaf, W.H. (1983) *The British Political Tradition, Vol. 2, The Ideological Heritage*, Methuen.
Hill, B.W. (1976) *The Growth of Parliamentary Parties 1689–1742*, Allen & Unwin.
Hill, C. (ed.) (1973) *The Law of Freedom and other writings of Gerrard Winstanley* Harmondsworth: Penguin Books.
Ingle, S. (1987) *The British Party System*, Oxford: Blackwell.
Lees, J.D. and Kimber, R. (eds) (1972) *Political Parties in Modern Britain*, Routledge.
Liberal Party (1928) *Britain's Industrial Future*, Liberal Party.
Lindsay, A.D. (1943) *The Modern Democratic State*, Oxford University Press.
McKenzie, R.T. (1955) *British Political Parties*, Heinemann.
Rose, R. (1980, 1984) *Do Parties Make a Difference?*, Macmillan, p. xxiii.
Sked, A. and Cook, C. (1986) *Post-war Britain — a political history*, Harmondsworth: Penguin Books.
Taylor, A.J. (1972) *Laissez-faire and State Intervention in Nineteenth-century Britain*, Macmillan.

Thomas, W. (1979) *The Philosophical Radicals*, Oxford: Clarendon Press.
Ullman, W. (1965) *History of Political Thought: The Middle Ages*, Harmondsworth: Penguin Books.
Woolrych, A. (1987) *Soldiers and Statesmen — the General Council of the Army and its debates 1647–1648*, Oxford: Clarendon Press.

Part one

Parties and Ideologies

Chapter two

The Left: The Ideology of the Labour Party

John Callaghan

The British Labour Party never subscribed to a systematic ideology and even its friends have complained of its lack of creed as its 'gravest weakness' (Tawney 1981:55–6). Most of its leaders, however, have found this eclecticism convenient, and some of them have justified it as a reflection of a healthy scepticism in British popular culture (Gaitskell 1955:922). The party has often expressed pride in its ideologically inclusive character. Yet this 'broad church' has sometimes seemed to contain ideological enemies intent on mutual destruction. On other occasions the internecine disputes which characterize periods in the party's history have receded and the party has been led by mere pragmatists.

This chapter will attempt to explain these variations and paradoxes by an examination of the ideological currents within the Labour Party in their historical context — from the party's origins to the period of disorientation and ideological volatility of the present.

The Critique of Capitalism

In common with their continental counterparts, the socialists who helped to form the Labour Representation Committee(LRC) in 1900 were moved by a deep sense of the social injustice which they believed to be endemic to capitalism; and it was their declared intention to eradicate it. Ramsay MacDonald, Labour's first Prime Minister, and widely regarded as a leading authority on socialist theory, argued that capitalism offended against the national interest because it was a system which could even find profit in the degradation and deterioration of the people. Socialism sought to end this exploitation and this fact, he wrote, 'sets the bounds to the ownership of private property' (MacDonald 1911:95, 130). Thus land, natural monopolies, and industrial capital needed to be 'socialized'. In this way MacDonald believed that the protective capacity of the state could be extended into economic and social affairs where otherwise a destructive Darwinian struggle of the fittest held sway. MacDonald was not alone in finding the 'free' market at loggerheads with a system of

23

ethics. Indeed, this was the central conviction of the ethical socialists of the Independent Labour Party (ILP), one of the affiliates to the LRC. Their leader, Keir Hardie, pointed to the poverty-stricken millions as an affront to the fellowship taught by Christ (Pelling 1954:201). This was what Bruce Glasier sought to convey when he argued that:

> The great wrong of existing social conditions does not lie in the mere circumstance that many are poor while few are rich but in the injustice and degradation, in the assertion of superiority and inferiority, in the denial of brotherhood which these conditions imply.
>
> (Pelling 1954: 364)

This was the message of the most popular socialist idiom in Britain at the turn of the century. Of course, these ILP socialists also railed against the waste and disorder of capitalism and represented socialism as the application of science to society. But it was not their most distinctive emphasis. The appeal to facts was more characteristic of the Fabian Society.

The Fabian Society saw itself as an intellectual aristocracy devoted to social analysis and policy-making in the service of collectivist values. Under the leadership of Sidney and Beatrice Webb, the society defined socialism as the 'economic side of democracy', and purported to see every extension of the state's powers and responsibilities as proof of a collectivist trend leading irresistibly towards socialism. The Webbs argued that the complexities of industrialism and the democratic forces in society were the twin dynamos compelling the growth of the state. Under these pressures it had 'silently changed its character . . . from police power to merely housekeeping on a national scale' (Webb, S. and B. 1920:13). This process had led to successive reforms designed to register, inspect and control the private economy. The Fabians wanted to make people more conscious of these developments and to accelerate the trend by which, as they saw it, the national interest was beginning to supersede sectional interests. By the First World War — and after a lengthy period in which they had tried to 'permeate' the established parties with their ideas — the Webbs were persuaded that the Labour Party was the best available vehicle for the realization of these ambitions. The Fabians expressed the socialist case in the language of national efficiency, but their objectives clearly overlapped with those of the ethical socialists.

The ILP and the Fabian Society agreed that socialism in Britain would be realized by peaceful, democratic reforms through the existing parliamentary institutions with only slight modifications. They rejected the Marxist theory of class struggle — which was 'nothing but a grandiloquent and aggressive figure of speech', according to MacDonald — and any idea that the state was simply an instrument for the suppression of the working class. Instead they took the view, as Tawney later expressed it, that 'the state is simply an instrument which can be used sensibly by sensible men or foolishly by fools' (Tawney 1981:97). Because they saw socialism as the growth of society linked inextricably with the growth of democracy, the major trends in British socialism had no time or need for revolution. Marxism was briefly present in the new-born LRC in the crude apocalyptic form given to it by the Social Democratic Federation (MacIntyre 1980:17). Far more influential was the idea of New Liberal provenance that the state can be a factor promoting cohesion and that true individual liberty requires an active interventionist state to remove or at least greatly modify the inequalities created by capitalism. Nevertheless, Marxist ideas have never been wholly absent from the Labour Party and have frequently influenced the views of leading figures within it.

Until 1918 the Labour Party was little more than a pressure group in Parliament. The socialist minority within the organization was dwarfed by the trade unions with their Liberal sympathies, qualified only by their commitment to independent parliamentary representation. Naturally the more prominent socialists within the party were those whose views came nearest to the concerns of the trade union leaders. The dominant ideology in the new party was therefore Labourism — a fusion of trade union assumptions concerning the efficacy of free collective bargaining, and the Liberal conviction that parliamentary reforms were all that was required to create a more just society (Saville 1973).

In terms of foreign policy this balance of ideological forces within the party was demonstrated by Labour's unwavering support for the First World War. The trade unions saw Britain's involvement as a necessary defence of the national interest. Only a tiny minority within the socialist organizations opposed the war as a manifestation of imperialism and contrary to the interests of workers everywhere. Others, slightly more numerous though equally marginalized within the party, could not support the war on pacifist grounds and believed that open diplomacy together with closer economic and political ties between nations could prevent future wars. After 1918 these minority views gained ground in the Labour Party in as much as they informed its faith in the League of Nations and its opposition to rearmament.

Clause Four

The First World War exercised a radicalizing influence in Britain that was reflected in constitutional changes adpoted by the Labour Party in 1918. In particular the party now adopted socialist goals for the first time as contained in the famous Clause Four of the new draft:

To secure for the producers by hand or by brain the full fruits of their industry, and the most equitable distribution therof that may be possible, upon the basis of the common ownership of the means of production and the best obtainable system of popular administration and control of each industry or service.

The party also adopted specific nationalization policies in its manifesto *Labour and the New Social Order* (1918), which called for state ownership of coal, steel, railways and life assurance, as well as a deliberate policy of full employment through state action and a more progressive system of taxation. But did these changes signal that the party had now been converted to socialism? The answer must be no. Undoubtedly Sidney Webb's carefully chosen words made Clause Four appeal to socialist sentiment in the party and also gave the fledgling organization a firmer identity. But the unions were the main beneficiaries of the constitutional changes (and that was the real point of the 1918 reorganization) since their power was actually increased within the organization (and that of the ILP diminished) by the new rules. The unions were given more representation on the party's executive while the ILP's monopoly of Labour's individual members was broken (henceforward new recruits were able to join the party's own local organizations directly instead of those of the ILP). When account is taken of the fact that there was still talk of a trade union secession and the danger of a separate Trade Union Party in 1918, it is evident that there had been no wholesale conversion of the unions to socialism (Cole 1948:48). The specific measures which were advocated in *Labour and the New Social Order* were perfectly compatible with the established goals of trade unionism and those of the advanced wing of Liberalism. Yet in all essentials this was to remain the Labour agenda until 1945–51.

Socialist Theory and Labour Practice

Immediately after the First World War socialist thinking both inside and outside the Labour Party became more sensitive to the dangers of state bureaucracy which the Fabian and ILP stress on nationalization foreshadowed. The war economy had been run with a high degree of state intervention but in the service of capitalism. It seemed after this experience that socialism had need of the emphases on decentralization and industrial democracy which found voice in the shop stewards' movement and guild socialism in Britain, and in the emergence of soviets, or workers councils, in Russia. Harold Laski, R.H. Tawney, and G.D.H. Cole were the most prominent of those in the Labour Party who took up these arguments. Both Cole and Laski argued that 'no political democracy can be real that is not the reflection of an economic democracy' (Laski 1919:38; Cole 1920:31). But the corrective which state socialism called forth was not only a revived interest in decentralization and participatory democracy, but also a renewed interest in socialism as a moral force, which R.H. Tawney did most to champion. In Tawney's view socialists had to restore to society the lost insight that the significance and measure of institutions and economic activities was the common end to which they were related (Tawney 1921:17; Wright 1987). Under capitalism individual rights bore no relation to social duty and very often conflicted with it. Great inequalities were allowed to corrupt and debilitate individuals and society alike. Under such circumstances as these Tawney advocated public ownership as a means of undermining selfish materialism and of promoting the ideal of public service. But this particular form of collectivism was not sought for its own sake; it was only ever intended as a means to higher socialist ends.

While socialist theory in the 1920s contained much that was important, it fell short of the mark as a practical guide to action. The mass unemployment which set in after 1921 undermined any base there might have been for the aims of the guild socialists and pluralists; and although two minority Labour governments were formed in 1924 and 1929–31 they achieved little. They did, however, demonstrate the tensions which existed between a Labour government claiming to represent the national interest and the interests of its own supporters which could be depicted as merely sectional and selfish. Ramsay MacDonald seriously considered the use of the armed forces under the provisions of the Emergency Powers Act in order to break a London bus strike in March 1924. Ernest Bevin, the leader of the union concerned, was at that time of the opinion that the political work of the Labour Party was 'subordinate to and dependent on the industrial strength of the Labour Movement organised in the trade unions' (Bullock 1960:235). But while this episode was merely embarrassing, the second MacDonald government ended disastrously, seemingly paralyzed before the rising unemployment which followed the Wall Street Crash, and divided over the proposal that a foreign loan should be financed out of the pockets of the unemployed and state employees. The stiffest resistance to MacDonald's policy came from the unions, leading Sidney Webb (by then a Cabinet member) to comment: 'the General Council are pigs, they won't agree to any cuts of unemployment insurance benefits or salaries or wages' (Bullock 1960:485).

Faced with a major international slump and the rise of Fascism, some Labour socialists were converted to an explicitly catastrophist perspective. John Strachey, for example, concluded that 'the capitalist system is dying and cannot be revived, the age of individualistic freedom is very nearly over' (Strachey 1935:163–4). For many socialists in the 1930s the Soviet Union 'was the only hope in an age of hopelessness' (Koestler 1945). Though membership of the British Communist Party remained small, the Soviet Union' sympathizers and apologists multiplied in response to the apparent successes of the first Five Year Plan and the USSR's commitment to collective security against Fascism. But the great majority of British socialists retained their faith in the future socialist commonwealth arising out of the parliamentary gradualism to which they had always subscribed. For them, the democratic idea had still to be tested since no Labour majority had yet tried and failed. Even those who now questioned the compatibility of capitalism and democracy — such as Stafford Cripps and Harold Laski — preferred to believe in the exceptional strength of democratic traditions in Britain. Indeed, the major ideological effect of the 1931 political crisis was that it served to focus the minds of the Labour leadership on the need for a programme of reforms which could be implemented within the lifetime of the next Labour government. After 1936 the hand of moderates within the party was greatly strengthened when J.M. Keynes provided a persuasive economic theory which showed how a private enterprise economy could be managed by the state in the public interest.

In foreign policy, also, the 1930s was a time when socialists within the Labour Party emphasized their distinctive approach and their mistrust of imperialism. Clement Attlee, the party leader, declared that:

> There is a deep difference of opinion between the Labour Party and the Capitalist parties on foreign policy as well as on home policy because the two cannot be separated. The foreign policy of a Government is the reflection of its internal policy. Imperialism is the form which capitalism takes in relation to other nations.
>
> (Attlee 1937:226)

Even after the advent of Hitler this mistrust of capitalist governments prevented the party from taking an unequivocal stand in favour of re-armament. But the rise of the Fascist dictatorships ultimately strengthened political realism at the expense of socialist internationalism within the Labour movement; and by the end of the Second World War the great majority of the party's leaders were practitioners of power politics in defence of the 'national interest'.

Labour in Power

It is generally agreed that the Second World War played a large part in creating the mood for social reform which swept Labour to power in 1945 (Calder 1965; Addison 1977). By now socialism had come to mean a programme of nationalization and social service provision under the aegis of a Welfare State. Though economic planning had occupied a prominent place in socialist debate in the 1930s, there was no mention of it in the 1945 manifesto *Let Us Face The Future*. Similarly, Labour had dropped some of the more militant nationalization proposals — such as land, banking, and engineering — and focused instead on targets that had allegedly 'failed the nation' against the efficiency criterion promoted by the early Fabians. Since the adoption of Labour's *Immediate Programme* in 1937 the party's agenda, indeed, resembled once again the tasks adopted in 1918. Coal, railways, and the 'natural monopolies' of electricity and gas could be regarded as 'overripe' for nationalization by Tories and Liberals as well as Labour people. In fact, public ownership in these industries as well as road transport, airlines and the Bank of England excited little parliamentary opposition. Such measures did not exceed the reforms advocated by many industrialists and their natural political allies in the inter-war years (Smith 1976). Nor did Labour's rationale for public ownership depart from the consensual national efficiency logic of the progressive Tories and Liberals.

Furthermore, the form nationalization would take was settled by the corporate model championed by Herbert Morrison in the 1930s. This proposed that a board of public officials should replace the private capitalists in the industries concerned without changing the basic power relations between managers and workers. In the absence of a powerful movement for workers' control within British trade unionism, this technocratic model completely dominated Labour's thinking until complaints about 'bureaucracy' began to be heard in the late 1940s. Thereafter the left of the party invoked the idea of workers' participation to deal with these shortcomings, while arguing that state ownership needed to 'embrace every industry' which either exercised 'a hold over our national economy' or 'which cannot be made efficient in private hands' (Crossman, Foot and Mikardo 1947:11). By the 1950s the party leadership around Hugh Gaitskell had also come round to the idea of industrial democracy as a means of inspiring a public service ethic and greater productivity from the workforce. These were benefits which an earlier generation of Labour leaders had naïvely expected to accrue from the mere fact of public ownership.

Despite these differences, it needs to be emphasized that the whole party perceived the reforms of 1945–51 as having effected major structural changes within the economy which shifted the balance of power away from private industry to the wage-earners and their paternalistic state. Similarly, the National Health Service was thought to embody the socialist principle of equal rights irrespective of the ability to pay. It was also believed that the government's reforms had moved Britain towards a more egalitarian income and wealth distribution and had taken major steps in the elimination of poverty and slum housing. However, even as these reforms were enacted, the question of what Labour would do next began to arise.

It should be noted here that foreign policy 'evoked far more controversy and division than did domestic disputes over the precise balance between "consolidation" and socialist advance or such detailed matters as National Health Service charges or public ownership' (Morgan 1984:234). There had been some talk of a 'socialist foreign policy' during the 1945 election campaign but the Labour government took for granted that Britain's Great Power status would continue, and that this involved maintenance of its imperial role. Indeed the government's 'almost fanatical promotion of the Commonwealth' was based on the perception that it was 'essential to the survival of Britain and . . . her position as a world power' (Fieldhouse 1984:88). It was, however, the government's perception of the Soviet Union as a major threat and of the United States as a force for good which aroused most controversy within the party. Against this polarization of international affairs some of the parliamentary left advocated a 'third force' policy which envisaged Britain leading Europe on a road independent of the superpowers. It cannot be said, however, that the Labour left was able to elaborate a general theory of socialist foreign policy at this time capable of challenging the 'realist' assumptions which actually held sway within the party; but some of them were deeply troubled by the smooth continuities between Ernest Bevin's time at the Foreign Office and the policies of his Conservative predecessors.

Rethinking Socialism and Capitalism

The evidence of these years suggests that the fulfilment of the party's original goals left it exhausted and directionless as early as 1947-8. A minority within the parliamentary party wanted to regard the government's reforms as but the first step towards socialism. The leadership, however, was for 'consolidation'; and in a very real sense the reforms of 1945-51 represented the culmination of a tradition of social reform for men such as Attlee and Morrison rather than the beginning of an assault on capitalism. Nevertheless, once it became plain that the Conservatives were reconciled to the new mixed economy, all opinion within the party was obliged to recognize that Labour could not find ideological distinctiveness merely by defending institutions which had become part of a new consensus.

Thus the intellectual initiative within the party passed to those who sought to redefine Labour's objectives in the light of the changes effected by the post-war Attlee governments. Since the late 1930s Labour economists such as Gaitskell, Douglas Jay, and Evan Durbin had been converted to the Keynesian view that management of the economy did not require comprehensive state ownership of industry. By means of monetary and fiscal controls, it was now argued, the government could achieve traditional socialist (and indeed Liberal) objectives such as full employment and a more egalitarian distribution of incomes without massively increasing state power. This theory was all the more attractive to those who were appalled by the example of Soviet socialism, which combined total state control of the economy with inequality and tyranny. Management of a mixed economy could be represented as a way of avoiding the threat to individual liberty posed by the Big State; and this was an idea which was always likely to appeal to the intellectual leaders of the Labour Party coming (as many of them did) from the traditions of English liberalism. Once it became clear that even a modest programme of nationalization had generated complaints of bureaucracy but little evidence of support for a second instalment, Gaitskell and his co-thinkers were persuaded that nationalization was an electoral liability.

Tawney expressed a widely held sentiment when he acknowledged that 'the danger of a top-heavy bureaucracy and remote control is . . . genuine' (Tawney 1952:127). But the party was divided over the issue of where this oligarchical power chiefly lay and of how it was to be dealt with. Anthony Crosland, a major Labour thinker of the post-war period, believed that the state was now strong enough to pursue socialist ends by Keynesian means. He argued in 1952 that sustained full employment would also limit the power of private business by promoting the counter-vailing power of the trade unions whose negotiating strength had been enhanced. Furthermore, successful management of the mixed economy by ensuring economic growth and full employment would reinforce the ideological shift to Welfarism which the war years and the Attlee governments had encouraged. The pre-war system of permissive free enterprise had therefore been morally exposed and intellectually discredited in Crosland's view; in fact, he believed it was beyond recovery, particularly since the private sector itself had changed in structure and motivation.

Here Crosland outlined a theory which pointed to the existence of a post-capitalist society in Britain. The ownership and control of large private firms were now in separate hands. While the shareholders, greatly increased in number, were naturally pre-occupied with company profits, Crosland believed that the managers who controlled the firms were disposed as professionals to consider a variety of corporate goals other than mere profit maximization. Not only, then, was the old style capitalist who both owned and controlled the firm a thing of the past, but the modern elite in indus-try could also be expected to work sympathetically with their counter-parts in the state towards the solution of common problems such as improved labour relations, mutually beneficial regional policies and new investment programmes (Crosland 1952:35–42).

31

The Bevanite Analysis

As far as Crosland was concerned 'the national shift to the Left with all its implications for the balance of power may be accepted as permanent' (Crosland 1956a:28–9). Yet this was not how Aneurin Bevan and the Labour left (organized around the journal *Tribune*) saw the matter. According to Bevan: 'The issue . . . in a capitalist democracy resolves itself into this: either poverty will use democracy to win the struggle against property or property in fear of poverty will destroy democracy' (Bevan 1952:23). Here Bevan was expressing the Marxist conviction that such limited democracy as Britain already possessed could not be placed on a secure footing until it was greatly extended against the capitalist autocracy in industry. This is why, writing in *Tribune*, Bevan argued that public ownership remained central to the socialist strategy of democratizing society. Those who would revise this estimation were simply 'frightened by the administrative difficulties which accompany the nationalisation of major industries. These are problems of transition and should be seen as such' (*Tribune*, 13–26 June 1952). The remedy for these problems, in Bevan's view, was 'probably' industrial democracy — an opinion shared by Richard Crossman when he argued that: 'plans for nationalisation which do not satisfy the aspirations to workers' control are the technocrats' perversion of our socialist ideal' (Crossman 1956:13).

Indeed, Crossman argued that 'the enemy of human progress is the managerial society and the central coercive power which goes with it' (Crossman 1952:12). Crosland and Gaitskell expressed similar sentiments during the 1950s, but where they focused attention on the sort of over-weening state bureaucracy associated with the Soviet Union, the left in the party saw the same type of threat coming from the giant corporations of modern capitalism (Crossman 1952:27). They also drew attention to oligarchical power within the Labour Party itself and in the trade unions. These overlapping bureaucracies often conspired in the 1950s to marginalize the Bevanites and, not surprisingly, it was the left of the party who called for their democratization. Thus, when Crossman defined 'the main task of socialism' as reversing the trend towards oligarchy and distributing responsibility, and enlarging freedom of choice, he had more in mind than just industrial democracy (Crossman 1952:27).

But the Labour left (dubbed 'fundamentalists' by their opponents in the party) never found a programme of reforms to reflect this ambition; nor was this ambition itself consistently fought for. Instead, the left adopted a mainly defensive posture which simply asserted the importance of public ownership and the need for more of it. Its advocacy of industrial democracy was similarly routinized. To all intents and purposes new thinking was the preserve of the so-called revisionists around Gaitskell and Crosland.

Equality Versus Public Ownership

The Gaitskellites emphasized that Labour's supreme goal was equality and the abolition of the class system. Nationalization was merely a means — and a poor means at that — to the realization of that end. Fiscal policy, it was argued, was a better means of achieving a more egalitarian distribution of incomes and wealth; social policy was a superior instrument in the elimination of poverty; and educational reform was a more useful measure against the deleterious influences of class. By comparison with these routes to equality, public ownership was allegedly a blunt instrument indeed.

It is important to recognize that in talking about equality and the abolition of class, the revisionist emphasis was not simply or even mainly on the economic factors that might be thought to bear on these issues. Crosland was of the opinion that the redistribution of income and wealth from the rich to the poor 'would make little difference to the standard of living of the British people'. This 'main prop of traditional egalitarianism has . . . been knocked away by its own success' (Crosland 1956b:5). The case for equality must now rest, he argued, 'on certain value or ethical judgements of a non-economic character' (ibid.:5).

Crosland perceived 'a marked equality in the distribution of incomes' arising from the achievements of the Welfare State (ibid.:7). Poverty had been beaten back and was on the way to extinction in Britain. However, in his view, an enormous number of social problems stemmed from the consciousness of class distinctions of a non-economic character — especially those associated with differences of status. This is one of the principal reasons why Crosland attached significance to educational reforms and those reforms designed to increase participation in decision-making, particularly in industry. Both types of reform were expected to break down barriers to social mixing and social mobility and hence to promote classlessness.

Educational reform was for these reasons 'of infinitely greater significance' in the pursuit of equality than the redistribution of wealth (Crosland 1956d:27). Here was an arena in which real social equality could be achieved. To those who feared that such equality would only engender a hyper-competitive social system, Crosland recommended an inspection of the United States of America — 'a fluid equal opportunity society, unrivalled in the degree to which its schools promoted co-operation and adaptability rather than rivalry and competition' (Crosland 1956c:43).

By comparison with social democratic Sweden, and even capitalist America, British society was seen to be enfeebled by status divisions associated with class. As Gaitskell put it in 1956:

We regard as unjust a class structure in which a person's income, way of living, education, status, and opportunities in life depend on the class into which he is born. We reject a society in which one man is regarded as superior or inferior to another, regardless of personal qualities, again simply because of the section of society to which his parents happen to belong.

(Gaitskell 1956:3)

Therefore:

the society we wish to create is one in which there are no social classes, equal opportunity . . . a high degree of economic equality, full employment, rapidly rising productivity, democracy in industry and a general spirit of co-operation between its members.

(Gaitskell 1956:5)

On this last point, Crosland complained of a society in which there was:

so much resentment, so many unofficial strikes, so many touchy, prickly, indignant and frustrated citizens in politics and industry with grudges against society and grievances at work sending telegrams and passing angry resolutions, flocking to meetings not with badges but with chips on their shoulders, peevishly waiting for someone to knock them off.

(Crosland 1956b:7)

Such was Britain as the revisionists saw it in the mid-1950s; a society in which great strides had already been taken economically, but in which such progress was fundamentally 'out of alignment with the class or social hierarchy' (Crosland 1956b:7).

The Labour left had no quarrel with much of the detail of these arguments. Bevan and his followers simply insisted that the mixed economy needed to have a much larger public component than that with which the revisionists were satisfied. Otherwise planning was held to be inconceivable, for unless there was extensive state ownership of industry there could be no effective control over it. The reliance on indirect fiscal and monetary controls advocated by the revisionists was, on this view, no substitute for the direct control which public ownership allowed.

Bevan saw the revisionist emphasis on taxation as a source of political weakness in a society based on individualism. Politics would degenerate to the issue of a penny on or off the standard rate of income tax and its burden would fall on those least able to evade it — the wage-earners and those least able to pay extra taxes. While the revisionists assumed that economic growth would obviate the need for income tax increases, Bevan was far more pessimistic about the alleged taming of the capitalist economy. He envisaged rising taxation as a source of inflation, individual frustration and discontent (Bevan 1952:136). Socialism would become synonymous with high taxation, since this was the likely outcome of a strategy of equality based on the continuing existence of an over-whelmingly private economy. The alternative, in Bevan's opinion, was to take over industries and firms and use the surpluses they create for public purposes. In this way, planning and stable prices could both be achieved as long as wages were also planned (Bevan 1952:138; Mikardo 1952:144).

Although both sides in this doctrinal dispute purported to abhor state-centred bureaucracy, neither was able to show how greater state direction over the economy would operate alongside the parliamentary control, public participation, and industrial democracy which they both advocated. For example, the Bevanites were keen to plan wages. Mikardo even argued that when Labour was in power 'every strike was a blow against their own Government and their own party' (Mikardo 1952:144). But how could wages be planned from the centre in order to prevent such anti-socialist action while the unions remained sensitive and responsive to the demands of their members? Such complex issues were never really addressed. The danger of bureaucracy, however, was also contained in the revisionist programme in so far as it promoted the proliferation of indirect controls over the economy in accordance with its Keynesian preferences. The work involved in state management of the mixed economy — even if the mix was predominantly private — would create problems of democratic control and accountability in relation to the organizations and committees entrusted with its day-to-day implemen-tation. The Labour left has argued that this approach incorporates organizations such as the trade unions into the state, and threatens to transform them from democratic bodies into instruments of state policy. This corporate bias of the Keynesians could be argued to subvert both parliamentary control and rank-and-file democracy within the state-integrated pressure groups. Yet it must be concluded that the left, while aware of the bureaucratic shortcomings of the revisionists, was even more statist and generally insensitive to the problems associated with planning from the centre. Thus a *Tribune* editorial could assert in 1959 that Russia's space technology demonstrated in practice the superiority of an economy which is 'one hundred per cent nationalised' and argue that this rendered the theoretical debate with the revisionists superfluous (*Tribune*, 23 October 1959).

Constitutional Change?

The revisionists drew on a different kind of empirical evidence, though it was perhaps equally tendentious. Sustained economic growth and full employment and the maintenance of the Welfare State under the

Conservatives underlined their contention that the old capitalist system was dead. The ideologies which had arisen to defeat and defend capitalism were accordingly redundant, and Labour in particular was seen as in need of modernization. By 1959 Gaitskell could plausibly explain three consecutive electoral defeats by reference to the growth of an affluent society and with it the decay of the old working class. 'Capitalism', he told Labour's annual conference in that year, 'has changed significantly largely as a result of our own efforts'. The new type of worker, according to this reasoning, was frankly repelled by Labour's cloth cap image and the outmoded ideas of the fundamentalists.

As party leader Gaitskell now sought to emulate the German Social Democrats who had dispensed with their own outmoded ideas (in relation to public ownership and the party's Marxist programme) at Bad Godesberg earlier in the year by making appropriate constitutional changes. Both Jay and Crosland argued for constitutional changes in the Labour Party soon after the electoral defeat of 1959. Jay even suggested a change of name to symbolize the fact that the unions (and the party activists) would exercise less influence under the new arrangements. However, Gaitskell ignored this advice and decided to concentrate his fire on Clause Four of the party's constitution, which ostensibly committed the party to a programme of comprehensive nationalization. He accepted that there were very few in the party who believed that the implementation of Clause Four was desirable, but he calculated that it was an electoral liability and served a mischievous function as the emblem of discredited and anachronistic theories.

In fact, Gaitskell underestimated the party's sentimental attachment to Clause Four, as well as the problems its excision would pose to particular unions which had similar commitments in their own constitutions. He was compelled to abandon his plans and submit instead a new statement of principles, which the 1960 conference adopted merely as a 'valuable expression of the aims of the Labour Party in the twentieth century' but without constitutional significance. These seven principles have been summarized as:

> concern for the worst off; social justice; a classless society; equality of all races and peoples; belief in human relations 'based on fellowship and co-operation'; precedence for public over private interest; freedom and democratic self-government.
>
> (Williams 1982:324)

Gaitskell's initiative provoked only a sterile response from the party and a valuable opportunity for a thorough rethink of Labour's goals was missed. The response of the *Tribune* left, as we have seen, amounted to little more than an assertion of the centrality of public ownership and — with the exception of its advocacy of unilateral disarmament — not much in the way of new thinking came from this source. Such evidence as exists suggests that Labour's activists were little influenced by the revisionist initiative in relation to public ownership (Minkin 1978:80).

Socialism and Modernization

It could be argued that the coalition of interests and ideologies within the Labour Party was threatened by the very fact that some attempt was made in the 1950s to introduce doctrinal clarity into the organization. Certainly unity was restored to the coalition after Harold Wilson took over the party leadership in 1963, utilizing a language which was sufficiently vague to appeal to almost all factions in the organization. Detailed policy remained revisionist in origin and intent, but it was dressed in radical rhetoric which spoke of the need to 'harness Socialism to science and science to Socialism' — one of the main themes of the party programme *Signposts for the Sixties* (1961). Supported by a new public awareness of Britain's relative economic decline, Wilson was able to scoff at the affluent society image which the revisionists had largely embraced in the 1950s. These were now dubbed the 'stagnant fifties', productive only of 'a pathetic economic performance' (Wilson 1964:11, 16). Wilson counterposed 'thirteen wasted years of Conservative misrule' to the promise of a future prosperity under Labour. He appealed to the left through his emphasis on the ills of British capitalism and to the revisionists because he seemed to share their priorities.

Wilson asserted that 'if any press or television interviewer asks a Labour leader what is our first priority the answer is invariably the restoration of Britain's economic dynamic' (Wilson 1964:11). In fact, together with Tony Benn and Peter Shore, Wilson gave Labour technocratic goals which were often couched in a patriotic language. Thus it was argued that: 'The supreme test of the relevance of contemporary British socialism lies in its ability to restore to Britain a sense of purpose and the ability to carry it out' (Wilson 1964:28).

Using an idiom now associated with Mrs Thatcher, Wilson lamented that the British people had been forced to witness 'a great nation unnecessarily accepting a state of economic growth and world status lower than its real abilities and needs would dictate' (ibid.:17). Britain, he argued, 'is a world power or it is nothing'; and Labour's principal task was to restore it to greatness by clearing the obstacles of privilege, amateurism, and snobbery from the path of scientific progress.

Wilson's critique of nepotism, aristocracy, and amateurism has a long pedigree in the history of Labour's indictment of British capitalism. The attack on rentiers, financial speculators, and other 'parasites' (a line of attack which Wilson made his own) had served in fact to obscure the ambivalence with which this tradition had always viewed the efficient capitalists and their managerial representatives. By championing meritocracy, expertise, and professionalism against 'the well-born and well-connected amateurs in the company boardrooms' (Wilson 1964:22–3), Wilson made these attributes seem the embodiment of socialist values. Whereas the left had bridled when Crosland wrote approvingly of qualified professional managers, *Tribune* applauded Wilson when he complained that Britain did not have enough of these people. Of course it was easy to equate socialism with the progress of science and technology in Britain precisely because British capitalism seemed to stifle their development; but there is no doubt that, when Wilson attacked the backwardness of British capitalism, many on the left believed that he meant to replace it with socialism rather than a more efficient variety of free enterprise.

But although planning was a central feature of the party's message in the early 1960s, definite public ownership proposals were absent from the Wilsonian agenda. Instead, Wilson's speeches referred to the need to induce private industry to co-operate with a Labour government by means of changes in the tax system and the provision of financial incentives. This type of policy had been denounced by Bevan in the 1950s on the grounds that it made Parliament the handmaiden of private interests, but it escaped the notice of his followers in the 1960s (Bevan 1952:50–1). Indeed, both sides to the doctrinal dispute of the 1950s overlooked the fact that Wilson tended to marginalize questions of socialist values altogether.

In his overriding concern to make Labour the natural party of government, Wilson moved to an essentially pragmatic position which was revealed as soon as his first government encountered economic difficulties. Planning became merely 'a permissive incantation without instruments of implementation' (Howell 1976:253). Modernization in practice often amounted to no more than a familiar rationalization with its associated loss of jobs. Steering the ship of state became its own justification, and both revisionists and Tribunites could find little to celebrate. Significantly, Wilson later reflected on his time as Prime Minister in three large books 'all without once discussing even rhetorically theories, doctrines, or values of any kind (let alone socialist)' (Crick 1984:13). Wilson's great talent was to hold the coalition of interests and ideologies within the Labour Party together, and yet his first six years as Prime Minister created enormous strains between its leadership and its rank-and-file members, and between its political and industrial wings.

Voluntary wage restraint was succeeded in 1966 by a statutory incomes policy which remained in force until the TUC and Labour conferences of 1968. But no sooner had these conferences voted for a return to free collective bargaining than the government began to prepare legislation introducing compulsory strike ballots and measures against unofficial strikes. The White Paper *In Place of Strife* which contained these and other proposals divided the party from top to bottom and was opposed virtually unanimously on the General Council of the TUC. The strife which continued until Barbara Castle was compelled to withdraw her policy document did much to undermine the party's credibility as the voice of consensus and the national interest. In 1970 Labour lost the general election and the Conservatives were able to introduce an Industrial Relations Act designed to achieve much the same reforms as *In Place of Strife*.

Moving Leftwards

As we have seen, much of revisionist thinking was premissed on sustained economic growth. However, when Crosland came to survey the performance of the first two Wilson governments between 1964 and 1970 he was obliged to acknowledge that there was 'very little sign of a coherent, overall, egalitarian, strategy' (Crosland 1974:21). Economic performance had been worse than expected and 'extreme class inequalities remain, poverty is far from eliminated, the economy is in a state of semi-permanent crisis and inflation is rampant' (ibid.:26).

Moreover, the standard rate of income tax had risen from 8 to 20 per cent of the pay of manual workers in the period 1960–70, and Labour had made virtually no progress in the redistribution of income. Crosland retained his faith in the revisionist conception of socialism until his untimely death in the mid-1970s, but by then its Keynesian foundations were so undermined that the Callaghan government had effectively abandoned it altogether.

With this exhaustion of revisionism arising from the inability of British capitalism to achieve rapid economic growth, the intellectual initiative passed to the left, and public ownership proposals came back on to the agenda after 1970. The annual conference of 1973 was dominated by the demand to nationalize the twenty-five largest companies in the country (which produced 50 per cent of output between them) as part of a bid to restructure the British economy. Largely due to the theoretical efforts of Stuart Holland, the left was persuaded that this measure would avoid many of the bureaucratic problems associated with nationalization of whole industries and focus reform at an intermediary or 'meso' level of the economy which, it was argued, is where real power lies in conditions of modern oligopoly and the multinational company — a phenomenon virtually ignored by the revisionists (Holland 1975). *Labour's Programme 1973* argued that:

The experience of Labour Government has made it increasingly evident that even the most comprehensive measures of social and fiscal reform can only succeed in masking the unacceptable and unpleasant face of a capitalist economy and cannot achieve any fundamental changes in the power relationships which dominate our society.

The left was convinced that such fundamental changes would only be brought about by means of sweeping measures of nationalization supported by statutory planning agreements in the private sector and selective import controls. This Alternative Economic Strategy (AES), as it was known, also stressed the need for a greatly enlarged public expenditure, steeply progressive income tax, and the introduction of a wealth tax. Though Wilson personally vetoed the specific proposal to take over the top twenty-five companies (and thereby fuelled demands for constitutional changes in the party designed to make the parliamentary leadership accountable to the membership and annual conference) these ideas informed the manifesto of 1974 which pledged the party to: 'bring about a fundamental and irreversible shift in the balance of power and wealth in favour of working people and their families'.

Since the beginning of the 1970s a growing number of activists in the Labour Party were concerned to democratize the organization. In the 1960s the mass party had suffered from neglect and disillusionment and thousands of members had been lost. When it began to revive again, as it did in the 1970s, the new recruits were typically young white-collar workers with experience of the radical movements which had developed during the previous decade. They brought a commitment to CND, public ownership, and participatory democracy into the local Labour parties, and readily supported the objective of internal constitutional reform which was championed by the Campaign for Labour Party Democracy (CLPD) from 1973. It was an objective which harmonized with the left's revitalized concern to make other centres of irresponsible power — such as the multinational companies — subject to some form of popular control. Even members of the parliamentary left of the Labour Party — notably Tony Benn — wanted democratic reform to extend into the British state itself, though this had been something which the old *Tribune* left had never thought necessary. Certainly as early as 1970 Benn was already looking 'beyond parliamentary democracy' and towards various forms of direct democracy (Benn 1970). In rejecting the technocratic collectivism which he and Wilson had championed in the 1960s, Benn's views chimed in with the enlarged and disparate left outside the Labour Party. The demand for democratic decentralization was prominent in the arguments of feminists, students, environmentalists, the revived nationalist movements in Scotland and Wales, and those active in 'community politics'. The left inside the Labour Party was joined by activists from these 'new social movements' and now contrived to fuse elements of this sort of radicalism with centralizing public ownership proposals.

Although Harold Wilson and James Callaghan did nothing to implement the more radical manifesto commitments of 1974, the leftward trend in the party continued through the 1970s and was reinforced by the sense of betrayal and the continued alienation of many trade unions. These had agreed with the party leaders to abide by a Social Contract by which the unions would moderate wage claims in return for the restoration of the legal immunities abolished by Heath's Industrial Relations Act, together with the implementation of measures designed to improve the social wage. Free collective bargaining survived between 1974 and 1979 under this agreement, but only because the unions observed three successive pay codes. However, this attempt to discipline sectional interests in the name of the larger community interest was not helped by the government's crisis-management of the economy which involved massive cuts in public expenditure and a corresponding inability to substantially promote the interests of the worst off; a fourth pay code foundered in the 'winter of discontent' of 1978–9, largely because of the action of unions representing the low paid (whereas the first pay code, with its flat rate rather than percentage increases, had alienated skilled workers from Labour). These tensions were undoubtedly exacerbated by the deflationary budgets of 1976 and 1977 which the Chancellor, Denis Healey, was obliged to introduce at the behest of the International Monetary Fund. Thus cuts in public expenditure were the price Labour was forced to pay in order to raise a loan, but once again a stagnant economy (accompanied during this period by high inflation) had been allowed to undermine the party's manifesto commitments.

The lugubrious performance of the Labour government between 1974 and 1979 strengthened the argument that revisionism was now dead. By 1978 the Tribune Group of MPs was more than double its original size, with eighty-six members, but it was also more amorphous. Some of its members were now active in the Labour Co-ordinating Committee, which Michael Meacher and Frances Morrell established in 1978 to act as a socialist think-tank. Within a year it had developed an alternative manifesto and detailed policies based on the AES to counterpose to official positions with which James Callaghan fought and lost the 1979 election. The LCC wanted the Labour Party to become a mass campaigning organization and, unlike the old Bevanites, was highly sceptical of the value of purely parliamentary action. It argued that:

> Britain is not as democratic a country as is often assumed. Our society is dominated by the class system: it has a ruling class who run financial and big business enterprises, the civil service, and the media. They have common interests in keeping elected government weak so

that it does not interfere in their financial and industrial operations.
So we must redistribute power as well as wealth and income
(Seyd 1987:93)

This Marxist analysis was also being put by the Militant tendency
and a number of other less conspicuous Trotskyist groups, such as the
Socialist Organizer Alliance, and the Socialist League, which joined the
Labour Party after 1978. The very fact that these groups, no doubt
impressed by the growth of Militant, came into the Labour Party at this
time is testimony to the changed intellectual milieu within the organization which was far more congenial to Marxists than ever before and (since
1973, when the list of proscribed groups was abolished) far less
authoritarian. Thus the organized Marxists did not cause the shift to the
left after 1970, they merely benefited from it.

With the victory of Mrs Thatcher in 1979, the proponents of class
struggle within the Labour Party were strengthened. The real choice
according to Benn was between democratic socialism or the bleak
prospect of monetarism or corporatism. Both monetarism and corporatism
could be shown to have authoritarian implications, while Benn's preferred
alternative — democratic socialism — became associated with a package
of reforms designed to open up the parliamentary Labour Party, government and Parliament to more democratic control and scrutiny.

Michael Foot became leader of the party in November 1980 — a month
after the annual conference had voted for the AES, industrial democracy,
a 35-hour week with no loss of pay, withdrawal from the EEC, cuts
in arms expenditure, abolition of private education and health services,
the introduction of a wealth tax, and a number of other radical measures
including the removal of US military installations from Britain and
unilateral nuclear disarmament. At the same time the party agreed to
introduce regular reselection procedures for MPs and to extend the
franchise for electing the party leadership. In January 1980 a special
Wembley Conference voted to create an electoral college for deciding
the party leadership, and it was after this event that twenty-eight MPs
left the party to become members of a breakaway Social Democratic
Party.

Meanwhile, the new Labour left was emerging as a force in local
government. By 1982 the Greater London Council (GLC), Inner London
Education Authority, six London Boroughs, and the councils of
Merseyside, South Yorkshire, Manchester, Sheffield, Stirling, and
Walsall were under the control of the radicals. Many of these Labour
councillors had served their political apprenticeships in the new social
movements of the 1960s and this was often reflected in their policies,
which gave a new priority to the concerns of feminists, gays, anti-racists,
environmentalists and other radical groups. The new style of politics

also involved staffing council committees with militants drawn from these movements and promoting such groups by means of council grants. Over 1,000 groups received such assistance from the GLC, and in the financial year 1984–5 it dispensed aid worth £47 million. In Liverpool, where Militant was influential, these policies were derided as middle-class distractions from the class struggle. Here power was as centralized as Militant could make it, and council policies focused on the creation of jobs and council houses. Nevertheless, such ideological differences were unobtrusive for as long as these councils seemed to function as centres of resistance to the Thatcher government.

Tensions within the Labour left began to surface between April and October of 1981 when Tony Benn, a very recent convert to the Tribune Group, tried unsuccessfully to become Deputy Leader of the party in a contest with Denis Healey, a stalwart of the right. Foot publicly appealed to Benn not to stand against Healey in the interests of party unity, and other members of the Tribune Group actually voted against the left candidate or abstained. The ideological divisions within the Labour left also led to open conflict when Foot decided to support an inquiry into the entrist activities of Militant, and when he declared that Peter Tatchell, the adopted candidate for Bermondsey, who had spoken of the need for extra-parliamentary struggle, would never be endorsed by the Executive. Another early argument between Benn's supporters and members of the old Tribune Group began in May 1982 when a Bennite, Chris Mullin, became editor of *Tribune* itself and promptly used the journal to attack the conservatism of the old Tribunites.

It would be wrong to suppose that the division between the 'hard' (Bennite) and 'soft' (old Tribunite) lefts was a division between Marxists and their opponents; there was nothing so coherent about the Bennite left. In an attempt to identify 'democratic socialism' Benn was prepared to invoke a most eclectic legacy:

> Its roots are deep in our history and have been nourished by the Bible, the teachings of Christ, the Peasants Revolt, the Levellers, Tom Paine, the Chartists, Robert Owen, the Webbs and Bernard Shaw who were Fabians, and occasionally by Marxists, Liberals, and radicals who have all contributed their analysis to our study of society.
>
> (Benn 1979:146)

The policies of the Bennite left were correspondingly syncretic, reflecting the coalition of ideological positions to be found within it. Alongside the call for democracy and decentralization of power, the left fought for a very large extension of state power over the economy. These statist measures sat in unresolved tension beside the call for 'power to the people', and Benn's advocacy of industrial democracy, shop stewards' initiatives, and workers' co-operatives, as well as his critique of Prime

Ministerial patronage and the irresponsibility of quangos and other non-elected organs of state.

The tensions between the populist and statist elements of the Bennite programme initially helped to maintain the broad Bennite coalition. Benn had helped to refashion Labour's issue-base to accommodate new sources of vitality on the left, and to harness them for the Labour Party. Leftists previously marginal to the party's ideological preoccupations now found their concerns prominent in the Bennite discourse. Enthusiastic advocates of the new emphasis on democracy criticized Labour's old paternalism, even where it was at its most successful (as in the NHS), as destructive of the solidarity and self-activity of the working class:

> The mutual support networks working-class communities previously had to evolve to survive have . . . been undermined by centralisation, by insensitive planning and public housing policies and by an increasingly privatised culture. In this sense 'statism' and 'privatisation' have gone hand in hand with not only social but also political consequences; socialist values of mutual co-operation and mutual aid have been eroded.
>
> (Hain 1983:78)

Champions of participatory grass roots politics such as Peter Hain imagined that a significant degree of extra-parliamentary politics, harnessing the energies of a plethora of radical cause groups demanding a say in community politics, would shift the balance of power in society to the people. But, as we have seen, the new stress on public ownership and extra-parliamentary action also appealed to a number of Trotskyist groups — notably Militant — which also rallied to the Bennite left. Among these vanguard organizations there was little commitment to the pluralism advocated by Hain. Militant, for example, had no sympathy with the priorities of feminists or environmentalists. It backed Benn in so far as he stood for an extension of the state-owned sector of the economy, and mobilized opposition to Labour's social democratic leadership, but insisted that nothing less than the nationalization of 'the top 200 monopolies' would do. It was left to others within the Bennite left to observe that: 'There is no example to point to of a genuinely democratic socialist society in which more than 50 per cent nationalisation actually works' (Hodgson 1981:205).

The assumption that state ownership was some sort of socialist panacea went far beyond the tiny Trotskyist groups, however, and influenced a good deal of opinion within the constituencies. It was one of the reasons why Militant could legitimately claim to be an authentic expression of the Labour tradition (Callaghan 1987). Many elements within the Labour left also rallied to the new emphasis on class-based politics. This could unite the entrist groups with a much broader coalition of interests than anything they had had access to before. Clearly this was an idiom in which Marxist and Trotskyist ideas could exercise more influence than they had been used to in the Labour Party since the 1930s.

The Labour Party fought the 1983 election with *The New Hope For Britain*, a thoroughly Bennite document in which the party restated its commitment to the elements of the AES and the other policies adopted at the 1980 conference and those that followed it. It was not until the party was crushingly defeated on these policies that the latent tensions within the left were translated into fundamental differences of policy orientation. Henceforward the Campaign Group of MPs (formed in December 1982 with twenty-three members) around Benn would seek to maintain the policies of 1983 and the radical alliance which supported them, while former Bennites joined Neil Kinnock (who was elected Leader of the party in October 1983) in the so-called 'soft' left which was persuaded that these policies were responsible for the party's electoral failure and that a new kind of revisionism was required, together with changes in the party's image. The attempt to present the party as a moderate and responsible organization involved the leadership in a campaign against Militant and the policies pursued by the Liverpool council in its opposition to the government's rate-capping tactic. The hard left was weakened by the defeat of the miners's strike in 1985 and the decision to set a legal rate which was taken by all the Labour councils except Liverpool in the same year. By 1986 emphasis on class struggle confrontation was discredited by the results this had obtained in Liverpool and in the coal industry, although the hard left regrouped in that year, on a smaller basis than in 1978-9, to form Labour Left Liaison consisting of the Campaign Group, the CLPD, the Labour Party Black Sections, Socialist Action, Socialist Organizer, Labour CND, the Labour Campaign for Lesbian and Gay Rights, the Labour Committee on Ireland, and the Labour Women's Action Committee.

Just before Labour lost its third consecutive general election in 1987, Kinnock argued that Labour needed 'a shift in attitudes and presentation not a change in principles'; and he went on to describe Labour as the party of efficiency, industry, and patriotism as well as justice, compassion and equality (Kinnock 1986:2). It was to be distinguished from social democracy because:

> The essence of social democracy is that it is not concerned with the structure of property ownership or the transfer of economic power . . . not of eradicating inequality but relieving its most gross manifestations. Always charity never parity.
>
> (Kinnock 1986:9)

But Labour had lost in 1987 with a manifesto — *Britain Will Win* — which had jettisoned the AES and the commitment to withdraw from

45

the EEC, and which had greatly scaled down the pledges made in 1983 to reduce unemployment, increase public expenditure, and fundamentally alter the distribution of power and wealth in Britain. The only major radical policy which remained was the ambition to remove American nuclear missile installations and move Britain towards a non-nuclear defence policy. After the election Labour's defence policy was the issue most frequently cited as the cause of the party's defeat, and within months the previously clear commitments in this area became subjects for equivocation again within the leadership (no doubt in part because of the apparent success of the superpowers to reach agreement on arms reductions by multilateral negotiations). Within months of the 1987 election the party was involved in a wide-ranging policy review process, the first phase of which produced the documents *Statement of Democratic Socialist Aims and Values* and *Social Justice and Economic Efficiency*.

Here the party restated its conviction in the relevance of a positive conception of freedom where rights have meaning because people have the economic and political strength to exercise them. While these documents show the interdependence, in this view, between national efficiency and individual fulfilment, as well as the needs of groups with specific injustices to overcome, the central problem which emerges concerns the precise role of the British state in this enterprise.

Labour now rejects something which it refers to as 'the intrusive state' in favour of an 'enabling state'. But it is a state, to judge by these documents, which will have all the old problems to contend with — many of them reminiscent of Wilson's project of modernization from the early 1960s — in a context where socialist programmes which are purely national are severely constrained by the more integrated global economy of the present, and where old forms of state intervention command less popular support and intellectual credibility. Nevertheless, Labour believes that its policies 'clearly require a greater sector of the economy to be socially owned', though it repudiates the 'Morrisonian form' of public ownership because of deficiencies in respect of consumer interests and workforce participation, and now acknowledges a central role for the market. The party still wants to achieve equality and to 'banish want and poverty from Britain' but is now more receptive to political reforms designed to pass power 'outwards and downwards'. The key issue is how this project can be achieved in an economy increasingly susceptible to decisions taken beyond its shores, and in a party where ideological coherence is notoriously difficult to achieve.

Further Reading

Useful collections of British socialist thought can be found in:

H. Pelling, *The Challenge of Socialism*, London: Black, 1954, and
A. Wright, *British Socialism*, London: Longman, 1983. The latter
contains a long introductory essay that is well worth reading. There are
many histories of the Labour Party. Critical accounts can be found in
R. Miliband, *Parliamentary Socialism*, London: Merlin, 1973, and
D. Howell, *British Social Democracy*, London: Croom Helm, 1976.
Revisionism is the subject of A. Warde, *Consensus and Beyond*,
Manchester University Press, 1982, and S. Haseler, *The Gaitskellites*,
London: Macmillan, 1969. Interesting accounts of the internal politics
of the Labour Party can be found in M. Jenkins, *Bevanism: Labour's
High Tide*, Nottingham: Spokesman, 1979, L. Minkin, *The Labour Party
Conference*, London: Allen Lane, 1978, and H. Wainwright, *Labour:
A Tale of Two Parties*, London: Hogarth Press, 1987. The history of
ideological controversy in the Labour Party is covered in G. Foote, *The
Labour Party's Political Thought*, London: Croom Helm, 1985. Some
of the more recent debates about the future of socialism can be found
in B. Pimlott (ed.) *Fabian Essays in Socialist Thought*, London:
Heinemann, 1984, B. Gould, *Socialism and Freedom*, London: Mac-
millan, 1985, R. Hattersley, *Choose Freedom: the Future for Democratic
Socialism*, London: Michael Joseph, 1987, and R. Plant, *Equality,
Markets, and the State*, Fabian Tract 494, 1984.

Bibliography (place of publication London unless otherwise stated)

Addison, P. (1977) *The Road to 1945*, Quartet.
Attlee, C. (1937) *The Labour Party in Perspective*, Gollancz.
Benn, T. (1970) *The New Politics: A Socialist Reconnaissance*, Fabian
    Tract 402.
Benn, T. (1979) *Arguments For Socialism*, Cape.
Benn, T. (1982) *Parliament, People, and Power*, New Left Books.
Bevan, A. (1952) *In Place of Fear*, Quartet.
Bullock, A. (1960) *Ernest Bevin Vol. 1: Trade Union Leader*, Oxford
    University Press.
Calder, A. (1965) *The People's War*, Cape.
Callaghan, J. (1987) *The Far Left in British Politics*, Blackwell.
Cole, G.D.H. (1920) *Guild Socialism Restated*, London.
Cole, G.D.H. (1948) *History of the Labour Party since 1914*, Routledge &
    Kegan Paul.
Cole, G.D.H. (1950) *Socialist Economics*, Gollancz.
Crick, B. (1984) *Socialist Values and Time*, Fabian Tract 495.
Crosland, C.A.R. (1952) 'The transition from capitalism', in R.H.S.
    Crossman (ed.) *New Fabian Essays*, Turnstile Press.
Crosland, C.A.R. (1956a) 'About equality (1)', *Encounter*, July.
Crosland, C.A.R. (1956b) 'About equality (2)', *Encounter*, August.
Crosland, C.A.R. (1956c) 'About equality (3)', *Encounter*, September.
Crosland, C.A.R. (1974) *Socialism Now*, Cape.

Crossman, R.H.S. (1952) 'Towards a philosophy of socialism', *New Fabian Essays*, Turnstile Press.

Crossman, R.H.S. (1956) *Socialism, and the New Despotism*, Fabian Tract 298.

Crossman, R.H.S., Foot, M., and Mikardo, I., (1947) *Keep Left*, New Statesman.

Fieldhouse, D.K. (1984) 'The Labour Governments and the Empire-Commonwealth', in R. Ovendale (ed.) *The Foreign Policy of the British Labour Governments 1945-51*, Leicester, Leicester University Press.

Gaitskell, H. (1955) 'The ideological development of democratic socialism in Great Britain', *Socialist International Information* 5, 52-3:24.

Gaitskell, H. 1956) *Socialism and Nationalisation*, Fabian Tract 300.

Gyford, J. (1985) *The Politics of Local Socialism*, Allen & Unwin.

Hain, P. (1983) *The Democratic Alternative*, Harmondsworth: Penguin Books.

Hodgson, G. (1981) *Labour at the Crossroads*, Martin Robertson.

Holland, S. (1975) *The Socialist Challenge*, Quartet.

Howell, D. (1976) *British Social Democracy*, Croom Helm.

Kinnock, N. (1986) *The Future of Socialism*, Fabian Tract 509.

Koestler, A. (1945) *The Yogi and the Commissar*, Cape.

Labour Party (1988) *Social Justice and Economic Efficiency*, Labour Party.

Laski, H. (1919) *Authority in the Modern State*, Yale University Press.

MacDonald, R. (1911) *The Socialist Movement*, Williams & Norgate.

MacIntyre, S. (1980) *A Proletarian Science: Marxism in Britain 1917-33*, Cambridge University Press.

Mikardo, I. (1952) 'Trade unions in a full employment economy', in R.H.S. Crossman (ed.) *New Fabian Essays*, Turnstile Press.

Minkin, L. 1978) *The Labour Party Conference*, Allen Lane.

Morgan, K.O. (1984) *Labour in Power 1945-1951*, Oxford University Press

Pelling, H. (1954) *The Challenge of Socialism*, Black.

Saville, J. (1975) 'The ideology of Labourism' in R. Benewick, *et al.*, *Knowledge and Belief in Politics*, Allen & Unwin.

Seyd, P. (1987) *The Rise and Fall of the Labour Left*, Macmillan.

Smith, T. (1976) *The Politics of the Corporate Economy*, Martin Robertson.

Strachey, J. (1935) *The Coming Struggle for Power*, New York: The Modern Library.

Tawney, R.H. (1921) *The Acquisitive Society*, Brighton: Wheatsheaf, 1982.

Tawney, R.H. (1952) 'British socialism today', *Socialist Commentary*, June.

Tawney, R.H. (1981) 'The choice before the Labour Party', in *The Attack and Other Papers*, Nottingham: Spokesman.

Webb, S. (1889) 'Socialism historic', in *Fabian Essays*, London.

Webb, S. (1890) *Socialism in England*, London.

Williams, P. (1982) *Hugh Gaitskell*, Oxford University Press.

Wilson, H. (1964) *The Relevance of British Socialism*, Weidenfeld & Nicholson.

Wright, A. (1987) *R.H. Tawney*, Manchester: Manchester University Press.

Chapter three

The Right: The Conservative Party and Conservatism

Martin Durham

The Nature of Conservatism

With the collapse of the post-war consensus and the rise of the New Right, interest in conservatism as a political ideology has grown. In particular, the nature of Thatcherism and its relationship to previous forms of conservatism have become a matter of sharp debate. In this chapter I shall be examining the development of conservatism in recent years as a contribution to a larger understanding of the role of ideology in British politics. Some writers have taken the view that there is no set of core concepts within conservatism. Thus, for one writer, the suggestion that conservatism rests on a conception of unchanging human nature or of British character founders on the impossibility of such notions. Classical Toryism, it is claimed, could at least plausibly assert that society did not change. But this is impossible for modern conservatism, fated to exist in a continuously changing industrial society. Rather than resting on a coherent philosophy, then on this view conservatism is concerned essentially with securing continued political dominance (Harris 1972:262–3). A similar view is contained in the argument, drawn from the Conservative political philosopher Michael Oakeshott, that conservatism should not be studied as a body of ideas but as a set of beliefs about governing (Gamble 1974:1–2).

Contrary to such interpretations, it has been argued that at least modern conservatism rests on a particular concept of human nature (Barker 1981:30–2). Yet this argument does not go far enough. Modern conservatism, as will be seen, may well have a claim to being more overt in its usage of ideological themes and more concerned with ideological disputation than earlier forms of conservatism. However, I want to suggest that conservatism as such is ideological and organized around a number of crucial concepts. What makes it conservatism is its core concepts; what makes for different kinds of conservatism is how these concepts are combined and with what other concepts they are interrelated.

There have been a number of efforts to define what is meant by conservatism. Two recent examples are illustrative. One view argues that conservatism rests on a conviction that humans are morally and, more importantly, intellectually defective. As a result of their proneness to evil they need government; because of their propensity to error they need guidance from the collective wisdom of the community. It is this latter belief which is said to be specific to conservatism and from which three principles flow. First, Conservatives are traditionalists; they revere established customs and institutions and oppose radical change. Second, they hold an organic view of society, in which humans are not merely individuals but are part of a rooted order. Finally, Conservatives are political sceptics, believing that society is too complex to be understood by abstract theory (Quinton 1978:13–17).

Similarly, it has been suggested that conservatism is essentially 'the defence of a limited style of politics, based upon the idea of imperfection'. The radicalism that conservatism came into existence to combat believed that political action could fundamentally transform the human condition. Burke and later Conservatives, by contrast, hold that the world imposes limits upon what can be achieved without destroying the basis of society. For one school of conservatism, the impossibility of drastically changing the human condition comes from the conception that the world is organized on a divine plan in which men are sometimes tempted to defy their rightful place. Although this notion occasionally surfaces in modern Conservative thought, a more important source of Conservative doubt about radicalism, particularly in Britain, comes from a profound scepticism as to what politics can achieve and a sense of trepidation concerning the difficulty of sustaining individual liberty. According to Conservatives, in pursuing the impossible dream of human perfectability and trying to tear society up by the roots in the process, radicals are ignoring the inherited wisdom of generations and the clear evidence that society can only answer human needs if it does not descend into chaos (O'Sullivan 1976:5, 9–27).

Thus conservatism is concerned with human fallibility and the need to rely on tradition. Even for Oakeshott, despite his claim that conservatism is merely a disposition, it is concerned with a defence of continuity and a rejection of abstract rationalism (Oakeshott 1962:5, 169–70). But are such views to be found within the writings of Conservative politicians, as distinct from academics? Compared with socialism or liberalism, conservatism is a relatively unreflective doctrine and Conservatives often congratulate themselves because they take their beliefs to be an expression of 'common sense' as against others' rootless abstractions. But at particular points in time, especially of danger, Conservatives have felt the need to restate their basic principles in order to renew their party and its values. One such moment, discussed shortly, was in the aftermath of the party's electoral defeat in 1945. By examining an important text from this period, we can begin to see to what degree academic portrayals of conservatism match those offered by Conservatives themselves.

For the Tory MP Quintin Hogg, writing in the wake of 1945, 'the signs and symbols which have guided the lives of men for centuries' had suddenly become 'unreliable and obscure'. Truth was lost in general darkness and in such obscurity false ideas flourished and charlatans multiplied. 'In these mad times', he wrote, 'Conservatives needed to challenge falsehood and restate what politics could and could not do' (Hogg 1947:7–12).

Society, he argues, should be seen, not as a machine, but as an organism, and as such it could not be changed at will. Conservatism did not deny change for, as Burke had observed, a state that could not change could not survive. But Conservatives argue that 'a living society can only change healthily when it changes naturally — that is, in accordance with its acquired and inherited character, and at a given rate'. There most certainly had been revolutions but they had led to tyranny, and the lessons that Conservatives drew from this were, first, that reform is a guarantee against revolution and, second, that 'the happy history of our country' since the English Revolution derived from the adoption of a constitutional framework 'sanctified by traditional authority and institutions' (Hogg 1947:24–7). At the core of conservatism is patriotism. Where socialists derive their inspiration from the injustices that have existed since time immemorial:

> Conservativism begins from the opposite end . . . the underlying unity of all classes of Englishmen, their ultimate identity of interest, their profound similarity of outlook, the common dangers and difficulties they have shared in the past, and with which they are still faced, and the necessity for unity as the true means of meeting them together. This does not mean that Conservatives are insensitive of the differences and injustices upon which Socialists love to dwell. It simply means that Conservatives consider superficial an analysis of politics which treats these differences as ultimate, or of the same importance as the unity of the nation. The nation, not the so-called class struggle is therefore at the base of Conservative political thinking.
>
> (Hogg 1947:31–2)

Hogg's account of conservatism upholds both authority and liberty. Authority, he proclaims, is central to a Conservative. Civilization is sustained and barbarism warded off by the establishment of government, and Conservatives accept established authority as a virtue in itself. But liberty is also central to a Conservative, it is argued, and can be reconciled with authority, for only under the rule of law and a settled government can liberty be enjoyed (Hogg 1947:44–7, 68).

In his discussion Hogg makes it clear that the contentions alluded to earlier — humanity's imperfection and the need for tradition — are crucial for Conservatives. Each generation, he states, should not start from scratch but, instead, should begin where their forebears left off. In relying on a country's collective wisdom, Hogg is at pains to warn of the fate that may otherwise await it. He writes:

> The Conservative does not believe that the power of politics to put things right in this world is unlimited. This is partly because there are inherent limitations on what may be achieved by political means, but partly because man is an imperfect creature with a streak of evil as well as good in his inmost nature.

> (Hogg 1947:11)

Needing to restate British conservatism in a period of crisis, Hogg sets down a doctrine which is recognizably that outlined by the scholarly accounts referred to earlier. As we examine the development of conservatism, we can explore the mutations it has undergone as the conditions of British politics have shifted.

The Conservative Tradition

However, in order to understand the conservatism of the last forty years, it is necessary briefly to set it in a larger context. As its adherents are more than willing to remind us, modern conservatism is the inheritor of a long tradition. The term itself only entered British politics in the early 1830s, but the tradition's origins can be traced to the writings of Edmund Burke some forty years earlier (although, it should be noted, some writers view earlier figures, such as Viscount Bolingbroke in the early eighteenth century, as anticipating Conservative arguments). Although a Whig rather than a Tory, in juxtaposing to the idealism of the French Revolution an organic society that changes only gradually, and in ways consonant with its nature and the nature of its human material, Burke laid down the founding tenets of British conservatism. As with some forms of conservatism on the Continent, there was a risk that such a view would prove unable to adjust to the new tensions of nineteenth-century society and could have become mere reaction, the doomed protest of countryside against city. Two figures were crucial in ensuring that this did not occur. By his response to the 1832 Reform Act, Sir Robert Peel broke with more intransigent elements in the party and acknowledged the claims of social forces that might have been lost to conservatism. In his Tamworth Manifesto (1834) Peel made clear the Conservative acceptance of reforms if they involved, not a 'perpetual vortex of agitation' and the adoption of 'every popular impression of the day', but instead entailed 'a careful review of institutions' and 'the redress of real grievances' while continuing 'respect for ancient rights' and for authority (O'Gorman 1986:134). The party subsequently split over the famous (or infamous) Corn Laws, and leading Peelites passed over to Liberalism. But it was the most forceful figure of those opposed to Peel who nevertheless was to restore the party's ability to adjust to change and renew its electoral appeal. In his celebrated 1872 Crystal Palace speech, Benjamin Disraeli set down the 'three great objects' of the party. The first was the maintenance of national institutions; the second was the upholding of the Empire; while the third was 'the elevation of the condition of the people'. Tories, he argued, had introduced the Factory Laws and favoured reforms of working conditions and of housing, whereas Liberals had opposed state intervention (O'Gorman 1986:150–1, 154).

'Conservatism in the late Victorian era', it has been observed, 'was an ideological response to the steady march of democracy' (O'Gorman 1986:36) and where Lord Salisbury, the party's leader from 1885 to 1902 and Prime Minister for much of that time, emphasized the dangers that democracy posed to property, his *bête noire*, Lord Randolph Churchill, sought to claim Disraeli's heritage and urged the party to reach out for popular support and incorporate it within a 'Tory Democracy'. If Churchill ultimately achieved little, and Salisbury's contribution to conservatism was arguably more to its electoral achievement than to its ideological development, the most important figure in conservatism in the late nineteenth and early twentieth century came from outside the party and came closer to destroying the party than to reshaping it. Following his break with the Liberal Party over Irish Home Rule, Joseph Chamberlain's battle to win the Conservative Party to Tariff Reform was unable to defeat inner-party resistance or persuade working-class voters that it did not represent a threat to their living standards. Addressing issues that would constantly recur for later Conservatives, Chamberlain drew attention to the threat posed to British pre-eminence by the rise of German and American competition but was unable to reverse it.

Unable to fend off economic decline, the party did prove itself capable of adjusting to immense changes in the political landscape. Rather than being crippled by the rise of Labour, the extension of the franchise and the loss of Ireland, conservatism instead was able to dominate politics from the early 1920s for the next twenty years, and, as Schwarz has shown, underneath the deceptive banality of his bucolic imagery, the Conservative leader, Stanley Baldwin, was remarkably successful in renewing conservatism's ideological appeal (Schwarz 1984).

But, without denying the importance of other figures, it is the three we first focused upon — Burke, Peel, and Disraeli — who are the most important for Conservative ideology. When we consider them we encounter themes which frequently recur in post-1945 conservatism. Burke, with his belief in an ordered and rooted communiuty, is often invoked by Conservatives of different persuasions. Peel's Tamworth Manifesto, an adaptation to change that some might well prefer not to have occurred, is a potent image for modern Conservatives faced with comparable developments in their own time. Finally, Disraeli, with his emphasis on Tory reform, is a key figure in the so-called 'progressive' or 'one-nation' Tory tradition, which passes through Randolph Churchill in the 1880s, to Harold Macmillan and his 'Middle Way' in the 1930s, and on into the post-war period.

This reference to Macmillan leads us naturally to the period immediately before the Second World War. Inter-war Conservative governments have been presented as 'do nothing' administrations, content to allow the market to go its own way and let mass unemployment disfigure the country. Closer examination shows a more complicated picture. Free trade, cuts in government expenditure, and hostility to state controls were the product of an individualistic stance championed by the Conservative Party. Yet the government in the 1930s also promoted structural changes in the economy, adopted protectionist measures, and regulated prices. For Macmillan, on the left of the party, the government was doing too little and what was needed was a thoroughly regulated capitalism, in which private enterprise coexisted with a major extension of state responsibility for industry and basic necessities. It cannot really be claimed that his argument was the 'decisive intellectual inspiration' in 1930s conservatism (O'Gorman 1986: 44–6, 190–1). The government's move in the direction of collectivism was half-hearted, obscured by anti-statist rhetoric, and as such generally deplored by Macmillan rather than motivated by him. But when the long-threatened war actually came and Conservatives moved more overtly towards utilizing the powers of the state, there were major aspects of inter-war conservatism from which Tory thinkers could claim continuity.

The Reshaping of Conservatism

War, as might be expected, turned government in an increasingly collectivist direction. The need to mobilize all the nation's resources was paramount, and planning was much in favour. In addition, the dominant forces in the wartime coalition were committed to a programme of social reform involving, most importantly, full employment, social security, family allowances, education and a National Health Service. The forces responsible for this programme were threefold in character. The Labour Party was crucial, while the two most important figures of wartime economic and social reform — Keynes and Beveridge — were Liberals. However, given the balance of forces in the coalition, significant

Conservative opposition could have derailed serious possibilities of social reform. What was crucial — and the third significant element in the reform programme — was that sections of the Conservative Party amenable to reform were in a position to speak and act in its name. Of particular importance was the party's Post-War Problems Committee, chaired by R.A. Butler, although an even more striking sign of Conservative sympathy for reconstruction was to be seen in the creation of the Tory Reform Commmittee in 1943.

Formed by thirty-six MPs, the committee included Quintin Hogg, Peter Thorneycroft and Lord Hinchingbrooke, the latter being particularly vociferous in arguing that during the inter-war period the country and the party had been seriously damaged by '"individualist" businessmen, financiers and speculators'. For 'the Progressive Right', he proclaimed, the grip of big business had to be broken, and planning and social purpose displace 'the old ways of laissez-faire' (Gamble 1974:34; Greenleaf 1983:255-6). There was resistance within the party, with MPs on the right forming a rival grouping, the Progress Trust, and Hinchingbrooke's language was surprisingly extravagant in its denunciation of business and pre-war conservatism. Hogg's arguments, however, were to be of more lasting importance. If we looked to the past, he argued, we could see how Disraeli had reacted to a similar situation, where the emergence of a new society had found conservatism wanting. The party had faced annihilation but Disraeli had realized that if it played a leading role in reform rather than opposing it, then it could become 'the effective instrument for applying a new political philosophy and developing a new conception of the mission of the British peoples' (Hogg 1944:42-3). It would be Butler (and Macmillan) rather than the Tory Reformers who would be central to the revitalization of conservatism after the war. But through Hogg's involvement in post-war policy-making, and his authorship of *The Case for Conservatism*, the heritage of the wartime Tory Reformers continued as one of the tributaries of the New Conservatism that emerged strongly after the party's 1945 defeat.

As Butler notes in his memoirs: 'The overwhelming electoral defeat of 1945 shook the Conservative Party out of its lethargy and impelled it to re-think its philosophy and re-form its ranks with a thoroughness unmatched for a century' (Butler 1971:126). Churchill had not wanted to draw up detailed policies in the aftermath of the defeat but for Hogg what was needed was a new Tamworth Manifesto. Butler concurred, believing that, as in Peel's time, the party had to adjust its policies to fundamental social change. Early in 1946, at the party's political education conference, Butler urged the elaboration of an alternative to Labour's policy, an alternative which would include the rejection of *laissez-faire* in favour of a society in which the state would be seen as trustee for the community (Butler 1971:133-4).

To press such a view on the party necessitated outmanoeuvring the Tory right with its accusations of 'pink socialism', but for Butler such a change was not a rupture with Toryism but its continuation. He later declared;

I had derived from Bolingbroke an assurance that the majesty of the State might be used in the interests of the many, from Burke a belief in seeking patterns of improvement by balancing diverse interests, and from Disraeli an insistence that the two nations must be one.
(Butler 1971:134)

The 1946 party conference demanded that policy be reformulated, and Butler, Macmillan, and others were appointed to an Industrial Policy Committee. A 'great deal of the intellectual background' of the celebrated *Industrial Charter* that resulted derived from Macmillan (Butler 1971:144). What the Charter did was establish that, while still favouring free enterprise, a modernized conservatism also accepted 'central direction' of the economy. The Charter pledged support for a full employment policy, accepted the nationalization of coal, rail, and the Bank of England, and called for the humanization of industrial relations. On closer examination it was not as radical as it first appeared — road transport was to be denationalized, the humanization of industry was more wishful thinking than a commitment to legislation (Hoffman 1964:149–51). For the Tory right, though, it went too far.

Despite the fury of Tory diehards and the *Daily Express*, the Charter overwhelmingly passed the 1947 party conference (in Macmillan's view, while Whigs and Liberals within the party opposed the Charter, 'the true Tories accepted it with growing enthusiasm' [O'Gorman 1986:204]). When the party produced its policy statement *The Right Road for Britain* in the run up to the 1950 election, it incorporated the Charter's proposals although in a more muted form, for as the 1940s came towards their end and discontent with Labour controls grew, so economic liberalism enjoyed a resurgence in the party. The virtues of free enterprise were espoused with greater confidence, and slogans such as 'Set the People Free' were used to good effect. Yet while 1947 was a high-water mark for Tory collectivism, and the tide fell back somewhat, it had effectively conquered the party. As Butler wrote in 1950, conservatism now had to be based on 'the acceptance by authority of the responsibility for ensuring a certain standard of living, of employment, and of security for all' (CPC 1950:3).

Pragmatism in Power

While the party had renewed its ideological appeal, the thirteen years of office that followed its 1951 victory owed much to economic good fortune. The austerity and controls associated with Labour were succeeded by a period of rising living standards and social mobility. Conservatism lost its association with the economic failure of the 1930s and acquired an identification with the 'affluent society' of the 1950s. Macmillan's famous (and often misquoted) comment that 'most of our people have never had it so good' summed up the confidence of the party during a period in which it defeated Labour in three successive elections. 'The great thing', Macmillan wrote in his diary, 'is to keep the Tory party on *modern* and *progressive* lines' (Gamble 1974:66). The Labour Party meanwhile was depicted as the old-fashioned party, trapped in the nineteenth century. While Labour fell to blows over Clause Four, Conservatives prided themselves on being the successful pragmatists, ostensibly free of ideology.

However, there were strains in the Conservative ranks. The increasing withdrawal from Empire generated widespread resentment from within a party which from Disraeli onwards had so emphasized the importance of colonial possessions. More significantly for the future development of the right, the revival of economic liberalism in the late 1940s sat uncomfortably with the reality of economic management by the 'progressive Tory' leadership, and rumblings were to be heard at party conference and in party periodicals over the tax rate, the level of spending, and the 'appeasement' of the unions by Conservative Ministers of Labour unwilling to disturb the industrial peace. If on the right of the party the forces of dissent were still weak, among the progressive wing there was questioning about the direction the government was taking. For the Bow Group, the progressives' 'think-tank', conservatism had not gone far enough down the road to modernity and when, in the early 1960s, the balance of payments crisis, pay restrictions, and concern about the rate of growth damaged the government's credibility, Bow Groupers urged a move in the direction of planning, pointing to France as a success story. The government did make moves in this direction but, troubled by divisions and refused entry into the Common Market, it became associated with a general loss of economic direction and went down to defeat to a Labour Party now pledged to technological revolution and the revival of economic growth.

As with the mid-1940s and the mid-1970s, so Conservative defeat in 1964 pressed the party to reconsider how to win popular support. The fact that in 1965, for the first time, the party leader was elected is an indicator of party discontent and Edward Heath's victory was intended as a clear sign that a conservatism which spoke the language of modernization needed a recognizably modern leader at its head. For Heath, the core of party policy was to create an economy that would be thoroughly competitive. By encouraging productivity agreements, reforming trade union legislation, and pressing to join the Common

Market, Britain could be made a modern economy. Alongside this, Heath envisaged restraining state expenditure and pursuing a more selective policy on social welfare. How is this programme to be seen? It has been suggested that Heath's approach was still that of the progressive right, but at a time when such an approach was becoming politically exhausted. Because Heath had no answer to the problem of how to make the policies he favoured genuinely popular, there was an ideological vacuum — one that more right-wing elements were keen to fill. While they could not displace Heath as Leader, they were successful in shifting the party to the right (Gamble 1974:91–2).

Some of this shift came from within the progressive right, from elements who believed that the conservatism of the 1950s had bent too far in the direction of the trade unions. However, in its approach to the 1970 election, Tory policy also showed the impact of what was becoming known as the New Right, a diverse bloc ranging from those discontented with what they saw as the bloodless and technocratic approach of the party hierarchy, to groups such as the Monday Club which objected to the leadership's policies both at home and abroad, and believed that post-war conservatism had succumbed to 'creeping socialism' and stripped the country of its 'monetary, military and moral defences' (Gamble 1974:107). For much of the New Right a potential alternative leader, capable of renewing the party's ideological appeal, had already emerged in the form of Enoch Powell.

The Challenge of Powellism

Two quotations from Powell give us clues to the nature of what became known as Powellism. The Tory Party, he argued at one point, is 'the nationalist party par excellence' (Wood 1972:168). Elsewhere, he declared that whatever else the party stood for, it had no role to play unless it was 'the party of capitalism' (Powell 1969:18). As with Thatcherism later, Powellism combined these two concerns for national identity and economic liberty. Unlike Thatcherism, however, Powellism as a popular ideology foregrounded the former and made little headway with its defence of economic individualism.

Powell's nationalism focused above all, on race. Speaking in Walsall in February 1968, he had used the image of a white girl alone in a class of immigrants to evoke a sense of helplessness in the face of immigration. But it was his speech in Birmingham in April of that year ('Powell's Bombshell', as one paper called it) which brought to the surface antagonisms long excluded from mainstream politics. One of his constituents, he declared, had told him that if he had the money he would leave Britain because in 15 to 20 years the black man would have the whiphand over the white. Continued immigration, Powell claimed, was reducing the indigenous population to the status of 'strangers in their own country' (Powell 1969:281–2, 286, 290). He was immediately sacked from the Shadow Cabinet, while polls showed extensive popular support for his views. Attacked in the media, Powell's level of support subsequently fell but remained strong, and the Heath leadership took a more restrictionist stance on immigration than it might otherwise have done.

While Powell returned to his anti-immigration views on a number of occasions, his 1968 speeches were crucial in establishing Powellism as a popular force. But while race was the cutting edge of his appeal, it needs to be seen in the context of his overall concern with national identity. In one of his most important speeches, made in the early 1960s, he argued that the life of nations is lived largely in the imagination. Within the nation nothing is more important than the picture of its own nature, its past and its future. The matter of this imagining, he went on, is largely historical, and the stateman's task is to offer the people what he called good myths and save them from harmful ones (Powell 1969:324–5). As commentators have suggested, Powell's belief that, with the passing of Empire, England needed to find a new identity, led him to find it in a defence of Englishness against what he saw as its disruption and dilution by the significant influx of immigration. (It was this concern with national identity that was to lead him to campaign against entering the Common Market and, ultimately, took him out of mainstream politics into the political quicksands of Ulster Unionism.)

If Powell's support was based on racial tensions and — more broadly — on a yearning for national identity, Powellism as an ideology was more ambitious. Powell made efforts to connect his argument with an overall notion of the people, threatened by an all-powerful enemy, most notably in his June 1970 speech in Northfield, Birmingham. Students were destroying universities and terrorizing cities, he declared, mob demonstrations were making governments tremble, disorder was undermining government in Ulster, the race problem was being inflamed with deliberate intent, and the recent campaign against the South African cricket tour, he said, gave many a glimpse of the enemy within (Wood 1970:104–12).

Powellism was also centrally concerned with economics. There comes a time in the life of a party, Powell argued in 1964, when it has to say what it stands for, and such a moment had arrived for the Conservatives. This meant above all making clear its support for capitalism. In part this was because of its material achievements. More importantly, though, it was because capitalism was a good society. Where people were economically free they were free in other areas. State socialism, by contrast, was incompatible with freedom and Conservatives, therefore, championed capitalism, both as a means of generating wealth and as a free way of life (Wood 1965:25–6). The Conservative, he stated elsewhere, 'in principle denies, in practice minimises, Government intervention' in the economy (Phillips 1977:107). Yet while he argued neo-liberal views over a long period, Powell never succeeded in making them as popular, as central to what we mean by Powellism, as he was to do with race.

The Failure of the Heath Government

Under pressure from Powell and the strengthening New Right, the 1970 election campaign took a strongly rightist tinge. The Shadow Cabinet's deliberations at the Selsdon Park Hotel in February 1970 achieved a great deal of publicity for its law and order and trade union proposals. Shortly after, Lord Hailsham (formerly Quintin Hogg), striking a note which would recur in Conservative polemic, attacked Labour for presiding over a massive crime wave: 'the permissive and lawless society', he argued, was 'a by-product of Socialism' (Hall, *et al.* 1978:275). Significantly, there is evidence that support for Powell was crucial for Tory victory, particularly in the Midlands and the North, but, despite its stance on immigration, the Conservative leadership did not focus on race. Instead, at the core of the Heath strategy was the belief that the only way out of economic stagnation was through a break with interventionism and the unleashing of entrepreneurial energies. If talk of shedding state responsibilities and strengthening market forces was welcomed on the right, it was regarded with abhorrence by political opponents. For Harold Wilson, 'the new Toryism is a return to the old Toryism, not just pre-1964 but pre-Macmillan, pre-Butler' (Wood 1970:78). Yet the experience of the Heath government was not to be the sustained break with the post-war consensus it initially appeared. Instead, battered by the economic winds and harried by the unions, the government went down to defeat in 1974 and Heath's leadership lasted little longer.

It came to an end for three reasons. Heath was certainly unpopular because of his leadership style, but he was also criticized heavily on policy grounds, and for the party's electoral fate under his leadership. He had been elected on a manifesto which announced 'We utterly reject the philosophy of compulsory wage control'; but under the pressure of events the government carried out a complete U-turn and pursued just such a statutory policy. The government had come to power committed to market forces. Companies that failed because of inefficiency, it was promised, would not be bailed out. However, when faced with such a situation, the Heath government nationalized Rolls Royce, bailed out the Upper Clyde shipyards, and passed the 1972 Industry Act that empowered it to pursue extensive state intervention. For many Conservatives, Heath had betrayed the policies that he had been pledged to implement — relapsing into collectivism rather than retaining the determination to push back the boundaries of the state. Led by Heath, the party had lost not one, but two general elections in 1974. Under pressure, he agreed that the leader should face annual election. The election was destined to be an important moment in the ideological development of the party.

The Rise of Thatcherism

The initial candidate favoured by inner-party critics was Sir Keith Joseph. A collection of essays he published in 1975 makes clear how deep his disagreements went. Significantly entitled *Reversing the Trend*, it argued that the levels of state intervention, taxation, welfare and public spending since the war had resulted in economic decay. 'It was only in April 1974', he wrote, 'that I was converted to Conservatism. I had thought I was a Conservative but I now see that I was not really one at all' (Joseph 1975:4). But some doubted his ability to lead the party, and his credibility was fundamentally questioned by a speech he made in Birmingham in October 1974. The family and civilized values, he declared, the foundation on which the nation was built, were being undermined. Socialism was taking responsibility away from families, divesting parents of their duty to provide. People had become irresponsible and, as a result, while living standards had risen, crime was on the increase, illiteracy was rife, and educational standards were in decline. All of this was part of the New Right's critique of post-war Britain and a growing current in Conservative ideology, drawing together in one argument anxieties over law and order, the criticisms of schooling associated with the 'Black papers' of the time, and the fears over the family and the home expressed by such campaigners as Mary Whitehouse, praised by Joseph in his speech. However, he went on to allude to the birth-rate among poorer families and parents of low intelligence, arguing that this was a threat to 'the balance of our human stock' (Joseph, 1974). The uproar that followed resulted in his withdrawing his candicacy and the standard of the New Right passed to Margaret Thatcher. She represented a new departure for a twice-defeated party, appealing beyond those MPs convinced of the New Right's arguments. On 11 February 1975 she became the new leader.

In the subsequent rise of Thatcherism the need is to set it against the background of the emergence of middle-class movements in the mid-1970s, protesting against Heath's 'betrayal' and the power of the unions. Numerous organizations sprang up — the National Federation of the Self-Employed, the Middle Class Association, the National Association for Freedom, and others — with their talk of overbearing trade union commissars, Labour going Leninist, and inflation destroying the middle-class backbone of the country.

Much of this ferment was only of transient importance, although significant for an understanding of the period. More important were two other organizations, one set up in 1974, the other dating back to the 1950s. The Centre for Policy Studies, set up after the collapse of the Heath government, saw its project as attaining a 'fuller understanding of the methods available' to improve British society 'with particular attention to social market policies', as economic liberalism was now known. Its founders, significantly, were Sir Keith Joseph and Margaret Thatcher (Behrens 1980:25). The older organization, the Institute of Economic Affairs, had spent a long time in the wilderness defending a seemingly vanquished doctrine of unleashing market forces and rolling back the state. However, in a time of raging inflation, Conservative government failure and the crisis of Keynesianism, the IEA's indictment of collectivism became increasingly attractive among Conservatives and others critical of the state of Britain (and the British state) in the 1970s. Much of the work of popularizing the New Right's ideas was carried out by politicians and political commentators writing in the columns of a wide range of publications, from *The Times*, the *Financial Times*, and the *Economist*, to the *Daily Mail*, the *Express* and the *Sun*. Also symptomatic of the time were books warning of the 'collapse of democracy', describing social democracy as 'the experiment that doesn't work' and urging a fight in 'defence of freedom' (Moss 1975; Tyrrell 1977; Watkins 1978). Of this array of tomes one of the most striking was the Tory MP Patrick Cormack's collection, *Right Turn: Eight Men Who Changed Their Minds*. The book opened:

> The authors of these essays have turned right because they believe there is a real risk that our society will be the sort of materially, intellectually and spiritually impoverished tyranny that so many millions suffer under . . . in Eastern Europe, if the Labour Party prevails at the polls.
>
> (Cormack 1978:ix)

Of the eight, seven were ex-Labour, one ex-Liberal, and they had all concluded that the Conservative Party was the only hope of saving freedom. As Lord Blake has pointed out, here was a crucial difference in the situations which faced Heath in the late 1960s and Thatcher a decade later. Margaret Thatcher was arguing against the backdrop of an intellectual shift to the right; Heath, for his part, had challenged a consensus which still remained dominant among 'the opinion-formers' (Blake 1985:310–11).

The Nature of Thatcherism

What then — against this background — do we mean by Thatcherism? Most importantly, it is economic liberalism, in the revivified post-war variant pioneered by F.A. Hayek, Milton Friedman and the Institute of Economic Affairs. Markets, it is argued, are more conducive to liberty than planning, and the state should restrict its activities to guaranteeing the market's ability to function (for instance by its property laws and monetary policies), and a limited number of other tasks, mainly law and order, defence and a minimum standard of welfare.

Yet this is only one aspect of Thatcherism, which has been well described as:

> A rich mix. It combines the resonant themes of organic toryism — nation, family, duty, authority, standards, traditionalism — with the aggressive themes of a revived neo-liberalism — self-interest, competitive individualism, anti-statism . . . 'Free market, strong state': around this contradictory point . . . the authentic language of 'Thatcherism' has condensed'.
>
> Hall, in Hall and Jacques 1983: 29–30)

It is the character of the combination, and of the contradiction, which is most significant of all.

In many ways there is a remarkable consistency in the Thatcher position. Speaking to the Conservative Political Centre in 1968, she argued that what was needed was 'a far greater degree of personal responsibility and decision, far more independence from the government, and a comparable reduction in the role of government' (Kavanagh 1987:10–11). In arguing for rolling back the state, Thatcherism contrasts the free society with the horrors of socialism. Thus in speeches in the late 1970s she portrayed a society in which people had the right to property and to achieve success to the best of their abilities. This, she argued, could only be achieved by a conservatism determined to combat a Labour Party 'now committed to a programme which is frankly and unashamedly Marxist' (Behrens 1980:61).

In subsequent speeches and interviews, Thatcher continues to see her political project in such terms. Thus in one interview towards the end of her first administration she explained how the government offered 'a complete change in direction — from one in which the state became totally dominant in people's lives and penetrated almost every aspect' to one 'where the state did do certain things, but without displacing personal responsibility. I think we have altered the balance between the person and the state' (Riddell 1983:1). Speaking shortly after the 1983 victory, she remarked that the government should be remembered because it 'decisively broke with a debilitating consensus of a paternalistic Government and a dependent people' (Kavanagh 1987:252). And, of course, more recently, she has proclaimed her intention to eliminate socialism as a force in British politics (Owen and Rutherford 1986).

However, in the complex way that Hall suggests, this talk of getting the state off the people's back and putting statist forces to rout is combined in Thatcherism with an equivalent emphasis on the restoration of authority. This was strongly evident in the 1979 election manifesto with its pledges to reassert the powers of government over irresponsible trade unions and rising crime, and was epitomized in the mid-1980s by Norman Tebbit's celebrated Disraeli Lecture denunciation of the permissive society. Socialism, he argued, had engendered 'economic failure and personal irresponsibility' but this had been compounded by attitudes which undermined moral standards and damaged family life. Violence and pornography had become part of the media, he declared, but a backlash was inevitable, and at the forefront of the 'campaign for a return to traditional values of decency and order' would stand the Conservative Party which alone understood 'as does no other party that the defence of freedom' involved a stand against licence (Tebbit 1985:6, 15–16).

Thatcherism's combination of libertarian and authoritarian themes has been crucial in securing support for modern conservativism. But the inevitable tensions which result present serious problems to Thatcherism in power. Not only do the priorities of office sit uneasily with New Right zealotry, but the New Right itself is not a homogeneous force. That-cherism's amalgam of neo-liberalism and old Toryism dominates the New Right but does not define it; and while some elements have restricted themselves to criticizing particular policies, others argue that authority and liberty have not, and perhaps cannot, be pursued in tandem and that one must be victorious over the other. For some, in such bodies as the Libertarian Alliance or the recently dissolved Federation of Conservative Students, a free market policy could well extend to the sale of drugs or of sex. Conversely, for others, writing in such publications as the *Salisbury Review*, the Thatcher government has been guilty of elevating economic liberalism over the Conservative values of 'order, authority, tradition' (Ellis-Jones 1985:43–7). So far, however, it has been the critics of particular policies who have been the most troublesome. For the Adam Smith Institute, the Committee for a Free Britain and others, whose concerns are with removing powers from the state and extending the market as far as possible, Thatcherism in power has sometimes been seen as insufficiently radical. The continued existence of the National Health Service, British Rail, and other objects of New Right scorn, the failure to take up education vouchers or to privatize the prison system, have all come under fire from elements on the libertarian right. But for others, whose feelings are articulated by such figures as Rhodes Boyson or, more recently, by the Conservative Family Campaign, or some of the publications of the Social Affairs Unit, the crucial failings of the government have been less a matter of leaving too much of the state in place than of neglecting to use its powers against 'the enemy within'. The continued rise in the crime rate, the teaching of peace studies and anti-racist education in the classroom, homosexuality, the divorce rate and other 'family' issues, have all been targets of the more authoritarian elements on the Tory right (Edgar 1984; Durham 1985, 1989).

There are signs that the government's third term will go some distance in meeting the demands of both sets of critics. Market liberalism, although slower than some would like, is continuing its inroads into the public sphere while, according to recent reports, the Prime Minister believes that collectivism has been decisively beaten on the economic front and the government can now turn its attention to a social programme that can restore the bonds and the certainties destroyed by 'the permissiveness of the sixties'. Young people, she has stated, want 'rules by which to live', a firm discipline 'in the family, and at school and at work'. Although this cannot be attained by Act of Parliament, she argues, it could be achieved by an extended educational effort aimed at discouraging crime, encouraging parental responsibility, and restoring social cohesion (English 1988; Hughes and Brown 1988).

This development will not satisfy many of the 'pro-family' campaigners, angered at the government's refusal to support legislation restricting abortion and its apparent postponement of legislation on the emotive issue of human embryo research. The government's new turn will also risk alienating those market liberals who extend libertarian principles to the social sphere and who are hostile to right-wing moralizing. Above all, it is difficult to imagine it meeting with success. It will, however, certainly enable the government to continue a sense of movement and dynamism, that it is engaged in a vital and long overdue transformation of the nation which is at the same time radical and conserving. Finally, and not unimportantly, it will deal a severe blow to the efforts of Thatcherism's opponents to portray it as solely economic individualism. Alighting on her recent comment that 'there is no such thing as society', only individuals and their families, opponents of the Prime Minister have argued that Thatcherism has no sense of social cohesion and is incapable of responding to the widespread doubts about the government's encouragement of an uncaring 'Loadsamoney' society. If Thatcherism was indeed suffused with the view summed up in the Prime Minister's rhetorical attempt to refute collectivism, it would be impossible to explain the recent turn towards social issues. Instead, Thatcherism combines contradictory ideological elements and that Thatcher can deny the existence of society while at the same time trying to restore it is testimony to how difficult the holding together of such a contradictory yet potent doctrine can be.

When we consider the government's actions since 1979, then, it must be set against the background of a conservativism unusual in its ideological fervour. Privatization and the spread of share ownership, council house sales and legislation enabling schools to secede from local authority control, are all policies which a merely pragmatic Conservative administration would not have pursued. Nor would most such governments have abolished the GLC, banned unions at GCHQ and come into conflict with the BBC, the Church of England, trade union officialdom and local government. This is not to say that the government's record has merely been the unfolding of some preordained scheme. Privatization, for instance, only took shape gradually, and originally had far more to do with cutting state expenditure than it did with carrying through Conservative notions of a 'property-owning democracy'. Nor has the government been as successful in challenging the Welfare State as it would wish. As opinion polls make clear, a majority of voters continue to favour social spending over lower taxation, and while the third term may see greater inroads into public welfare, this is an important pointer to the as yet still partial nature of Thatcherism's ideological success. But, while falling short of a full-blooded New Right programme, it has none the less been a highly ideological administration with an explicit ideological mission.

There are those, both Conservatives and non-Conservatives, who argue that Thatcherism is not conservativism at all but, on the contrary, that it represents a break from the true Conservative tradition. Writing in the *Guardian* in the October following the 1983 General Election, Sir Ian Gilmour, a former member of the Thatcher Cabinet, argued that it was perfectly possible for the Conservative Party to be in power while jettisoning the distinctive features of the authentic Tory tradition. These features included, he suggested, the 'realisation of the State's duty to protect the weak', support for public expenditure, rejection of dogmatism and confrontation and 'a readiness to use the power of the State to guide the economy and a refusal to leave the steering to market forces alone' (Gilmour, 1983). Such themes were not new for Gilmour. Writing in the late 1970s, he had warned against the allure of Hayek and suggested that, for the party to move right, or to uncritically embrace the market, would be to break with Tory tradition (Gilmour 1978:117–33). In his view, then, Thatcherism is not Toryism. Instead, as he put it more recently, it is 'Manchester liberalism minus the idealism and plus a centralising State' (Critchley 1987).

For another inner-party critic and former Cabinet minister, Francis Pym, the right approach to politics is 'the Disraelian tradition' or 'One Nation Conservatism'. Pym argued that, even though at the moment intolerance and dogmatism ruled, in the future someone would again take up the banner of 'traditional Conservatism'. He claimed that there were three political views of society — the Marxist, the *laissez-faire* and the paternalist — and it was the last of these, 'the least fashionable', which he espoused. Conservatism, in his view, abhorred *laissez-faire* and was opposed to ideology (Pym 1984:x–xi, 129, 188). Other Conservatives, notably Peter Walker, have also criticized Thatcherism as a break from real conservatism. Similar views can be found in the writings of academic commentators. Thus one writer on 'the Conservative tradition of thought' describes a defence of the free market as 'neo-liberalism masquerading as Conservatism' (Bennett 1977:21).

Nor do such characterizations come only from so-called 'wet' critics of Thatcherism and certain academics. They also emanate, more surprisingly, from two other directions. First, some admirers of the Prime Minister have wanted to describe her in this way. Thus Milton Friedman, in an interview in 1982, observed that 'Margaret Thatcher is not in terms of belief a Tory. She is a nineteenth-century Liberal' (Leach 1983:9). Sir John Nott agreed: when a member of her Cabinet he characterized himself as a nineteenth-century Liberal, adding that so too was the Prime Minster and, indeed, that was what the government was all about (Riddell 1983:11).

Other supporters of Thatcherism have taken a very different view. Troubled by its affection for market liberalism, they have sought to rescue it for a more statist variant of rightist politics. In recent years, as we have seen, this school of thought has found a forum in the pages of the *Salisbury Review*, but its views were already being articulated even before Thatcherism's accession to power. Writing in the late 1970s, in the dying days of the Callaghan regime, Peregrine Worsthorne argued that Thatcher was wrong to criticize Labour for its attack on individual liberty. On the contrary, he argued, what was wrong with Britain 'was not so much the lack of freedom as its excessive abundance'. Notions of 'setting the people free . . . so dear to Mrs Thatcher' were not what was wanted, he declared:

> The urgent need today is for the State to regain control over 'the people', to reassert its authority, and it is useless to imagine that this will be helped by some libertarian mish-mash drawn from the writings of Adam Smith, John Stuart Mill, and the warmed-up milk of nineteenth-century liberalism.
>
> (Cowling 1978:145-9)

Writing shortly afterwards, Roger Scruton likewise expressed concern over the party's view of itself as defender of the individual against the state. What this potentially entailed, he feared, was 'the wholesale adoption of the philosophy which I shall characterise . . . as the principal enemy of conservatism, the philosophy of liberalism' (Scruton 1980:15–16). For Worsthorne and Scruton, as for Gilmour and Pym, the problem is liberalism. For both camps, what is at stake is community and an ordered society. For the latter grouping, however, the problem with individualism is that it is insufficiently compassionate and thus weakens social bonds; for Worsthorne and Scruton, individualism corrodes authority.

From a number of different political stances, then, Thatcherism has been chastised as a cuckoo in the Conservative nest. But how justified is this? One answer, strongly argued from within the Thatcherist redoubt, is to assert its Conservative credentials and to brand its critics as the heretics. We have already referred to Joseph's view that, until 1974, he had not been a Conservative at all, while Nigel Lawson, writing in 1980 on 'The New Conservatism', was concerned to show that the politics he advocated were firmly in the Conservative tradition. In the twenty-five years that followed Churchill, he claimed, social democracy had gained ascendancy over conservatism. Its belief in government action and in 'equality' had eclipsed Conservative distrust of officialdom, of abstract ideas and Utopianism. What the New Conservatism had done, he continued, was to 'return to the mainstream' and re-establish the 'old consensus'. They had turned to Hayek and Friedman because these writers were in the tradition of Burke and Adam Smith and because they were able to explain the failures of post-war economic policy. Rather than being an alien creed, the New Conservatism was very much 'the politics of imperfection' with its faith in tradition, its scepticism about the state, its inclination to gradualism. To those who saw recent developments as an incursion of liberalism, Lawson's riposte was that this obscured the 'fundamental consensus on economic policy' of Tory and Liberal in the previous century. For those concerned at the seeming victory of theory over pragmatism, Lawson pointed to the changed circumstances which meant that Conservatives, as never before, had to wage a battle of ideas. The ideas were old and Conservative, he concluded; what was new was that Conservatives were seeking to re-educate the people in these old truths and dispel the myths of big government (Lawson 1980:2–3, 15, 18).

One possible approach, then, is to see Thatcherism as conservatism restored. But an examination of Thatcherism as an ideology need not conclude that it is the authentic bearer of the Tory tradition any more than an invader of the Conservative sanctum. Instead of having to choose between the claims of Thatcherism and the 'wets', it is feasible to see both (and other strands too) as forms of conservatism. As Greenleaf and others have argued, Conservatism has long had an ambiguous attitude towards the state. While one strand is collectivist, the other is libertarian (Greenleaf 1973). Other writers, distinguishing between the two strands, have used the terms Tory and Whig, but the point is the same. If we examine the history of conservatism, what we see is shifts in the balance of forces between tendencies. Further, not only has a strand of conservatism been hostile to economic intervention since Burke (a co-thinker of Adam Smith on this question), but there is also the fact that conservatism as a party experienced infusions of free-market Liberals in the late nineteenth and early twentieth centuries. As Liberalism declined, so it splintered, some adding their forces to conservatism. As Labour rose, so the emphasis for conservatism for much of the twentieth century has been on fighting statism not individualism. To assert the legitimacy of liberal argumentation within conservatism does not necessitate seeing Thatcherism as the true conservatism. As Arthur Aughey has argued, the roots of Thatcherism lie deep within the Conservative Party but it is not the only voice of conservatism (Aughey 1983:395).

Conclusion

In considering the development of post-war conservatism, it is necessary to consider it both as a political party and a political ideology. At times its finely-tuned instrumentalism has all but blocked out ideological considerations, and the conservatism of the 1950s is a crucial case of this. Having disagreed earlier with one study which was sceptical about the existence of a Conservative ideology, it is worth noting in this regard that the study in question was focused on just the period that conservatism was at its most pragmatic (Harris 1972). However, even in the 1950s Conservative ideological themes infused the party's practice.

At other points in the party's history the role of ideology has been far more evident. The rethinking of conservatism after the 1945 defeat, the emergence of the New Right, the challenge of Powellism and, finally, the rise of Thatcherism (and the ineffective 'wet' counter-attack), all testify to the importance of ideology in moments of crisis. Faced with the trauma of electoral defeat, forced to grapple with social change and economic decline, post-war conservatism has on three occasions turned back to its ideological roots. In 1945, swept out of office by Labour, and chastened by the popular support for a collectivism it had seemed to oppose in the election campaign, the party built on its wartime Coalition commitments, and summoned up its long tradition of using the state to promote national solidarity. The New Conservatism was impressively successful in restoring the party's fortunes, but by the 1960s it was increasingly politically exhausted. Heath's attempt to lead it to the right miscarried, while Enoch Powell's more radical effort to create a Conservative populism also failed. Yet out of the Heath government's failure came an opening for the right to succeed where Powellism had failed.

Powell's combination of a neo-Liberal stance on economics and an authoritarian line on crucial social questions had sketched the outlines of a politics which could revitalize conservatism, but in his case the economic argument failed to find a popular echo. A decade later, though, with the economy in dire straits, there was a new opportunity for an approach which could popularize Liberal economics. Invoking images of the housewife's budget, tapping discontent with the Welfare State and the power of the unions, Thatcherism succeeded where Powellism had not. It is not possible, therefore, to agree with Peregrine Worsthorne's vivid 1983 argument that both Powellism amd Thatcherism served up 'bitter tasting market economics . . . rendered palatable . . . by great creamy dollops of nationalistic custard', the difference being that the Falklands campaign proved more conducive to popular support than a blatant appeal to race (Edgar 1984). While it is important to recall how unpopular the government's economic policies were for much of its first term, to accept Worsthorne's comparison would be to obscure the crucial fact that Thatcherism — unlike Powellism — has made market arguments themselves popular.

All three of these important moments in the history of modern conservatism gave Conservative answers to questions about authority and liberty, economy and polity. The first of these moments drew on the 'middle opinion' of the 1930s and emphasized shared ground with the moderate left; the later trends, faced with more desperate circumstances, turned to a liberalism that had long been present in the party to give answers where the progressive right was no longer convincing. Conservatism prides itself on being non-ideological, but Thatcherism should not be regarded as some unique moment where it has fallen from grace. Instead, conservatism itself is an ideology — the most successful one in modern British politics.

Further Reading

For general discussions of conservatism as an ideology, see Noel O'Sullivan, *Conservatism* (Dent, 1976) and Robert Nisbet, *Conservatism* (Open University Press, 1986). On British Conservatism, see Philip Norton and Arthur Aughey, *Conservatives and Conservatism* (Temple Smith, 1981), Robert Blake, *The Conservative Party from Peel to Thatcher* (Fontana, 1985), Frank O'Gorman, *British Conservatism* (Longman, 1986), and the relevant section of W.H. Greenleaf, *The British Political Tradition*, vol. 2 (Methuen, 1983). For an excellent discussion of post-war British conservatism up to the early 1970s see Andrew Gamble, *The Conservative Nation* (Routledge & Kegan Paul, 1974).

A valuable account of the refurbishment of British conservatism in the late 1940s can be found in J.D. Hoffman, *The Conservative Party in Opposition 1945-51* (MacGibbon and Kee, 1964). Nigel Harris, *Competition and the Corporate Society* (Methuen, 1972) is useful on conservatism in the 1950s and early 1960s, as is Gamble, *op cit*. For Powellism, Douglas Schoen, *Enoch Powell and the Powellites* (Macmillan, 1977) and Ken Phillips, 'The Nature of Powellism', in Neil Nugent and Roger King (eds), *The British Right* (Saxon House,

1977) are both valuable, while Tom Nairn, 'English Nationalism: The Case of Enoch Powell', in his *The Break-up of Britain* (NLB, 1977) is a *tour de force*.

For the 1970s, Stuart Hall, *et al.*, *Policing the Crisis* (Macmillan, 1978) is an evocative account of the political anxieties out of which Thatcherism arose while, on Thatcherism itself, see the essays by Hall and Gamble in the Stuart Hall and Martin Jacques collection, *The Politics of Thatcherism* (Lawrence & Wishart, 1983).

Of the different studies of the New Right, see in particular Norman Barry, *The New Right* (Croom Helm, 1987), Andrew Gamble, *The Free Economy and the Strong State* (Macmillan, 1988), and two earlier essays by Gamble, 'The Free Economy and the Strong State', in *Socialist Register 1979* (Merlin, 1979), and 'The Political Economy of Freedom', in Ruth Levitas (ed.), *The Ideology of the New Right* (Polity Press, 1986). For a defence of 'one-nation' conservatism see Ian Gilmour, *Inside Right* (Quartet, 1978), while for a selection of essays from the *Salisbury Review* see Roger Scruton (ed.), *Conservative Thinkers* and *Conservative Thoughts* (both Claridge, 1988). David Edgar explores the ideological tensions within Thatcherism in two essays, 'Bitter Harvest' in James Curran (ed.), *The Future of the Left* (Polity Press, 1984) and 'The Free or the Good', in Levitas, *op. cit.* Finally, on Thatcherism in power (and, indeed, the post-war period in general), see Dennis Kavanagh, *Thatcherism and British Politics* (Oxford University Press, 1987); but also see Bill Schwarz, 'The Thatcher Years' in *Socialist Register 1987* (Merlin, 1987).

Bibliography (place of publication London unless otherwise stated)

Aughey, A. (1983) 'Mrs Thatcher's philosophy', *Parliamentary Affairs* (Autumn) 36:389–98.

Barker, M. (1981) *The New Racism*, Junction Books.

Behrens, R. (1980) *The Conservative Party from Heath to Thatcher*, Saxon House.

Bennett, R. (1977) 'The Conservative tradition of thought', in N. Nugent and R. King (eds), *The British Right*, Saxon House, pp. 11–25.

Blake, R. (1985) *The Conservative Party from Peel to Thatcher*, Fontana.

Butler, R. (1971) *The Art of the Possible*, Hamish Hamilton.

Conservative Political Centre (CPC) (1950) *Conservatism 1945–1950*.

Cormack, P. (1978) *Right Turn*, Leo Cooper.

Cowling, M. (1978) *Conservative Essays*, Cassell.

Critchley, J. (1987) 'Sit vac: A leader for the "wets"', *Observer*, 9 August.

Durham, M. (1985) 'Family, morality and the new right', *Parliamentary Affairs*, 38, 2:180–91.

Durham, M. (forthcoming) 'The Thatcher government and "the moral right"', *Parliamentary Affairs*.

Edgar, D. (1984) 'Bitter harvest', in J. Curran (ed.) *The Future of the Left*, Polity Press, pp. 39–57.

Ellis-Jones, A. (1985) 'The politics of economics', *Salisbury Review* 3, 3:43–7.

English, D. (1988) 'This is my new crusade?', *Daily Mail*, 29 April.

Gamble, A. (1974) *The Conservative Nation*, Routledge and Kegan Paul.

Gilmour, I. (1978) *Inside Right*, Quartet.

Gilmour, I. (1983) 'Gilmour asks: is conservatism dead?', *Guardian*, 13 October.

Greenleaf, W.H. (1973) 'The character of modern British conservatism', in R. Benewick, *et al.* (eds) *Knowledge and Belief in Politics*, Allen & Unwin.

Greenleaf, W.H. (1983) *The British Political Tradition* vol. 2, *The Ideological Heritage*, Methuen.

Hall, S., Critcher, C., Jefferson, J., Clarke, J., and Roberts, B. (eds) (1978) *Policing the Crisis*, Macmillan.

Hall, S. and Jacques, M. (eds) (1983) *The Politics of Thatcherism*, Lawrence & Wishart.

Harris, N. (1972) *Competition and the Corporate Society*, Methuen.

Hoffman, J.D. (1964) *The Conservative Party in Opposition 1945–51*, MacGibbon and Kee.

Hogg, Q. (1944) *One Year's Work*, Hutchinson.

Hogg, Q. (1947) *The Case for Conservatism*, Penguin.

Hughes, C. and Brown, C. (1988) 'Thatcherism's focus faces radical change', *Independent*, 11 August.

Joseph, K. (1974) 'Sir Keith calls for "remoralisation" and reassertion of civilised values', *The Times*, 21 October.

Joseph, K. (1975) *Reversing the Trend*, Centre for Policy Studies.

Kavanagh, D. (1987) *Thatcherism and British Politics*, Oxford University Press.

Lawson, N. (1980) *The New Conservatism*, Centre for Policy Studies.

Leach, R.F. (1983) 'Thatcherism, Liberalism and Tory collectivism', *Politics*, 3, 1:9–14.

Moss, R. (1975) *The Collapse of Democracy*, Temple Smith.

Nairn, T. (1977) *The Break-up of Britain*, NLB.

Oakeshott, M. (1962) *Rationalism in Politics and Other Essays*, Methuen.

O'Gorman, F. (1986) *British Conservatism*, Longman.

O'Sullivan, N. (1976) *Conservatism*, Dent.

Owen, G. and Rutherford, M. (1986) 'Two more terms to eliminate socialism', *Financial Times*, 19 November.

Phillips, K. (1977) 'The nature of Powellism', in N. Nugent, and R. King (eds) *The British Right*, Saxon House.

Powell, J.E. (1969) *Freedom and Reality*, Elliot Rightway Books.

Pym, F. (1984) *The Politics of Consent*, Constable.

Quinton, A. (1978) *The Politics of Imperfection*, Faber.

Riddell, P. (1983) *The Thatcher Government*, Martin Robertson.

Schwarz, B. (1984) 'The language of constitutionalism', in *Formations of Nation and People*, Routledge & Kegan Paul
Scruton, R. (1980) *The Meaning of Conservatism*, Penguin.
Tebbit, N (1985) *Britain's Future, A Conservative Vision*, CPC.
Tyrrell, R.E. (ed.) (1977) *The Future that Doesn't Work*, Doubleday.
Watkins, K.W. (ed.) (1978) *In Defence of Freedom*, Cassell.
Wood, J. (1965) *A Nation Not Afraid*, Batsford.
Wood, J. (1970) *Powell and the 1970 Election*, Elliot Rightway Books.
Wood, J. (1972) *Still to Decide*, Batsford

Chapter four

The Centre: Social Democracy and Liberalism

Robert Behrens

In *The Acquisitive Society*, published in 1921, Tawney suggested that extraordinary times demanded something more than a combination of intellectual tameness, practical energy and following the road (Tawney 1921:9). The recent histories of social democracy and liberalism illustrate the importance of this maxim. The twin resurgence of a hard-nosed, individualist conservatism, and a hidebound, illiberal labourism, created extraordinary times in British politics from the late 1970s. This presented the forces of the political centre with an unparalleled opportunity to sink their differences, and to set about constructing a populist idiom from the strands of social democracy and liberalism. No doubt this would be uncongenial to bustling, practical people (Tawney 1921:9), but it held out the prospect of the emergence of a strong, cross-class alliance to challenge the traditional class-based alignments of the major parties. With the birth of the Social Democratic Party in 1981, the emergence of a new third force looked distinctly possible, but by 1987 the possibilities receded as the political centre sank into unfraternal factionalism.

How do we account for this failure, and what part did ideological tensions play in it? To answer these questions it is necessary to follow Hobhouse in the view that:

> the onward course of a movement is more clearly understood by appreciating the successive points of view which its thinkers and statesmen have occupied than by following the devious turnings of political events and the tangle of party controversy.
>
> (Hobhouse 1911:31)

Such an approach reveals that the collapse of centrist politics was not the inevitable result of irreconcilable ideological conflict. Rather, it stemmed from the inability of centrist politicians to settle on an agreed political strategy, or transcend the divisions of competing party ethos and utilized a broad philosophical consensus to confront what Keynes (1931:299) had predicted would be a formidable adversary — the Conservative Party rejuvenated with a version of individualistic

74

capitalism (Keynes 1931:299). In this chapter a review of each of the traditions of social democracy and liberalism is followed by a discussion of Alliance and post-Alliance politics. A short conclusion discusses the prospects for the political centre in its present fragmented state.

Social Democracy

In their long march away from Marxism and towards centrism, social democratic thinkers have been preoccupied with the construction of a state form which generates greater social equality in the context of representative democracy. Historically, social democracy developed as a variant of socialism. Before 1914 'social democracy' primarily meant organized Marxism, but after Leninists seized power in Russia in 1917, the term began to be used to identify those socialists committed to the defence of democratic institutions, and opposed to Communist totalitarianism (Kolakowski 1982:16–17). Some of these social democrats described their own position as 'democratic socialist' to emphasize their rejection of undemocratic socialism and yet underline their commitment to a socialist reorganization of society which went beyond reformism (Wright 1987a:3–4).

In Britain, this democratic socialist stance was taken up and expounded by such figures as Durbin, Tawney, and Cole. Their socialism was distinguished by a number of common factors. They were agreed that the foundations of British socialism were essentially ethical, not economic (Cole 1943:9; Tawney 1964:155,167). Programmatically, they envisaged the use of democratic institutions to create a socialist commonwealth through a nationalization of the industrial system, a redistribution of income, and the introduction of economic planning (Cole 1920:391; Durbin 1940:255–321; Tawney 1964:148–64). They were also united by a practical bias, a commitment to factual enquiry and rational argument, and a willingness to compromise (Gaitskell, in Durbin 1940:9). This scepticism and rejection of grand theory arose out of a recognition that the challenge of democratic socialism was to reconcile the competing values of individual liberty and social equality. As Durbin summed it up: 'The problem of a just society is not the single problem of economic equality,but the much more difficult problem of achieving simultaneously in one society both liberty and equality' (Durbin 1940:269–70).

After the Second World War, social democracy developed in two important ways. First, it underlined its belief in parliamentary democracies by supporting the collective defence of the west through the North Atlantic Treaty Organisation (NATO). Second, it adopted a revisionism which stressed the potential for an accommodation between capital and labour in what was seen to be post-capitalist society. This revisionism was expounded with great clarity by Anthony Crosland in *The Future of Socialism* (1956). Crosland suggested that inter-war democratic socialist writing had been rendered obsolete by the achievement of the Labour government after 1945 in fundamentally altering the distribution of economic power in Britain (Crosland 1956:41). The creation of an extensive nationalized sector, comprehensive national health and insurance provisions, rising living standards, and full employment, had ushered in a post-capitalist era. This, Crosland called — and later regretted calling — 'statism' (Crosland 1956:58-9, 67, 75-6).

For Crosland, the ethical goals of socialism should reflect the concern for social welfare and the creation of a more equal, classless, society (Crosland 1956:112-13). This meant that the future of socialism was about social policy development. He took it for granted that Keynesian budgetary techniques would promote economic growth, and argued for generous, long-term public spending to ensure that opportunities were not tied to social class. The state must establish universal social services equal in quality to the best private provision (Crosland 1956:145-62, 208, 517). It should eschew a further rapid nationalization of large industries which would be 'bad for liberty and wholly irrelevant to socialism' (ibid.: 485, 496). Instead it ought to preside over a society in which ownership was thoroughly diverse, so that competitive public enterprise and effective profit-sharing could co-exist (ibid.: 496)

Crosland's formulations featured prominently in the thriving Keynesian social democratic practice of the 1960s, but his optimistic statism, and indeed the whole edifice of Keynesian social democracy, looked vulnerable to a number of serious challenges and criticisms in the 1970s. First, the emphasis on a more equal wealth distribution was based on the assumption that wealth creation and growth would be unproblematic. This assumption proved unrealistic as Keynesian demand management begat rampant inflation and negative growth. In these circumstances, environmentalists began to challenge the view that unlimited growth should be a foundation of policy even if it could be sustained (Emmett Tyrell Jr 1977:51; Owen 1981a:118-19; Marquand 1983:16).

Second, the greater equality strategy itself was seen to be overreliant on the activities of the state machine. The rapid expansion of central government bred corporatism and bureaucracy. These were expensive, since government expansion necessitated high public expenditure paid out of taxation at rates which stretched the tolerance of taxpayers (Luard 1979:32-6; Williams 1981:28-30; Owen 1981a: 38-55). They were also oligarchical and had an adverse effect on individual rights and liberties

(Luard 1979:32–6; Owen 1981a). Indeed, the outcome of the corporatist carve-up was systematic race and sex discrimination. Ethnic minorities were invariably viewed as 'pools' of labour not citizens with fundamental rights. Similarly, women faced occupational segregation and economic dependency brought about by male control of family wages and benefits (Rose 1981:497–8).

This discontent with existing social democratic practice stimulated, on one side, a resurgence of a populist democratic socialism which came to regard 'social democratic' as a term of abuse. Weary of the failure of Labour governments after 1964 to abide by party conference decisions, it opposed the leadership discretion inherent in the representative theory of party government, and argued that the parliamentary leadership must be directly accountable to conference. It was hostile to the European Economic Community (EEC), critical of the traditional social democratic support of NATO in the face of the deployment of medium-range nuclear missiles in Europe, and zealous in the pursuit of expanded public ownership and spending (Benn 1979; Byrd, in Paterson and Thomas 1986:66–94).

By the end of the 1970s, therefore, the productive, distributional, and representational strategies of social democracy were under severe attack and in need of reformulation. A contemporaneous leadership crisis added to the impression of disarray. Roy Jenkins had left British politics to become President of the EEC in 1976. Crosland himself died in 1977. A year later John Mackintosh also died. Mackintosh had been an eloquent exponent of social democracy who had spoken out strongly in defence of the EEC and in favour of an economic policy which emphasized private sector wealth creation. He had also championed representative democracy and questioned whether it was any longer compatible with the traditional, organic links between the Labour Party and the trade unions. (Marquand 1982:155–68, 202–22, 222–32).

The formation of the Social Democratic Party (SDP) in March 1981 has to be seen in the context of these crises. Three of the founders of the SDP — Shirley Williams, David Owen, and William Rodgers — served loyally in Labour governments until Labour's electoral defeat in 1979. Having initially come together in May 1980 to oppose Labour hostility to the European Community, they published a wide-ranging open letter to the Labour Party in the *Guardian* on 1 August 1980. Declaring that there could be 'no compromise with those who share neither the values nor the philosophy of democratic socialism', they outlined their commitment to the mixed economy, representative democracy and an international socialism which embraced multilateral nuclear disarmament. If Labour failed to stick to these principles, 'the argument may grow for a new democratic socialist party to establish itself'.

Although none of the books subsequently published by the 'Gang of

Three' constituted a serious analysis of the democratic socialist tradition in particular, it is interesting that each acknowledged a debt to it. For Shirley Williams, Tawney's concern for individual liberty and fraternity highlighted the centrality of persuasion in the social democratic variant of socialism (Williams 1981:23–4). For David Owen, Cole's rejection of forms of socialism that neglected liberty and fraternity in the quest for equality were important in developing a revised socialist philosophy that rejected corporatism and statism (Owen 1981a:4, 11; citing Wright 1979). Similarly, for William Rodgers, Durbin's *The Politics of Democratic Socialism* (1940) with its rejection of both Utopian socialism and totalitarianism 'remains for me the plainest declaration of one large part of my faith and purpose' (Rodgers 1982:4–5).

The use and exploitation of Tawney, Cole, and Durbin, by the Gang of Three was a good example of the ritual appeal to the authority of dead heroes, and the call for their restoration, that Nicholas Deakin has called (Deakin 1987:30–1) temperamental Jacobitism. It indicated where the Gang of Three had come from. It was also helpful in easing a painful passage out of Labour Party politics. If Williams, Owen, and Rodgers had to leave the Labour Party, at least they could take socialist giants with them (Wright 1987b:131). In this way it was possible to argue that the Labour Party and not the Gang of Three had left democratic socialism. Beyond this, however, the invocation of the democratic socialist giants had little prescriptive relevance. Although it took the Gang of Three a short time to come to terms with the fact, leaving the Labour Party also meant leaving democratic socialism and abandoning the aspirations and symbols of a socialist commonwealth. The ritual appeal to the likes of Tawney obscured this reality. In doing so, it clouded positional judgement, and postponed serious thinking about where the SDP would fit on the political landscape. Shirley Williams's round denunciation of centre party politics shortly before the birth of the centrist SDP (Bradley 1981: 76–8) is a good illustration of the dangers of political ritualism of this kind.

The fourth founder of the SDP, Roy Jenkins, though a participant in democratic socialist politics for decades, and a Labour Party member until 1980, had long rejected the label 'socialist' (Campbell 1983:197; Jenkins 1985:6). With this detachment from Labour politics and socialism, Jenkins was ahead of the Gang of Three in presenting his ideas in terms of 'strengthening the political centre' (Jenkins 1979:736). This was the theme of his Dimbleby Lecture, delivered on an excursion back from Brussels in November 1979. A strong political centre met the aspirations of the electorate. It was attainable through electoral reform and principled coalition within or between parties, and could bring talented individuals into political commitment. Britain needed the stimulus of the free market economy without the 'brutality' of its distribution of rewards or its indifference to unemployment (Jenkins 1979:736–7, 738). In June

1980, borrowing a phrase from Jo Grimond, Jenkins suggested that left and centre politics in Britain were 'frozen in an out-of-date mould' which was bad for national politics and economics alike. It was time to redraw the political map of Britain (Grimond 1963:311–12; Jenkins 1985:25–6).

There were, therefore, two main strands in the genesis of the SDP. The first looked back to democratic socialism, while the second was unambiguously centrist and appealed beyond the confines of existing political activists. The coming together of these strands was marked in personal terms by the creation of the 'Gang of Four', and in political terms by the publication of the Limehouse Declaration on 25 January 1981. This was a short prospectus for the revision of revisionism. In terms of British politics, it was an attempt to herald a parting of the ways between social democracy and democratic socialism.

The Limehouse Declaration briefly outlined the future hopes of social democracy. The aim would be to construct an open, classless, prejudice-free society through a realignment free of the dictates of the Labour movement. Its productive strategy would be rooted in a mix of stable and competitive private and public sectors. Distributionally, it would seek to eliminate poverty and create greater equality through a decentralized decision-making process responsive to people's needs. Statism was thus *passé*. Finally, it would be emphatically internationalist, working within the European Community, NATO, and the United Nations to negotiate disarmament and grapple with Third World poverty (Jenkins 1985:28). These aims were subsequently incorporated into the constitution of the new Social Democratic Party.

At the launch of the SDP Roy Jenkins proclaimed that: 'We offer not only a new Party, although it is that, but a new approach to politics'. This involved releasing the energies of people fed up with class confrontation and 'the old slanging match' (Jenkins 1985:29). This lofty moralism seemed to ignore the function of argument in constructing a new idiom, and attracted the jibe from the likes of Rumpole that people joined the SDP so that they could give up politics altogether (Mortimer 1987:116). Nevertheless, the majority of SDP members and its middle-ranking elite had not previously been members of any political party, even if the leaders came from the Labour Party (Doring 1983:351; Owen 1987b:232). Whether this new voice was heard in the articulation of the new social democracy is more doubtful. The influence on the party of the Gang of Four was 'excessive' (Owen 1987b:206). This was not least because of a constitution which combined democratic, one-member one-vote decision-making with wide leadership discretion (Drucker, in Paterson and Thomas 1986:119–122). In addition, the refusal of defecting Labour MPs (with one exception) to resign their seats and submit themselves to the hazards of re-election, not only sat uneasily with the vigorous avowal of representative democracy, but also ensured plenty of old wine in the new bottle.

Liberalism

If the history of social democracy has been preoccupied with the role of the state in ordering production and distribution, liberalism has focused on the rational individual as the basic unit of discourse (Winch 1970:48 in *Introduction to Mill, J.S.* [1848, new edition 1985] Dunn 1979:32). This focus has produced characteristic liberal scepticism about the role and size of the state, and about authority. It has also produced an enduring commitment to what Mill called 'The Art of Living' rather than 'the art of getting on' (Mill 1848:116), and a constitutionalism zealous to preserve individual rights and disperse power.

In classical liberalism, the more the individual received free scope for the play of his faculties, the more rapidly would society advance. In this view, unrestricted competition was the mainspring of progress. At home, an existing harmony of interests required only limited government to maintain order, enforce contracts, and protect individual property rights (Hobhouse 1911:33–4, 44, 54). Abroad, 'the spread of commerce and the diffusion of education' were more conducive to the maintenance of peace than 'the labours of cabinets and foreign offices' (Cobden, quoted in Taylor 1969:49). The Benthamite variant of this individualism was to assert that government action should conform to the principle of ensuring the greatest happiness to the greatest number of individuals. Paradoxically, the outcome was an interventionist and crudely majoritarian social policy careless of justice or rights because they were subsumed under the fiction of 'utility'.

John Stuart Mill transformed classical individualism into a liberal individuality (Freeden 1978:22–3). In *On Liberty* (1859) Mill argued that individual self-development was at the root of liberty. The cultivation and exercise of human capacities — thoughts and deeds, tastes and eccentricities — were safeguards against despotic custom and the collective mediocrity of public opinion (Mill 1859:125–36). This view of progress through individual self-development influenced both Mill's political and economic thought. He saw the choice of political institutions as determined in part by what they could promote in terms of further progress in life and culture (Mill 1861:168–70). On this criterion representative government was appropriate because participation in public affairs had educative value and proportional representation was an effective mechanism because it ensured the participation of those with minority views (Mill 1861:196–8, 247–71).

In the economic realm, although Mill saw the restriction of competition as an evil (Mill 1848:142), he was careful to subordinate economic objectives to ethical values. He emphasized 'the civilizing and improving influences of association' in the process of production. This made him an advocate of partnership through either profit-sharing or co-operatives (Mill 1848:128–33). He was also concerned about the quality of life, and not just material standards. A 'stationary state' of better distribution and with room for appreciating the spontaneous activity of nature was preferable to the endless increase of production and the eradication of wild flowers in the name of improved agriculture (Mill 1848:114–6).

Mill's overriding concern for individuality presented liberalism with ambiguous intimations about the role of the state (Condren 1985:214–17). He concluded *On Liberty* (1859) with the beguiling statement that:

A government cannot have too much of the kind of activity which does not impede, but aids and stimulates, individual exertion and development. The mischief begins when, instead of calling forth the activity and powers of individuals and bodies, it substitutes its own activity for theirs.

(Mill 1859:187)

Subsequent liberal discourse was a passionate argument about precisely when the mischief began. On the one hand classical liberals like Herbert Spencer saw most kinds of state activity as enervating and inimical to the individuality at the core of social evolution (Greenleaf 1983:59–82). On the other hand, from the late 1880s onwards Hobson and Hobhouse articulated a social liberalism which emphasized the role of the state in creating the conditions for individual self-development (Hobson 1909:97; Hobhouse 1911:83).

The ascendancy of social liberals over classical liberals owed a great deal to 'the manifest teaching of experience that liberty without equality is a name of noble sound and squalid result' (Hobhouse 1911:46). There were two central tasks on their agenda. Since liberty had a social and economic dimension, the first task was to create a social democracy to set alongside political democracy (Hobson 1909:107–10, 173–4; Hobhouse, 1911:16–23; Clarke, in Bogdanor 1983:28). The second task was to ensure that state intervention was subordinate to the goal of facilitating individuality, and did not become an end in itself (Hobson 1909:94).

Social liberalism had an important impact on party policy and strategy (see Bentley 1987:109–10, 144–5). The concern to separate the social from the individual factors in production, and to redistribute social factors through need-related welfare (Hobhouse 1911:91–108), underpinned the social reform programme of the Liberal government after 1906. This included limited schemes for old age pensions and national insurance paid (in part) out of redistributive taxation (Collini 1979:108–13). In addition, liberal recognition of the need to redress social and economic

81

inequalities opened up the possibility of an alliance with exponents of the social democratic varieties of socialism (Hobhouse 1911:115–16; Clarke, in Bogdanor 1983:33). Hobhouse, indeed, noted the potential for a democratic 'Liberal Socialism' which took account of common welfare without destroying either property or the market-based springs of initiative and energy. This he contrasted with an illiberal socialism which was contemptuous of humanity, and was an unremitting road to wholesale nationalization and state bureaucracy (Hobson 1909:172–3; Hobhouse 1911:88–108).

The prospects for a cross-party alliance between social liberals and social democrats diminished after 1916 as the Liberal Party split into personality-based factions. These sustained divisions debilitated Liberal electoral strength in the face of a burgeoning Labour Party, and caused Hobson and other liberal intellectuals to move over to Labour (Clarke 1978:195–214). Although this intellectual seepage was damaging, liberalism in the 1920s retained many vibrant qualities, as seen through the work of Liberal Summer Schools in general, and of Keynes in particular.

For Keynes, *laissez-faire* capitalism had produced an economic anarchy, in which undirected economic forces generated unemployment and great inequalities of wealth. The objective of liberalism was to control and direct these forces without paying obeisance to the selfish, sectional interests of trade unions, 'the beauties of the class war, or to doctrinaire State Socialism' (Keynes 1931:291–3, 305, 309–10). Towards this end, and under the patronage of Lloyd George, Keynes participated in the Liberal Industrial Inquiry which in 1928 published *Britain's Industrial Future*. This set out a programme to manage capitalism and reduce inequalities without resort to wholesale nationalization. Its cornerstone was a Board of National Investment established to direct capital investment towards labour-intensive reconstruction (Layton *et al.* 1928:111–14, 280–1). This was an anticipation of the larger theme in Keynes's general theory (Keynes 1936:378–80) that the public control of investment 'will prove the only means to an approximation to full employment' compatible with the wide exercise of private initiative and responsibility.

If these ideas dominated economic thinking for more than a generation, the Keynesian legacy was not unproblematic for liberalism. Keynes's emphasis on economic efficiency promulgated a political thought over-concerned with the technical knowledge of specialists and antithetical to values in the liberal tradition which emphasized the role of persuasion and democratic participation in policy-making (Keynes 1931:295–6, 311; Skidelsky, in Kilmarnock 1987:72; Marquand 1988:20–41). This technocratic elitism was also at the heart of William Beveridge's liberal social policy analysis. Like Keynes, Beveridge welcomed a selective extension of state responsibilities to overcome specific social evils (Beveridge 1945:8, 36–7). Liberty was not confined to 'freedom from the arbitrary power of other men . . .', as Hayek had maintained. It meant using the organized power of the community to secure freedom from the 'five giants' of want, disease, squalor, ignorance and idleness (Hayek 1944:19; Beveridge 1945:33–7).

In his official report, *Social Insurance and Allied Services* (1942), Beveridge proposed that the state should establish a system of social insurance to guard against the loss of earning power. It should operate as part of a comprehensive plan which would introduce child allowances, a national health service, and full employment (Beveridge 1942:9, 156–64). A non-means-tested benefit, calculated 'on a scientific basis' at subsistence level, would secure a citizen against want. This would leave room for voluntary action by individuals to provide more than that minimum for themselves and their families (Beveridge 1942:7–15). Although these plans formed the basis of social policy for more than thirty years, the erroneous 'scientific' assumptions about need, and the failure of governments to up-rate subsistence benefits stimulated the reappearance of additional, means-tested 'national assistance'. The result was a dramatic growth in state welfare fostered or tolerated by post-war governments in a way that undermined Beveridge's hope that his scheme would stimulate individual incentive and responsibility (Beveridge 1942:141–2, 146–7; Macleod and Powell 1952:30–5; Marquand 1988:28–33).

Post-war liberalism had therefore to ask itself difficult questions about how far individuality was compatible with both an interventionist state and technocratic elitism. Under the leadership of Jo Grimond the party began to re-work its social liberal inheritance. An iconoclastic public policy profile was developed as liberals seized the opportunity to think, unconstrained by the prospect of political office, and the dead-weight of official opinion. In this speculative climate the Welfare State was seen as a 'grandmother state' which dispersed 'endless' benefits (Grimond 1959:21–2). As Elliott Dodds noted (in Watson 1957:13–17), it was financed through heavy taxation, and operated as a bureaucratic machine stuffed with red tape and an army of officials. This was fundamentally illiberal because state-financed universal social services, free at source, perpetuated conditions under which individuals had no opportunity for exercising social responsibility for themselves (Peacock, in Watson 1957:118–20). What was needed was not a Welfare State but a welfare society in which social policy objectives were increasingly delivered through private endeavour and voluntary agencies (Dodds, in Watson 1957:18–26). Liberal social policy should facilitate a partnership between public and private provision, and it should not shy away from selectivity because of the stigmatic quality of Poor Law means testing (Peacock, in Watson 1957:120–30). This confidence in selectivity rested on over-optimistic expectations about the ability of full employment on its own to diminish poverty and social service provision (see Peacock, in Watson 1957:120–1; Grimond 1959:103). It also rested on a positive view of the market system. Although this offered advantages to too few people, it was the most efficient, satisfying, and democratic way of running the economy. Excessive inequalities should be reduced through co-ownership and partnership in industry (not nationalization), and a wider spread of private wealth and property (Grimond 1959:59–61, 76–86; 1963:24; 1979a:207–8).

To complement this critique of state welfarism, Liberals offered a critique of the British state which focused on the erosion of the constitutional checks and balances necessary to safeguard against executive dominance. Individuality required a clearer legislative definition of personal rights and their protection through a variety of administrative law and official secrets reforms (Skelsey, in Watson 1957:54–87). It also required a centrifugal dispersal of power. Inside Britain this would involve electoral reform, devolution, and a reform of local government (Grimond, in Watson 1957:27–53; 1963:10). Externally, Britain should pool her sovereignty, not only in NATO, but also in the early moves to construct a European political and economic union based on respect for the individual and parliamentary government (Deighton, in Watson 1957:255–74).

Across a broad range of issues then — the bureaucratic state, administrative law reform, decentralization, partnership in industry, and enthusiasm for European economic and political co-operation — this radical social liberalism of the late 1950s and early 1960s anticipated the later preoccupations of the mainstream political agenda. To consolidate liberal influence, Grimond simultaneously campaigned for a political realignment embracing the Liberal Party, some Tory voters and the Labour Party divorced from its illiberal socialist minority (Grimond 1963:309). Although there were discussions between Liberals and Social Democrats, these did not survive the revival in Labour Party fortunes in 1963. When Labour achieved office in 1964, 'with all the patronage and hope that went with it', Grimond's hopes for realignment were effectively ended (Wallace, in Bogdanor 1983:55–6, Grimond, 1979a:216, 218).

Revitalized social liberalism survived the trauma of the Thorpe leadership, and informed the political perspective of Grimond's protégé, David Steel, who became Liberal leader in 1976. Steel was a firm supporter of the EEC, and an exponent of industrial partnership. He combined support for NATO with traditional Liberal opposition to an independent nuclear deterrent (Steel 1980:1–5, 19–21; Steel and Holme 1985:6–7, 130–47). What divided Steel from Grimond was neither policy perspective nor belief in the urgency of realignment. It concerned their different views of the worth of Social Democrats as partners in bringing about political change. Grimond's abortive push for realignment led him to believe that, following Gaitskell's death in 1963, Social Democrats had not been prepared to fight for their convictions. By the late 1970s too many of them had abandoned the political battle field for 'the flesh-pots of the capitalist-socialist establishment'. Thus, when Roy Jenkins appeared from the flesh-pots of the European Commission to deliver his Dimbleby Lecture in 1979, Grimond's response was lukewarm (Grimond 1979a:199, 218, 257; 1979b:802).

Steel, however, was more enthusiastic. He had co-operated closely with Roy Jenkins over abortion law reform in the 1960s and in the pro-EEC 'Britain in Europe' campaign in 1975. Steel had also been encouraged by the experience of the 'Lib-Lab' pact after 1977. In the wake of this experience he called for 'a great alliance of progressives, radicals and social democrats with Liberal leadership, to change a rotten political system' (Steel 1980:11, 19–21, 152–3, 162). Thus, when Jenkins privately confessed his disenchantment with Labour politics after the 1979 general election, Steel encouraged him in his inclination not to join the Liberals, but to launch a new political party that the Liberals could do business with (Josephs 1983:10–12).

However, to the community Liberals, who sprang up in the party towards the end of the 1960s, the disposition of individual Social Democrats was less important than the statist philosophy with which they had long been associated.

Community Liberals looked back less to Hobhouse, Keynes, and the equality goals of social liberalism, and more to Mill and the anarchist Kropotkin, whom they saw as exemplars of libertarianism. This had an overriding respect for human personality and ensured an emphasis on both distributional and procedural questions in politics. Following Mill, community Liberals subordinated economic objectives to ethical values, and cherished participation, diversity, experimentation and spontaneity (Greaves, in Hain 1976:48; Hebditch, in Hain 1976:58–62; Meadowcroft 1980:7; Thompson 1985:8). They saw the pursuit of growth as compromising the right of individuals to a healthy environment, and thought democracy in its representative form something of an empty shell. Communities should be involved with decisions which affected their own lives. Through learning the habit of participation in single issue campaigns, communities could move on to a wider political control over institutions. In this way a mature participatory democracy would slowly evolve (Lishman, in Hain 1976:79–83; Bradley 1985:163–9).

The strategy of the community Liberals was endorsed at the 1970 party Assembly. Liberals voted to act both inside and beyond established political institutions. They would 'help organise people in communities to take and use power, to use political skills to redress grievances, and to represent people at all levels of the political structure' (Steed, in Cyr 1977:16–17; Wilson 1987b: 14–15). This was a sensible strategy for a party long on the periphery of the parliamentary scene. Tough-minded exponents of community politics constituted a cadre so sensitive to changes in local opinion that they became an electoral force to be reckoned with. Herein lay one of the reasons for the tense relationship that community Liberals enjoyed with the party leaders, some of whom they viewed as 'black-tie' politicians, corrupted out of radicalism through membership of the exclusive club of Parliament. Their libertarian bottom-up view of politics made them deeply sceptical of grand talk of leader-inspired realignment. Given that elitist politicians could not rise above a narrow concern for the trappings of power, realignment was 'the epitome of nothingness'. New coalitions could not be conjured into life at one wave of the leader's wand. They would have to emerge from 'modest and highly practical beginnings' of personal relationships built up through local action (Lishman, in Hain 1976:88–91).

The party that David Steel led to the Social Democratic-Liberal Alliance was therefore anything but monolithic. The traditional and common concern with individuality did nothing to mask the divisions between the revisionists of social liberalism and the libertarian, community Liberals. These tensions played an important part in undermining the Alliance's attempt to construct a distinct idiom.

The Alliance and After

The SDP-Liberal Alliance was the light that failed. It was conceived in 1981 by David Steel and Roy Jenkins as the coming together of two reforming traditions in a partnership of principle. Working together to rid the electoral system of class-based, adversarial politics, the Social Democratic and Liberal Parties would educate the nation in the virtues of partnership. In 1987, after six bold, gorgeous, years, the Alliance collapsed in a heap of old-fashioned, adversarial acrimony. The political centre was left demoralized and fragmented.

Sketching out his view of the Alliance after the foundation of the SDP, Roy Jenkins suggested that, although the two parties had different traditions, the policy disputes between them did not come readily to mind. No mere arrangement of convenience would suffice. A principled partnership was called for, and one committed to the mixed economy, electoral reform, and internationalism (Jenkins 1985:31–2). Spurred on by what he called 'the present mood of pulsating political excitement', Jenkins soon began to speak of this partnership as having the potential of a 'union of hearts' (ibid.: 33). This elevated tone pervaded Alliance publications. For example, *A Fresh Start for Britain* (SDP/Liberal

Alliance, 1981) derided 'the politics of contrived antagonism' which had undermined public confidence in parliamentary institutions. Similarly, *Working Together for Britain* (SDP/Liberal Alliance 1983) looked forward to a new politics of co-operation in which the Alliance would bring back idealism and hope. This claim to have invented a new co-operative kind of politics was trumpeted throughout the duration of the Alliance. For David Owen and David Steel, in *The Time Has Come — Partnership for Progress* (Owen and Steel 1987), partnership was a mechanism for creating change by consent. The Alliance parties had 'successfully applied the partnership approach to their relationship with each other', and wished to extend it across government, public policy and the wider community (ibid.: 27).

What this meant in terms of concrete proposals was spelled out in the two Alliance general election manifestos, *Working Together for Britain — Programme for Government* (SDP/Liberal Alliance 1983) and *Britain United — The Time Has Come* (SDP/Liberal Alliance 1987). These were written from the distilled wisdom of an assorted group of appointed committees set up astride the separate constitutional structures of the two parties. The manifestos included a number of central themes. First, they reiterated the commitment to partnership and loudly denounced the dogma and bitterness of class-dominated politics. Second, they outlined a package of constitutional change. Electoral reform through proportional representation was at the heart of both *Working Together for Britain* and *Britain United*. It encouraged non-dogmatic cross-party combination, and the greater representation of women and ethnic minorities. The incorporation of the European Convention on Human Rights into British law would safeguard individual and civil rights, and the creation of national and regional assemblies with vague, undefined powers would begin a process of the decentralization of the power of the state.

Third, the manifestos set out the Alliance plans to revive the economy without changing the balance of ownership between private and public. Capital investment targeted to key sectors of the national infrastructure would expand the economy and generate employment. Growth would be 'green' to ensure environmental protection and energy conservation. Profit-sharing, employee share ownership and works councils would promote partnership in industry. In social policy, poverty would be confronted by targeting and raising the value of basic state benefits, and increased investment in health, education and housing would assist a reversal of declining public sector standards.

Finally, the manifestos reaffirmed that the Alliance was staunchly internationalist, an enthusiastic supporter of the European Community, and firmly adherent to the principle of collective security through NATO. In carefully chosen words that concealed a crucial disagreement, *Britain United* declared that the UK should maintain 'with whatever necessary modernisation' a minimum nuclear deterrent until it could be negotiated away.

There are a number of important points to make about this programme which bear upon the failure of the Alliance to construct a populist idiom. First, it is possible to view the programme from two different perspectives. In one, it incorporated the tenets laid out in the Limehouse Declaration, in Jenkins's Dimbleby Lecture, and in the pronouncements of Crosland, Owen, and Jenkins, that egalitarian public policy should operate within the confines of stable boundaries between healthy public and private sectors. No doubt the partiality of Social Democrats for this perspective explains why Liberals sometimes thought them 'patronising' (Meadowcroft 1987:418), because, in another perspective, the Alliance programme was the embodiment of ideas rehearsed in the long history of social liberalism. The critique of class politics echoed Keynes's strictures in *Essays in Persuasion* (1931); the constitutional and environmental concerns drew on a liberal tradition going back to Mill; and the proposals to create employment and industrial partnership were an uncanny replication of the plans in the 1928 Liberal Industrial Inquiry, *Britain's Industrial Future* (Layton *et al.* 1928). The point about these two perspectives is not that one was more accurate than the other, but that across a broad range of public policy issues it is impossible to separate out completely the Liberal from the Social Democratic components. Given that the aim of social liberalism was to construct a social democracy, and that revisionist social democracy after 1979 embraced much of liberalism's political explanation of economic decline, this is hardly surprising.

Although this broad ideological consensus augured well for the construction of a distinctive Alliance idiom, beyond it were a number of particular issues upon which there was no consensus. These included defence, the use of nuclear power, the renewal of the Prevention of Terrorism Act, tenants' rights to buy council houses, and the redistribution of wealth through integrating tax and social security (Owen 1987b:228; Butler and Kavanagh 1984:76–7; 1988:83–4). To depict these as simple conflicts between social democracy and liberalism would be to ignore the broad spectrum of policy positions within each tradition. This is well illustrated by a review of the defence disagreement which proved by far the most politically significant of all the policy disagreements.

The spectrum of Liberal defence positions ranged from pacificism and Cobdenite suspicion of great power *realpolitik* at one end to conditional acceptance of deterrent theory at the other. Many libertarians had been in the vanguard of the Campaign for Nuclear Disarmament, but party policy under Jo Grimond and David Steel combined opposition to an independent British nuclear deterrent with support for participation in NATO. Post-war Social Democratic defence positions were less heterogeneous, but not monolithic. The collective defence of the west through NATO had been a central theme, making Labour's adoption of unilateral nuclear disarmament an important stimulus to the creation of the SDP. Nevertheless, a minority of Social Democrats supported unilateralism, and even some multilateralists were undecided about whether to replace the ageing deterrent, Polaris.

From this gamut of opinions the Alliance had to construct one policy. In 1983, Liberal Assembly and SDP differences over both the future of Polaris and the deployment in Britain of American nuclear missiles were accommodated within a form of words which expressed the hope that both would disappear through arms control talks. However, after 1983 the impending obsolescence of Polaris required a new equilibrium. In an attempt to construct one, an Alliance defence commission rejected in 1986 the more powerful Trident as a replacement for Polaris, and concluded that no immediate decision need be taken about whether to replace Polaris at all. In May, in advance of the publication of the commission report, and without consulting his colleagues, the SDP leader Dr Owen condemned the second recommendation as 'fudging and mudging'. Without a massive reduction in superpower weaponry the only way to defend the cancellation of Trident was to insist on Britain remaining a nuclear weapons state. The SDP had been founded on convictions and these should not be abandoned. Liberal fury knew no bounds. At their September Assembly at Eastbourne they welcomed a more effective British contribution to NATO providing it was 'non-nuclear'. After this, no amount of reassurance from Owen and Steel about a commitment to a minimum nuclear deterrent could erase the impression that the Alliance was split on defence.

The defence décâcle was an important reason why the Alliance failed to develop a characteristic idiom, but it was not the only reason. Beneath the bland assurances of partnership, it was possible to identify a number of conflicting political strategies. Here they are abstracted (and therefore corrupted) into three: social market and Owenite, Jenkinsite, and participative Liberal. The failure of the Alliance to settle on any one of these strategies added to public confusion about what the Alliance stood for and where it was going.

David Owen began to explore the potential of a 'social market' strategy after assuming the leadership of the SDP in 1983. The theme had been used in West Germany by conservative Christian Democrats in the Dusseldorf Principles of 1949 to outline a competition policy, and by Social Democrats when they took the revisionist road in their Bad Godesberg programme a decade later (Leaman 1988:50–8, 74–7). It had also been borrowed by Sir Keith Joseph for his revision of conservatism after 1974. For Dr Owen, the social market approach began with the belief that market discipline, 'the progenitor of change and progress', could not and should not be avoided if industry was to become competitive at home and abroad (Owen 1984:8, 66, 103, 178). Government must accept a more restrained view of its role. It should not attempt to override market forces, but anticipate market-place demands and accelerate adaptation to them. This could be done by stimulating technology and skills training, by tempering the social consequences of adjustment, and by bringing market discipline to the competitive public sector (Owen 1984:10, 18–27).

At the same time, social policy should aim to make generous provision for individuals who can not fend for themselves in a competitive society, since markets can only exist within a framework of policies for ensuring social rights to households (Owen 1984:119–20; 1987a:11). The challenge was to discover how to eliminate poverty and promote greater equality 'without stifling enterprise or imposing bureaucracy from the centre' (ibid.:108). To meet this challenge, Owen turned to the American liberal philosopher, John Rawls, and his persuasive attempt to reconcile liberty and equality. For Rawls (1973:83), 'social and economic inequalities are to be arranged so that they are . . . to the greatest benefit of the least advantaged'. Owen used this principle to propose a selectivist social policy that promoted the prospects of the worst-off without crude levelling or the universal provision of services (Owen 1984:108–10).

The merit of this approach was that it constituted a serious attempt to shift the emphasis of social democracy from the strategy of distribution which was dependent on economic growth, to a strategy of production which promoted economic growth. Furthermore, the combination of market liberalism and egalitarian social policy was capable of translation into the readily understandable themes 'tough and tender', competitiveness and compassion. This was the nearest the Alliance came to adopting a distinctive idiom, but it failed to win universal assent across the two parties. To understand why, it is important to see that the social market approach was tied politically to Owenism, a paradoxical phenomenon related to, but not synonymous with, the social market. Owenism was a form of charismatic, conviction politics which gave to itself the leading role in defining clear-cut positions, not only on the social market, but also on sound defence and the decentralized state. The perceived obstacles to these outcomes were a preoccupation with merger between the two Alliance parties, and the refusal of the Jenkinsites to confront important policy differences with the forces of soft-centred liberalism. Owenism saw coalition politics as the natural and desired concomitant of electoral reform, and its own policy imperatives of market-led recovery and strong, nuclear defence made post-electoral combination with Thatcherism a distinct possibility. This was a prospect Dr Owen entertained with equanimity in the 1987 general election campaign (Owen 1987b:216, 220–39).

For the duration of the Alliance, social democratic opposition to the social market and Owenism was *sotto voce*, and confined to the supporters of Roy Jenkins, the first elected leader of the SDP and 'father' of the Alliance. Although the Jenkinsites were no less 'top-down' in their view of decision-making, they were irritated by the charismatic quality of Owenism (Marquand 1988:12, 232–3) and sceptical about the social market. The reverence for 'natural' markets in which sovereign individuals supposedly exchanged goods and services free of government distortion was fetishistic. Markets were neither historically nor functionally prior to the state, and individual exchanges were often fashioned by corporate power. Thus, although advocates of a mixed economy, Jenkinsites saw the need for a developmental state which intervened 'on a significant scale to supplement, constrain, manipulate, or direct market forces for public ends' (Marquand 1988:10, 100–7, 152, 225–6). This was not the restrained role for government advocated by Dr Owen.

Jenkinsites also objected to the way Owenism drew a distinction between soft-centred liberalism and hard-centred social democracy. Roy Jenkins was prepared to recognize the tensions of competing party ethos, but he considered that Owenism exaggerated out of all proportion the minimal policy differences between social democrats and liberals. For Jenkins, social democracy and liberalism were divided by 'one of the narrowest ideological divides in the history of politics' (Jenkins 1985:32, 66–7). The exaggeration of this divide was symptomatic of the Owenite attempt to shun closer partnership with the liberals and create 'a sort of junior Thatcherite party' out of the SDP. The spirit and outlook of the SDP needed to be wholeheartedly opposed to Thatcherism, because 'Post-Thatcher the country will not want a sub-Thatcherite alternative' (Jenkins 1985:165–6).

In the Liberal party there was a widespread distrust of Dr Owen. Why was this the case? The paradox of Owenism was that it was decentralist in aim, but emphatically centralist (because charismatic) in method. This method was inimical to a prevailing liberal ethos which emphasized the participative, bottom-up, nature of decision-making. Even without Owenism, many liberals were suspicious of both the SDP and the Alliance itself. Community politics had grown as a direct reaction to the elitist, centrifugal politics of old-style social democracy, yet the SDP had acted as a refuge for its unreconstructed survivors, and through its use of leader-appointed policy commissions the Alliance had adopted its oligarchical methods (Meadowcroft, in Meadowcroft and Marquand 1981:5; Thomson 1985:22; Greaves 1986; Wilson 1987b:25). In the context of this ethos, even pro-Alliance liberals were disposed to view Owenism as an assault on liberal values. Owen's enthusiasm for the social market was non-liberal because it put a system before the individual (Andrews

1985:15), conviction politics translated itself into contempt for Liberals and 'obsession' about defence (Wilson, 1987b:195–6), and arms length approach to interparty co-operation became wilful obstruction of the Alliance. The years from 1983 to 1985 should have been spent projecting Alliance policy priorities and strategy. Instead, time was wasted as Dr Owen shunned joint policy negotiations and defined the social market. This lost opportunity was said to have cost the Alliance the 1987 election (Wallace 1987:9–10; Meadowcroft 1987:415). Lastly, liberalism could, *in extremis*, swallow a post-electoral pact with conservatism purged of what was seen as Thatcherite excess. However, as David Steel made clear during the 1987 general election, in a way which exposed a disagreement with Dr Owen and confused the electorate, the prospect of treating with Mrs Thatcher in person was anathema (Wilson, 1987b:197–200).

Plagued by policy disagreement and unable to agree on a political strategy, the Alliance impact was blurred in the general elections of 1983 and 1987. Although recording more than a quarter of the popular vote in 1983 and more than a fifth in 1987, the Alliance parties fell short of the 'total victory' that Roy Jenkins had thought (Jenkins 1985:42) 'perfectly possible'. Even the more realistic aim (Owen 1987b:229–30) of a balanced or 'hung' parliament proved elusive. In June 1987, in the wake of the second electoral set-back, and two days after David Owen had reaffirmed his commitment to a partnership of separate parties, David Steel unveiled proposals for 'democratic fusion' between the Liberals and the SDP. This prompted a sustained bout of mutual recrimination — utterly inappropriate coming from the apostles of partnership and co-operation. David Steel was judged 'a fixer' with a Jekyll-like personality; David Owen suggested the mergerites showed a lack of nerve typical of liberal-minded people in Britain; and Rosie Barnes dubbed the Liberals 'a sleepy party' inclined to do 'dotty things'. If, alongside this invective, the merger debate was ideologically significant in any way, it was because it highlighted contrasting views about the traditions of social democracy and liberalism and their relationship to each other.

The mergerites argued that the liberal and social democratic traditions were already inextricably intertwined. From a Jenkinsite perspective, Marquand (1987) explained that:

> Since 1906 . . . mainstream British liberalism has been social liberalism — as committed as social democracy to the values of community, fraternity and social equality and as determined to use the power of the state to redistribute resources to the disadvantaged.

This meant that there existed what social liberal, Richard Holme (1987), called 'an extraordinary degree of intellectual convergence', something likely to find clearer expression in a new, single party. Mergerites also disagreed with David Owen about the extent and nature of the policy differences between the two parties. To Lord Grimond (Grimond 1987:17) these were 'microscopic compared to the chasms in the Tory party', and hardly visible to most Alliance activists. In any event, differences had been exacerbated by the operation of two separate party structures, and existed within parties just as much as between them (Taverne 1987; Steel 1987). In consequence, fusion was the one acceptable political choice available. The failure to merge would undermine the credibility of two parties who had argued for partnership. It would also reduce the SDP into 'an Elysium where we could rest from the turmoil of political life or a narrow sect where we could talk endlessly to each other' (Rodgers 1987; Wilson 1987a). Heeding these arguments, the majority of members of both former Alliance parties supported the creation of a new, merged party, and the Social and Liberal Democratic Party (SLDP) duly appeared in March 1988.

To the Owenites, the presentation of the debate in terms of 'unity or bust' was defeatism. For Dr Owen, the strength of the Alliance as two separate parties had been that it allowed two different strands of political thought, one collectivist and social democratic, the other anarchic and liberal, to work together. The distinctive contribution which the SDP had brought to British politics should not be lost. Therefore, the redefinition of social democracy around the idea of the social market was vital. It would hasten the day 'when the SDP is seen to be closer to the heartbeat of this nation than any other party' (Owen 1987b:232, 226; 1988a; 1988b). In consequence, Dr Owen would have no truck with the merged party, and remained behind with a band of loyal supporters in a 'continuing' SDP.

Owen's decision to opt out of the merger talks helped to assure the fragmentation of the political centre at a time when Thatcherism, after its third successive electoral triumph, looked unassailable. Owen defended his determination to stay out of a merged party by reference to the different natures of social democracy and liberalism. He was proud of a career-long association with a consistent social democratic position which had begun in Gaitskell's Labour Party (Owen 1987b:239). He was also concerned to emphasize the anarchic flavour of the liberal tradition. No doubt both these positions were sincerely held and no doubt they contained important elements of truth. For example, there was nothing in Dr Owen's policy profile to match the tergiversation of David Steel and Robert Maclennan (1988) in hastily withdrawing their joint leaders' policy declaration, 'Voices and choices for all', during the merger negotiations. This declaration almost aborted the whole merger process when its proposals to retain Trident and extend VAT to food and children's clothing excited the scorn of the entire Liberal party. Few would dispute Owen's description of this episode as a 'ghastly mess', and it gave a fillip to his separatist party in waiting. Furthermore, the party ethos of liberalism was certainly anarchic. Even David Steel had referred to the Liberal Party as lacking discipline and behaving 'like a flock of flapping chickens in a hen-run at the appearance of a fox' (Steel 1980:8). Liberal faith in the perils of participative democracy contrasted sharply with the more disciplined, leader-orientated SDP, and this had caused considerable tension in the Alliance.

Nevertheless, Dr Owen's assertions were contestable in two important ways. First, as we have seen, social democracy has travelled a long way since Gaitskell and, in this history, consistency was not the salient theme. One of Dr Owen's characteristics has been his readiness to abandon positions in the face of changed circumstances, and it is not necessary to accept uncritically his own description of himself as a consistent Social Democrat. For example, the first edition of his *Face the Future* rejected certain aspects of the socialist tradition, not democratic socialism itself (Owen 1981a:5, 33, 56, 66, 71). Yet, only months later, in the revised edition, democratic socialism had to make way for a distinct social democratic philosophy. This would appeal to those 'who believe in the mixed economy' (Owen 1981b:3). By 1984, though, the mixed economy itself had become 'a portmanteau description to which virtually anyone can subscribe' (Owen 1984:8), and had to make way for the social market economy.

Furthermore, without descending into political ritualism, there were important procedural qualities in Gaitskellite social democracy missing from Owenism which deserve attention. Durbin wrote that politics in a period of economic complexity required not only intelligence and knowledge, but also charity (Durbin 1940:256). Of course, Dr Owen was blessed with an abundance of intelligence and knowledge. However, charity was never much in evidence. This is clear from his description of Roy Jenkins's 1979 Dimbleby Lecture as indulging in the 'luxury' of someone not involved in Labour Party battles, and from his suggestion that mergerites had 'chickened out' and reverted to the 'old politics' (Owen 1987b:163; Naughtie 1987). Another quality missing from Owenism, and stressed by Gaitskell himself, was the willingness to compromise, and the commitment to persuade and be persuaded. These were necessary attributes for any political leader aspiring to synthesize two related political traditions. For all its merits, therefore, Owen's conception of himself as a conviction politician seemed steadily to reduce his manoeuvrability, and to make him associate all compromise and persuasion with what he called 'mudge and fudge'. This was starkly illustrated in his decision to reject merger negotiations in advance of the SDP membership ballot, an uncomfortable position for the co-founder of a political party based on one-member, one-vote (Liddle 1987:7).

Second, as far as Owen's depiction of the liberal tradition as anarchic is concerned, his status as trenchant reinterpreter of the social market idea should not disguise the somewhat inchoate nature of his political thought. The description of liberalism as anarchic is scarcely adequate to describe a rich and contested political tradition, which (as we have seen) has social liberal and free market dimensions as well as a libertarian one. The aim of social liberals from Hobhouse onwards was to demonstrate both that the development of individual personality could not be divorced from collective action by the state, and that the challenge for economics was to equate social service with individual reward (Hobhouse 1911:107; Clarke 1978). These were themes to warm the cockles of Dr Owen's heart and indeed featured prominently in his own account of the social market. Dr Owen was perfectly entitled to reject merger, but not on the spurious ideological grounds that liberalism was essentially anarchic.

Conclusion

The division of the country's progressive forces in the face of conservatism has been a consistent liberal preoccupation from Keynes to Grimond and Steel. If the realignment achieved in 1988 was incomplete, it took a stage further a process begun with the foundation of the SDP in 1981. Social democracy, shedding its socialist pretensions at the beginning of the decade, found a long promised institutional union with liberalism at the end of it. The price paid for this union was high. It involved an unseemly public row which flew in the face of years of rhetoric. It also involved losing the services of easily the most formidable politician the Alliance had possessed, and a man with a competing vision of centre politics. In this there lay a portent of trouble to come.

The merger debate concentrated the minds of the political centre on the appropriate road to follow. As Tawney had warned, this was uncongenial but necessary. It necessitated the confrontation of political difficulties by recourse to principle (Tawney 1921:10). By deciding to merge, Social Democrats and Liberals expressed confidence that their traditions had sufficient in common to construct a broad, non-socialist alternative to Thatcherism. In doing so, Liberals said goodbye to the historic Liberal Party, and Social Democrats rejected a narrower commitment to redefine social market ideas ambiguous in their relationship to Thatcherism because of their emphasis on market-led recovery.

For all its venom, then, the political argument of 1987 and 1988 at least produced important decisions about the futures of social democracy and liberalism. However, this was the beginning not the end of difficulties. Merger did not, by itself, create a homogeneous political force. The publication of Marquand's *The Unprincipled Society* in 1988 heralded an important attempt to confront this problem and point the way to a distinct centrist governing philosophy. According to Marquand, Britain needed a 'developmental' state to influence and constrain market factors, but one whose directions were 'negotiated' between the state and its social partners. This could only be achieved through a cultural change which harmonized the ideas of power-sharing and class-collaboration. Politics would become a mutual education in which the preceptoral mode was adopted to work out common purposes and some notion of the public good (Marquand 1988:107, 111, 146, 163, 165, 216, 229).

The attraction of this approach was its recognition that a usable doctrine had to be 'hammered out in the give and take of a debate' and did not 'spring, fully armed, from a theorist's brow'. This left room for negotiation with Liberal libertarians who represented more accurately than anyone else in the new party what Marquand called the 'cultural mutation' in Britain which emphasized the values of 'autonomy and authenticity' (Marquand 1988:12, 201–2). However, preceptoral politics was not without its risks. How (for example) would the politics of mutual education cope with intransigent social partners of labour or business who were unwilling to engage in conversation? As Marquand well understood, the idea of constructing a progressive civic morality relied heavily on the optimistic belief that individual, class and corporate appetites were susceptible to *persuasion* (Marquand 1988:67–8). If this looked a bit like whistling in the dark in contemporary Britain, it was what had sustained historic liberalism and social democracy through previous sloughs of despond (see Hobhouse 1911:115). The challenge to the first SLD leader, Paddy Ashdown, was to deploy the rational discourse of preceptoral or some other general interest politics in a way which made the party's social liberal inheritance distinct and intelligible.

This would not be easy for, at the end of the 1980s, British politics had no shortage of opposition parties trying to construct a governing philosophy for post-Thatcher Britain. The social market Owenites were unlikely to go away and, as long as they survived, the collapse of the Alliance would continue to haunt the centre ground. The professed ideological stance of the Ashdown Democrats was firmly left of centre, and their strategic objective was thus to replace Labour as the main opposition to the Conservatives. This was a logically coherent stance, but whether it was politically plausible is a quite different matter. With the Kinnock Labour Party moving in the direction of market socialism, social liberalism was clearly embarked on a long, difficult, and crowded road. In these circumstances, the prospect of an effective progressive challenge to conservatism remained elusive.

Further Reading

Robert Eccleshall's Introduction to *British Liberalism: Liberal Thought from the 1640s to 1980s* (1986) is a clear, concise, and authoritative starting point. Michael Bentley, *The Climax of Liberal Politics: British Liberalism in Theory and Practice, 1868–1918* (1987) is a stimulating, scholarly and accessible account which places the development of liberal thought in a party political context. Vernon Bogdanor's *Liberal Party Politics* (1983) is the best account of contemporary British liberal politics. The chapter by Peter Clarke usefully summarizes his exemplary study *Liberals and Social Democrats* (1978). Of the primary texts, Hobhouse's *Liberalism* (1911) retains its passionate majesty, and Keynes's *Essays in Persuasion* (1931) elegantly illustrate liberal impatience with class-dominated politics.

William Paterson and Alastair Thomas, *The Future of Social Democracy: Problems and Prospects of Social Democratic Parties in Western Europe* (1986) stands alone as a comprehensive overview of contemporary European social democratic thought. Anthony Crosland's *The Future of Socialism* (1956), for all its statism, is still required reading. The incisiveness and humour of *John P. Mackintosh on Parliament and Social Democracy* (1982), edited by David Marquand, is testimony to the loss social democracy experienced with Mackintosh's early death. Marquand's recent contribution, *The Unprincipled Society: New Demands and Old Politics* (1988), bears comparison with Crosland.

Bibliography (published in London unless otherwise stated)

Andrews, L. (1985) *Liberalism versus the Social Market Economy*, Hebden Bridge: Hebden Royd Papers.

Benn, A.W. (1979) *Arguments for Socialism*, Jonathan Cape.

Bentley, M. (1987) *The Climax of Liberal Politics: British Liberalism in Theory and Practice, 1868–1918*, Edward Arnold.

Beveridge, Sir W. (1942) *Social Insurance and Allied Services*, Cmd 6404, reprinted 1966, HMSO.

Beveridge, Sir W. (1945) *Why I am a Liberal MP*, Herbert Jenkins Limited.

Bogdanor, V. (ed.) (1983) *Liberal Party Politics*, Oxford: Clarendon Press.

Bradley, I. (1981) *Breaking the Mould? The Birth and Prospects of the Social Democratic Party*, Oxford: Martin Robertson.

Bradley, I. (1985) *The Strange Rebirth of Liberal Britain*, with a foreword by the Rt Hon. David Steel MP, Chatto & Windus.

Butler, D. and Kavanagh, D. (1984) *The British General Election of 1983*, Basingstoke: Macmillan.

Butler, D. and Kavanagh, D. (1988) *The British General Election of 1987*, Basingstoke: Macmillan.

Campbell, J. (1983) *Roy Jenkins: A Biography*, Weidenfeld & Nicolson.

Clarke, P. (1978) *Liberals and Social Democrats*, Cambridge: Cambridge University Press.

Cole, G.D.H. (1920) *Guild Socialism Re-Stated*, Leonard Parsons.
Cole, G.D.H. (1943) *Fabian Socialism*, Allen & Unwin.
Collini, S. (1979) *Liberalism and Sociology: L.T. Hobhouse and Political Argument in Britain, 1880-1914*, Cambridge: Cambridge University Press.
Condren, C. (1985) *The Status and Appraisal of Classic Texts: An Essay on Political Theory, Its Inheritance, and the History of Ideas*, Princeton, NJ: Princeton University Press.
Crosland, C.A.R. (1956) *The Future of Socialism*, Jonathan Cape.
Cyr, A. (1977) *Liberal Party Politics in Britain*, with a foreword by Michael Steed, John Calder.
Deakin, N. (1987) *The Politics of Welfare*, Methuen.
Doring, H. (1983) 'Who are the Social Democrats?' *New Society* 65, 1086:351-3.
Dunn, J. (1979) *Western Political Theory in the Face of the Future*, Cambridge: Cambridge University Press.
Durbin, E.F.M. (1940) *The Politics of Democratic Socialism: An Essay on Social Policy*, with a foreword by the Rt Hon. Hugh Gaitskell, Routledge; 6th impression, 1965.
Eccleshall, R. (1986) *British Liberalism: Liberal Thought from the 1640s to 1980s*, Longman.
Emmett Tyrell, R. (ed) (1977) *The Future that Doesn't Work: Social Democracy's Failures in Britain*, New York: Doubleday.
Freeden, M. (1978) *The New Liberalism: An Ideology of Social Reform*, Oxford: Clarendon Press.
Greaves, A. (1986) 'The Tony Greaves Column', *Liberal News*, 12 September.
Greenleaf, W.H. (1983) *The British Political Tradition*, vol. 2 *The Ideological Heritage*, Methuen.
Grimond, J. (1959) *The Liberal Future*, Faber & Faber.
Grimond, J. (1963) *The Liberal Challenge*, Hollis & Carter.
Grimond, J. (1979a) *Memoirs*, Heinemann.
Grimond, J. *et al.* (1979b), 'Roy Jenkins's Dimbleby lecture: a symposium of views and reactions', *Listener*, 13 December.
Grimond, Lord (1987) 'Making capitalism work for everyone', *Independent*, 13 December.
Hain, P. (ed.) (1976) *Community Politics*, Platform Books.
Hayek, F.A. (1944) *The Road to Serfdom*, Routledge & Kegan Paul, 1976.
Hobhouse, L.T. (1911) *Liberalism*, with a new introduction by Alan P. Grimes, Oxford: Oxford University Press, 1964.
Hobson, J.A. (1909) *The Crisis of Liberalism*, edited with an introduction by P.F. Clarke, Brighton: Harvester Press, 1974.
Holme, R. (1987) 'The stark options for the Alliance', *Guardian*, 17 June.
Jenkins, R. (1979) 'Home thoughts from abroad', *Listener*, 29 November, 733-8.
Jenkins, R. (1985) *Partnership of Principle: Writings and Speeches on the Making of the Alliance*, selected and edited by Clive Lindley, The Radical Centre in association with Secker & Warburg.

Jenkins, R. (1987) 'Where we must go from here', *Observer*, 9 August.
Josephs, J. (1983) *Inside the Alliance: An Inside Account of the Development and Prospects of the Liberal-SDP Alliance*, foreword by Dick Taverne, John Martin Publishing.
Keynes, J.M. (1931) *Essays in Persuasion*, in *The Collected Writings of John Marnard Keynes* vol. 9, Macmillan and St Martin's Press for the Royal Economic Society, 1972.
Keynes, J.M. (1936) *The General Theory of Employment, Interest and Money. The Collected Writings of John Maynard Keynes*, vol. 7, Macmillan and St Martin's Press for the Royal Economic Society, 1973.
Kilmarnock, A. (ed.) (1987) *The Radical Challenge: The Response of Social Democracy*, Andre Deutsch.
Kolakowski, L. (1982) 'What is living (and what is dead) in the social democratic idea?' *Encounter*, 58, 2.
Layton, W.T., Simon, E.D., Lloyd George, D., Keynes, J.M., Masterman, C.F.G., Samuel, H. and Simon, J. (1928) *Britain's Industrial Future being the Report of the Liberal Industrial Inquiry*, Ernest Benn.
Leaman, J. (1988) *The Political Economy of West Germany*, Basingstoke: Macmillan.
Liddle, R. (1987) 'Democracy David Owen style: heads I win, tails I split the party', *New Statesman* 21 August.
Luard, E. (1979) *Socialism without the State*, London and Basingstoke: Macmillan.
Macintyre, D. (1987) 'Owen: why I refuse to merge', *Sunday Telegraph*, 12 July.
Macleod, I. and Powell, J. Enoch (1952) *The Social Services: Needs and Means*, Conservative Political Centre, No. 115.
Marquand, D. (1981) *Russet-Coated Captains: The Challenge of Social Democracy*, Open Forum 5, SDP.
Marquand, D. (ed.) (1982) *John P. Mackintosh on Parliament and Social Democracy*, Longman.
Marquand, D. (1983) 'Is there new hope for the Social Democrats?' *Encounter*, 60, 4:11-17.
Marquand, D. (1987) 'Unity of purpose for power and honour', *Sunday Times*, 28 June.
Marquand, D. (1988) *The Unprincipled Society: New Demands and Old Politics*, Jonathan Cape.
Meadowcroft, M. (1980) *Liberal Values for a New Decade*, Liberal Publication Department.
Meadowcroft, M. (1987) 'The future of the left: a liberal view', *Political Quarterly*, 58, 4:414-23.
Meadowcroft, M. (1988) 'Liberal leader with a risky strategy', *Independent*, 4 January.
Meadowcroft, M. and Marquand, D. (1981) *Liberalism and Social Democracy*, Liberal Publication Department.
Mill, J.S. (1848) *Principles of Political Economy*, books iv and v, edited with an introduction by Donald Winch, Harmondworth: Penguin Books, 1985.

Mill, J. (1959) *On Liberty*, edited with an introduction by Gertrude Himmelfarb, Harmondsworth: Penguin Books, 1985.

Mill, J. (1861) *Representative Government*, reproduced in *Three Essays*, with an introducton by Richard Wollheim, Oxford: Oxford University Press, 1975.

Mortimer, J. (1987) *Rumpole's Last Case*, Harmondsworth: Penguin Books.

Naughtie, J. (1987) '''Chickening out'' gibe by Owen', *Guardian*, 3 September.

Owen, D. (1981a) *Face the Future*, Jonathan Cape.

Owen, D. (1981b) *Face the Future*, revised edn, Oxford: Oxford University Press.

Owen, D. (1984) *A Future that Will Work: Competitiveness and Compassion*, Harmondsworth: Penguin Books.

Owen, D. (1987a) *Social Market and Social Justice*. The Tawney Society, Fifth Anniversary Lecture.

Owen, D. (1987b) *David Owen Personally Speaking to Kenneth Harris*, Weidenfeld & Nicolson.

Owen, D. (1988a) 'We're here to stay', *Campaigner*, February.

Owen, D. (1988b) *Sticking With It*, Campaign for Social Democracy.

Owen, D. and Steel, D. (1987c) *The Time Has Come: Partnership for Progress*, Weidenfeld and Nicolson.

Paterson, W.E. and Thomas, A.H. (1986) *The Future of Social Democracy: Problems and prospects of Social Democratic parties in Western Europe*, Oxford: Clarendon Press.

Rawls, J. (1973) *A Theory of Justice*, Oxford: Oxford University Press.

Rodgers, W. (1982) *The Politics of Change*, Martin, Secker & Warburg.

Rodgers, W. (1987) 'Why merger must take place', *Observer*, 21 June.

Rose, H. (1981) 'Rereading Titmuss: the sexual division of welfare', *Journal of Social Policy*, 10, 4:477–502.

SDP/Liberal Alliance (1981) *A Fresh Start for Britain*.

SDP/Liberal Alliance (1983) *Working Together for Britain; Programme for Government*.

SDP/Liberal Alliance (1987) *Britain United. The Time Has Come. The SDP/Liberal Alliance Programme for Government*.

Steel, D. (1980) *A House Divided: The Lib-Lab Pact and the Future of British Politics*, Weidenfeld & Nicolson.

Steel, D. (1987) 'The case for union now', *Observer*, 19 July.

Steel, D. and Holme, R. (eds) (1985) *Partners in One Nation: A New Vision of Britain 2000 presented by David Steel*, The Bodley Head.

Steel, D. and Maclennan, R. (1988) 'Voices and choices for all', *Guardian*, 14 January.

Taverne. D. (1987) 'Choice between fusion and fission', *Independent*, 22 June.

Tawney, R.H. (1921) *The Acquisitive Society*, Brighton: Wheatsheaf, 1982.

Tawney, R.H. (1964) in R. Hinden (ed.) *The Radical Tradition: Twelve Essays on Politics, Education and Literature*, Allen & Unwin.

Taylor, A.J.P. (1969) *The Trouble Makers: Dissent over Foreign Policy, 1792-1939*, Panther Books.

Thompson, D. (1985) *The Shocktroops of Pavement Politics: An Assessment of the Influence of Community Politics in the Liberal Party*, Hebden Bridge: A Hebden Royd Pamphlet.

Wainwright. H. (1988) 'Who's afraid of political activists?' *New Statesman*, 8 January: 11–13.

Wallace, W. (1987) 'The first and future steps', *New Statesman*, 26 June.

Wallace, W. (1988) 'How the Alliance was sundered', *The Independent*, 14 January.

Watson, G. (ed.) (1957) *The Unservile State: Essays in Liberty and Welfare*, Allen & Unwin.

Williams, S. (1981) *Politics is For People*, Harmondsworth: Penguin Books.

Wilson, D. (1987a) 'When two into one has to go', *Guardian*, 15 June.

Wilson. D. (1987b) *Battle for Power*, Oxford: Sphere Books.

Wright, A.W. (1979) *G.D.H. Cole and Socialist Democracy*, Oxford: Clarendon Press.

Wright, A. (1987a) *Socialisms: Theories and Practices*, Oxford: Oxford University Press.

Wright, A. (1987b) *R.H. Tawney*, Manchester: Manchester University Press.

Part two

Ideologies and Policies

Chapter five

Social Policy

Nicholas Deakin

The Context

In one of the best-known recent studies of social policy, Marshall defines the limits of the field in the following terms:

> social policy uses political power to supersede, supplement or modify operations of the economic system in order to achieve results which the economic system would not achieve on its own, and . . . in doing so is guided by values, other than those determined by open market forces.
>
> (Marshall, 1965)

In giving this definition Marshall assumes that the social policy objectives which he identifies can stand as separate goals which politicians will accept as such, and seek to implement through the political process. But in practice, the independence of social policy has by no means always been accepted by politicians or in public debate; and the willingness to override other considerations in setting policy priorities had consequently often been lacking. In order for the goals of social policy to be given the central place that Marshall (and others) wishes to give them, the ideas and values that underpin them also have to command acceptance, both among politicians and more widely.

The recent history of social policy, like a fever chart, displays evidence of rapid bursts of frenetic activity during the stages when these conditions are satisfied, followed by long periods of quiescence, during which new ideas are incubated, but either fail to find wider acceptance or are blocked because social policy issues are not being given priority on the general public policy agenda. Sometimes there is a time-lag; although ideas emerge into the arena of public debate coloured by the circumstances and values prevailing when they are first expressed, they may prove to have applications unsuspected at that period which give them durability. Others are children of their own times, whose relevance rapidly disappears when the policy context changes.

For these reasons, in particular, it is difficult to treat the debate on the ideologies of social policy within a strictly chronological framework. Ideas emerge, are debated, sink back into obscurity and then reemerge and capture the attention of politicians. Reading the Edwardian debates on the role of institutions and the proper division of responsibilities between the individual, the state and the market; or arguments about the problems of introducing and funding social programmes in a democratic system, it is possible to believe that very little has changed, at least in the vocabulary and content of debate. The issue of the autonomy of social policy and the extent to which it can be used to modify economic priorities, was debated as intensively after the First World War as it has been in the 1980s. Some critics would argue that the views expressed by Treasury ministers then have more than a little in common with those paraded in the past few years. Stripping off the contemporary clothing in which these ideas were paraded at different times often reveals resemblances of this kind, although it is important not to neglect the significance of the vast changes that have taken place over the past century in the structure of British society and its institutions, and the circumstances of individuals. With this caveat in mind, one of the most revealing common themes that runs through debates on social policy between and within political parties over the past century is the argument on the proper role and responsibilities of the state: how is state intervention justified and how effective can it be?

The Origins of State Welfare

Classical liberalism, in its pure, nineteenth-century form, conceived of the role of the state in highly restricted terms. The functions that could be legitimately assigned to it — the maintenance of law and order and the defence of the realm — impinged barely, if at all, upon the area of social policy. The Poor Law, with its rigid confining of relief to the minimum necessary to secure bare subsistence for those with no other recourse who were morally fitted to receive it, was the single chilly exception to this general rule. The common justification for these restrictions rested on two parallel arguments; first, the inevitable tendency of any intrusion, however benevolently intended, to diminish the liberty and self-sufficiency of individual citizens and, second, the inability of state invention to achieve the objectives for which it has been undertaken.

These propositions were most clearly articulated, in the context of nineteenth-century political debate by the philosopher and pioneer sociologist Herbert Spencer, in his polemic *The Man versus The State* (1969). His pessimism about the likely impact of state intervention was matched by an optimism about the capacity of individuals to manage their own lives and secure their welfare and that of their families. But the arguments he and others deployed in support of these propositions gradually ceased to command general acceptance once the economic depression of the 1880s undermined the claims of *laissez-faire* capitalism to have provided an infallible mechanism for rewarding the individual who had exhibited thrift and industry, and punishing profligacy and idleness. The revelations that followed about the extent of poverty among those who could not be categorized as 'undeserving', in part as as a result of the activities of social investigators like Spencer's protégée Beatrice Webb, undermined the moral case for *laissez-faire* at its most vulnerable point, and greatly strengthened the case for state intervention to correct those abuses left untouched by the operation of the economic system.

The argument about the form that such intervention should take was of particular significance for the Liberal Party, which had served for most of the century as the main vehicle for social reform. Within the party the intellectual dispute was intense; the main success of the so-called 'New Liberals' after the turn of the century lay in persuading a majority within their party that the state could now be trusted not merely to inspect, regulate, and control, but also to implement new social policies, beyond the manifestly inadequate minimum provision contained in the Poor Law. The anxieties articulated in their most extreme form by Spencer (a life-long Liberal) and the constitutional lawyer A.V. Dicey about the likely impact of such interventions on the rights and duties of citizens and their individual capacities, came to seem less important than the likely consequences of continued inadequacies in the education, housing, and health of the industrial working class. C.F.G. Masterman, in his comprehensive review of the state of the country before the First World War (*The Condition of England*, 1909) argued on behalf of the New Liberals for intervention from the state to rescue a society poised on the lip of the volcano. By acting in this way as the agent of the collectivity of citizens, the state would be reinforcing, not undermining, their liberties.

This acceptance of the case for state intervention extended beyond the Liberal Party. The Fabian Sidney Webb wrote in 1909:

> In every direction the individual finds himself, in the growing elaboration of organisation of the twentieth century State, face to face with personal obligations unknown to his grandfather, which the development of collective action both enables and virtually compels him to fulfil.
>
> (Webb 1916:44)

Dispute about the form that state intervention should take, the proper limits to be set to it, and even the terms that should be employed to describe it — collectivism, socialism — formed the subject matter of an extended debate. The legislative programme of the Liberal government in the decade before the First World War was the substantive outcome of this debate. The contribution of politicians in other parties — the recently formed Labour Party, individual Conservatives — or of those, like the Webbs, who were working outside the framework of conventional party politics, helped to ensure that the principle of reform was accepted, and priority for its implementation was secured.

However, these reforms took a partial — even ramshackle — form. A compromise was struck between individual and state responsibility for provision by adopting the insurance principle to address the problems of invalidity and unemployment. But substantive reform of the Poor Law, still the main expression of social policy through government, was not secured. In part this reflected the absence of a consciously evolved 'grand design' embodied in the electoral programme of one party (Thane 1982:98). In social policy Edwardian politicians were groping for ways of coping with a situation that was still only half understood and where the means,in the shape of effective administrative machinery, hardly existed, and the problems of implementation were only dimly glimpsed. But once the principle of state action had been accepted, the fluidity of the political situation, and the absence of complex institutional structures, worked in favour of action. As Douglas Ashford puts it 'the liberal welfare state in Britain was in many ways not the product of politics, but a product of political action that exploited the reflection and research of an entire generation' (Ashford 1986:77). It would be thirty years before another conjunction between ideas and action in social policy came about; and then the circumstances were very different, even if many of the ideas were not.

In the interval a number of important developments helped to recast the context in which ideas were debated. The Liberal Party suffered its 'strange death' and ceased to be a major force in conventional politics; but Liberal ideas survived. The 'liberal socialist' synthesis of the New Liberalism found an outlet through a series of policy documents prepared under the aegis of Lloyd George, as part of his vain attempt to recapture power, and incorporating the powerful advocacy of J.M. Keynes. As the Liberal Party's supplanter as the principal party of opposition to conservatism and inheritor of its role as the vehicle for transmmission of ideas on social reform, the Labour Party offered few refinements on the position that had been evolved before the First World War. The rational, orderly, rather bureaucratic approach evolved by the Webbs and their fellow Fabians, which had held an appeal to reformers of all parties, became the basis of Labour's subsequent approach. The appeal of the Fabian approach lay in the combination of a sound basis in well-researched analysis of social problems, with a systematic approach to their solution, in state-run services staffed by well-trained professionals. The adoption of this approach in local government, most notably in the

London County Council by the Progressive coalition of Socialists and advanced Liberals, appeared to provide the necessary proof that this technique — 'gas and water socialism', to its half-contemptuous, half-admiring critics — could pass the practical test of providing solutions to intransigeant social problems. A counter-current of concern on the left about the implications of entrusting too much power to a Prussian-style state apparatus whose officials (particularly those in central government) would be as unlikely as their predecessors in Poor Law administration to pay proper regard to the interests of working-class clients persisted, but failed to produce politically appealing alternative proposals.

The vast expansion of the machinery of government produced as a result of the four years of the First World War appeared to provide the opportunity to test out ideas for reform on a larger scale. But after flirting with reconstruction policies in health and housing, on the first signs of economic difficulties the post-war Coalition government opted for drastic retrenchment. The Treasury asserted itself to ensure that social policy objectives did not cut across economic policy goals, defined in traditional terms of strict economy and good book-keeping. Successive inquiries each led in turn to severe cuts in social programmes, the second of these contributing directly to the fall of the minority Labour government that had been elected in 1929.

But despite the clearest possible evidence that, to use Marshall's terms, social policy had been unable to establish and sustain its autonomy, the inter-war period was not wholly barren. The implementation of the pre-war Liberal government's reforms had generated its own momentum; a powerful new state apparatus had come into being, led by a generation of civil servants accustomed to the notion that a substantial public sector of welfare was a natural element in the machinery of government. Increasingly, centralization of these responsibilities limited the extent to which local authorities could undertake independent initiatives; but within the new constellation of forces they, too, had taken on a substantially enhanced role. A series of administrative reforms introduced by a Conservative minister, Neville Chamberlain, effectively gave the Poor Law its quietus, and created a recognizably modern apparatus for policy implementation. However, this apparatus was not employed to develop a coherent set of welfare policies. When the next test occurred, with the Great Depression of the early 1930s, and rapid growth in poverty and unemployment, the response of the new National government was to cut government expenditure on welfare and impose stringent means tests for beneficiaries.

For after 1931 the dominance of economic policy was total in domestic politics; experiments in welfare policy tried elsewhere, in Europe and in Australasia, were not attempted in Britain. But interest in the potentialities of these initiatives was great; and was linked to a new concern with the concept of planning. One lesson of war, it was suggested, was that the potentialities for co-ordination of effort and efficient use of resources, through systematic central direction which had been revealed through the development of military planning, could be applied in a civilian context. Interest in an 'Economic General Staff' employed in this way as a central planning capacity in government was reinforced by the apparent success of the Soviet Union's 'Five Year Plans' and President Roosevelt's use of expert advisers in his 'Brain Trust'. The pressure group, Political and Economic Planning (PEP) was created explicitly to explore the potentialities of this approach, and devoted considerable attention to its application to health and the social services. While the government was not persuaded, a considerable number of politicians of all parties, notably the young Conservative MP Harold Macmillan, who argued forcefully in a book published in 1938 for a 'middle way' in politics, were convinced that a new initiative was necessary. If, by the outbreak of the Second World War, social policy still failed to command a central place among the government's priorities, and new initiatives were left mainly to local authorities (notably the LCC under its Labour Leader Herbert Morrison), and to voluntary organizations, with some central funding, ample evidence about the viability of alternative approaches was to hand. But the occasion for implementing them was still lacking.

Enter the Welfare State

On any rational calculation, Britain had, by late 1940, virtually lost the war against Hitler. In view of the bleakness of the military outlook after the fall of France that summer, it would hardly have been surprising if social policy, which had failed to find a prominent place in the national policy agenda in peace, had been banished altogether from the scene for the duration of the war. But in fact the opposite was the case. In the week of Dunkirk, *The Times* had called for a wholly new approach. It proclaimed in a leader article:

> If we speak of democracy we do not mean a democracy which maintains the right to vote but forgets the right to work and the right to live. If we speak of freedom, we do not mean a rugged individualism which excludes social organisation and economic planning. If we speak of equality, we do not mean a political equality nullified by social and economic privilege.
>
> (1 July 1940, quoted in Calder 1969:137)

A ferment of activity broke out: committees and study groups of all parties and none; even, eventually, an altogether new political grouping, Common Wealth. Elaborate blueprints for the construction of what one latter-day detractor has satirically described as 'The New Jerusalem' were painstakingly put together, published and debated. Within government, Churchill's energies as Prime Minister were wholly taken up with the prosecution of the war: concentrating on everything necessary for its winning and leaving aside everything that was not. Other ministers, mainly Labour members of the Coalition, had different views and used the reconstruction machinery established within government to press them. All this activity found its focus in 1942 when Sir William Beveridge published his report on social insurance.

The Beveridge Report came to be regarded, at the time and subsequently, as the founding charter of the Welfare State. Yet to take it as the high-water mark of acceptance of state intervention in social policy is in many ways misleading. Beveridge himself as a young man had been partly responsible for the introduction by the Liberal government of an insurance-based approach to deal with unemployment. Although he had come under the influence of the Webbs, his intellectual roots were among the New Liberals. Thus, while he talked of his report as embodying all that he had learned from the Webbs, the lessons he applied were in practice those he had learned from the operation of insurance-based schemes in social security. 'All-in insurance' had been his motto; and this was the principle he adopted in his report.

Insurance, in turn, implied partnership between state and individual, sharing responsibility for providing welfare. Although Beveridge, himself a former senior civil servant, was prepared to accept that the state could be entrusted with the predominant role in the provision of welfare, he was at no stage an advocate of excluding other forms of delivery by agencies outside the state. His report contains a series of exhortations designed to reinforce the concept of individual responsibility; and, in a subsequent report, he was particularly concerned to emphasize the importance of a continued role for voluntary organizations in the field of welfare (Beveridge 1948). The term 'Welfare State' is not his; indeed, he cordially disliked it, preferring 'welfare society'. In this society, the stress was to be on equality of status and quality of service. Equality derived from the common basis on which all citizens participated in his scheme, paying equally in contributions for equal benefits, by virtue of their common citizenship. Beveridge did not allow for local variations in circumstance — rent levels, for example — which might put some individuals at a disadvantage; nor was he prepared to accept that equality should extend to the case of married women. But with these important exceptions, equality in outcome deriving from rights of citizenship is the key Beveridge value.

Quality of welfare provision raised more complex issues. Beveridge's thinking was strongly influenced by the social investigations of his youth, and in particular Booth and Rowntree's findings on subsistence levels in their studies of poverty. At the same time he was concerned to ensure that the stigma of the minimum standards applied under the Poor Law should be avoided in the new system. Benefits should accordingly be pitched at an adequate level, sufficient, in Beveridge's terms, to secure 'freedom from want'. In addition, Beveridge stipulated that three other conditions would have to be met in order to ensure that his proposed system would not be eroded at the outset, as the partial insurance schemes of the past had been. The first was that the government should, as an act of policy, guarantee full employment in peacetime circumstances; the second that a system of family allowances should be introduced to provide direct support for mothers in bringing up children; and the third that a comprehensive health service should be created.

Beveridge's proposals, therefore, went far beyond his ostensible terms of reference; taken together, they made up the 'grand design' for future social policy that had previously been lacking. But although they were instantly and resoundingly successful with the general public, they provoked serious anxieties in government. True to form, it was the Treasury that demurred; in the parliamentary debate on the report early in 1943, the Chancellor, Sir Kingsley Wood, expressed grave anxiety about the cost of the proposals and declined to commit the government to their full implementation. In doing so, he precipitated a major parliamentary revolt against the government, involving members on all sides of the House. It became clear that the political pressures would be too strong to withstand; and with evident reluctance the Prime Minister fell into line. Once, the Treasury would have held its ground; but its position was weakened in wartime, when the Chancellor was not a member of the War Cabinet, and had been subverted from within by the admission, as temporary civil servants, of Maynard Keynes and a number of his younger followers. Keynes himself had been consulted by Beveridge during the preparation of the report, and had advised him on how best to deal with Treasury objections; their formidable alliance, and their insider skills, were too much for the Treasury old guard. For the first time for thirty years the dominance of economic policy objectives over social policy was broken.

Once the breach in principle had been made, the rest followed. Beveridge himself had been excluded from the implementation process; but retaliated by threatening the government with a further report on full employment, funded from private resources. Thus began the once notorious 'White Paper Chase', in which the government struggled to anticipate its critics by producing reports on the key issues that Beveridge had identified for action. The 1944 Employment White Paper, with its ringing pledge committing the government to the maintenance of full employment was followed by legislation implementating Eleanor Rathbone's proposals for family allowances (although the Treasury managed to limit the cost by the exclusion of the first child) and by another White Paper with proposals for reform of the health service. Taken together with R.A. Butler's 1944 Education Act, which completely overhauled the secondary education system, the Coalition government had by the time it left office in 1945 gone a long way in the direction of meeting Beveridge's demands.

Seen in retrospect, the near-unanimity with which this exercise was undertaken seems surprising. The simplest, and not necessarily the worst explanation, is that wartime circumstances provided a unique opportunity. Common experience of adversity strengthened the sense of common citizenship; Beveridge's proposals appealed both to the instinct for change, offering, in his phrase, a 'British revolution', but also to the desire for continuity, with their roots in earlier forms of social insurance. Yet there was nothing inevitable either about the timing of the implementation or the form that the proposals took. The Treasury case for postponing the commitment to welfare expenditure until the shape of the post-war economic scene could be seen had a certain logic to it, though not as much as its latter-day celebrators now suggest (Barnett 1986). Wartime experience certainly contributed powerfully to a change of attitude, perhaps most markedly in making the state seem more trustworthy and its claims to be able to plan effectively more credible. But comparisons with other societies make the simple conclusion that modern war must necessarily act as midwife for welfare reform seem less convincing. Some countries which experienced war deferred their equivalent measures; others which did not none the less introduced new welfare systems, in many ways more radical than Britain's. For Beveridge's approach, though logical and comprehensive in its own terms, left many gaps and inconsistencies behind it, most notably in the case of women. That said, the introduction of the Welfare State, for which his report provided the foundation, was a remarkable episode; and its survival, in virtually unchanged form for a further thirty years testifies to the way in which it chimed in with other interests and values.

The Shape of the Post-War Settlement

The simplest way of characterizing the values on which the introduction of the post-war Welfare State was based is to say that they were collectivist, in the sense in which that term was used in the Edwardian social policy debate. But, as we have already seen, Beveridge (who was himself an active participant in that debate as a young man) was what has since been called a 'reluctant collectivist' (George and Wilding 1980), unwilling to abandon the concept of individual responsibility for welfare and building provision for personal contributions into the funding of his plan. Similarly, Keynes, whose discoveries in economic theory now appeared to provide governments with the essential capacity for planned direction of the economy which made up the other major contribution to the creation of the post-war settlement, was a life-long Liberal. Although he proclaimed, in a famous essay, 'The End of Laissez-faire', his concern for individual freedom led him to scepticism about the implications of full-scale state control (Keynes 1931).

For examples of full-blooded collectivism we must turn to the Labour politicians who assumed responsibility for the implementation of the remainder of the Welfare State agenda when they succeeded the wartime Coalition in power after their sweeping election victory of 1945. Here the key figure is Aneurin Bevan. The bulk of Labour's social legislation followed the lines defined during the coalition; the solitary and significant exception is in the field of health. Bevan's creation of the National Health Service cut sharply across the trend; it is tax-based and free at the point of delivery, and the administrative machinery is centralized under direct ministerial control, subject only to parliamentary scrutiny. There is no directly-elected local representation in its management. Bevan's concessions to professional interests, in the shape of the medical lobby, helped to mask the radical nature of the plans for the funding and management of the service he was creating; even so, they were too much for the Conservative opposition to swallow and health became the one major item of Welfare State legislation to be systematically opposed in Parliament.

For the rest, the Conservative Party not merely accepted what was being done, but claimed their share of credit for it. This approach was largely the creation of Butler, whose 'New Conservatism' was based on the acceptance of the principle of active state intervention in economic and social policy and of the viability of a planned economy in which trades unions would play an active part alongside employers. He spoke, in short, 'the language of Keynesianism' (Butler 1971:160). He was also anxious to stress at all possible opportunities the contribution that the Conservative Party had made to the introduction of the welfare legislation of the Coalition government, notably his own Education Act. Within the party, once Churchill's support had been made clear, there was little outright opposition, although some grumbling about 'pink socialism' could be heard. Outside it, the main criticism was of the encroachment of state powers on individual liberty and the most telling critique was the one made by Hayek in *The Road to Serfdom* (1944).

Hayek's polemic on the dangers of planning is an excellent example of a statement of a set of ideas whose relevance was not accepted at the time at which they were produced. A jeremiad about the dangers of totalitarianism produced at the end of the Second World War, when the Fascist dictatorships had just been soundly defeated, cut little ice. The very English variations on the theme of planning adopted by the two major parties did not appear to contain any very profound threat to liberty — although many citizens found the continuation of wartime controls and rationing irksome. Hayek himself was not a Conservative — and has never presented himself as such. Perhaps not surprisingly, his direct impact on British politics was for many years extremely limited, although some individual Liberals were responsive to the positive case for individualism that he subsequently began to deploy.

The informal political accord, of which the agreement on the introduction of the vast bulk of Welfare State legislation formed a crucial part, has come to be known as the 'post-war consensus', which is sometimes also termed 'Fabian' or 'social democratic'. As far as social policy goes, these terms suggest a general acceptance of propositions deriving from the Webbs: entrusting the state with powers of intervention to guarantee the stability of society and the relief of poverty, these powers to be exercised by state bureaucracies under political direction, funded from local and central taxation and staffed by properly trained professionals. This approach is egalitarian, in the sense that it is based on the expectation that state-provided services will be used by all citizens, and also redistributive. Taxation is a key instrument of policy, seen both as a means of providing the necessary resources for maintaining the social services, and also as a device for eliminating gross disparities of wealth.

In some senses this approach can be seen as a means of safeguarding as much as possible of the traditional order in the shape of a reformed capitalism; some of the subsequent criticism of the post-war settlement from the left is based on this premiss. It is certainly the case that part of the ready acceptance of the social legislation was based on this assumption: that, as Quintin Hogg put it, if you do not give the people reform they will give you revolution (Deakin 1987:45). On the other side some contemporary Conservatives represent this as the period when, as Margaret Thatcher has since observed, 'the Conservatives became too much influenced by the Socialists', accepting the continuation of an intrusive role for the state which could only be justified in circumstances of national emergency.

This might suggest that there was a conscious decision on both sides of politics to create a single set of policies that would stand apart from the general terrain of political debate. Much discussion of 'the post-war consensus' is conducted as if that did in fact occur; and to that extent it is misleading. What is true is that although there was very considerable dispute about social policy issues in the thirty years after the end of the Second World War, it was conducted largely around issues of implementation of welfare policies, not on matters of principle.

Travelling the Middle Way

The three main questions around which debate took place in the post-war period were the cost of welfare, the adequacy of provision, and the social consequences of introducing state-funded and state-managed welfare.

On the first, the terms of debate had been transformed by the conversion of the Treasury. Economic policy objectives had been broadened to accept the legitimacy of social policy goals and hence to make payment for welfare an early charge upon public revenues. The pessimism of the Treasury diehards during the wartime debate on the costs of Beveridge's proposals gradually faded from memory as the economy began to recover and the task of sustaining full employment proved less daunting than had been expected.

But shortly before Labour went out of office in 1951, however, the outbreak of the Korean war precipitated a new economic crisis and with it a violent dispute within the Labour Party itself about the decision of the Chancellor, Hugh Gaitskell, to impose charges in the health service. This led to the resignation of Aneurin Bevan and two colleagues (including the future Prime Minister, Harold Wilson). The debate was more symbolic than substantial; the sums involved were not large, and Bevan had previously accepted the principle of charges. What was at stake was the concept that social expenditure should be protected even at times of severe economic pressure. When Labour left office, the debate threatened to repeat itself on a larger scale; the incoming Conservative government had represented the economic situation to the electorate as being close to a national emergency, and drastic reductions in welfare expenditure seemed a logical option. Moreover, a device was conveniently to hand; the abandonment of universal benefits in favour of a return to a means-tested approach. This option was rather tentatively floated by two younger Conservatives, Iain Macleod and Enoch Powell (1952), but not taken up.

The decision not to disturb the broad terms of the post-war social settlement was a deliberate one; and (it appears) largely that of Winston Churchill, once again Prime Minister, but this time presiding over a wholly Conservative government. The election had demonstrated the popularity of Welfare State policies, whose protection had been a major feature of Labour's campaign; the economic emergency proved on closer examination to be less severe than had been feared. The National Health Service, when submitted to detailed scrutiny, proved to be not as profligate as its critics had supposed. In the event cuts were made in education spending, but the remaining programmes were left as Churchill put it, to 'bed down' undisturbed (Seldon 1981). However, fears about the likely costs of social security — and in particular the possible future 'burden' of pensions — led to funding of the benefits system being kept at a level well below that envisaged by Beveridge. This in turn rapidly produced a much higher incidence of dependence on the safety net of national assistance than had been anticipated, and provoked denunciation by Beveridge himself, now in the House of Lords after the briefest of interludes as a Liberal MP.

Fears about the cost of welfare and its place in expenditure programmes subsided steadily under the successful Chancellorship of Butler (1951–5), re-emerged during the stop-go years of the late 1950s, and subsided again in the early 1960s when Harold Macmillan responded to the latest in a series of crises by rediscovering his pre-war attachment to the concept of planning. The elaborate structure he created, modelled in part on the French system, provided an important place for new social programmes, to be funded from the dividend of economic growth. Conservative ministers in major spending departments, Enoch Powell at Health and Keith Joseph at Housing prominent among them, vied with each other to bring forward ambitious and costly new projects. Their Labour successors attempted an even more far-reaching enterprise; a National Plan with ambitious targets for economic expansion and expenditure.

These, if any, should have been the golden years for post-war social policy, with its autonomy fully accepted and the funding of substantial programmes of expansion guaranteed. That they were not was due to two factors. One was the continued indifferent performance of the economy both under the Conservatives and their Labour successors (1964–70). The stuttering of the engine of growth set restrictions on levels of expenditure and inhibited systematic planning of new developments (Abel-Smith 1966). The other was the character of the welfare provision actually funded.

This second major issue — the adequacy of welfare — came to the surface in the late 1950s and precipitated a number of critiques of welfare policy. One early criticism was that if welfare programmes were meant to redistribute resources in favour of the less well off, it seemed wrong that the main beneficiaries were not among those most in need (Abel-Smith 1957). The middle class had been quick to declare their discontent with the cost of supporting the Welfare State — a discontent expressed politically in two successive Liberal revivals — but analysis of the distribution of benefits from welfare programmes very soon showed how ill-founded their discontents were (Titmuss 1962). So, far from bearing a disproportionate share of the costs, the middle classes were among the major gainers. Chief among the other principal beneficiaries through the 1950s and early 1960s were the skilled working class. Helped to house ownership in the expansion of the building programme promoted by Harold Macmillan that was the Conservatives' main innovation in social policy in the 1950s, their children were simultaneously climbing the ladder of opportunity provided by the 1944 Act through the grammar schools to the newly expanding higher education sector. The defection of a substantial segment of this group to the Conservatives at the general election of 1959 had precipitated speculation about a permanent shift in their political allegiances. Michael Young's satirical glimpse of this social group as a new governing class, the 'meritocracy', came to be taken literally.

Those who had not benefited, as a new round of social investigations soon demonstrated, were the residual poor. The maintenance of full employment had provided for the majority; but social changes were beginning to produce a new underclass. This was made up of the victims of the perpetual housing problems of major cities, still unresolved by the new municipal housing programmes; dependent woman cast adrift by the breakdown of marriages; and immigrants from the New Commonwealth drawn in to make good labour shortages in the public services. These were, in the phrase then current, the 'casualties of the welfare state' (Harvey 1960).

As the structures and agencies of the welfare system were subjected to these new tests, the debate about the purpose that it was intended to serve was reopened. Rethinking social policy in opposition in the late 1950s, the Labour Party turned to a group of Fabian academics for ideas on the remodelling of the post-war settlement. Anthony Crosland, using some of the work done by this group as a basis for his review of the future of socialism, had reached the conclusion that 'Keynes-plus-welfare state' was not socialism (Crosland 1956). If the main objective of socialists, the achievement of greater equality, was to be attained, he argued, there would have to be substantial investment in education at all levels, as the social policy most likely to promote it. Crosland's analysis provided the core of the case made by the revisionists in the Labour Party during the inquests on the party's three successive defeats. But even among those who rejected the revisionist case in general, there was agreement that Labour would have to move beyond the 1945 agenda in the field of welfare. For example, Richard Crossman vividly described the impatience that he had come to feel with Beveridge's solutions and his desire for alternatives that would embody a different set of values (Crossman 1966).

On the opposite wing of politics, questions were being asked about whether persisting with universal state-provided services offered the best solution to these persistent problems. Liberal social policy resurfaced as an attempt to think beyond welfare based on state provision to Beveridge's concept of a welfare society and the forms of provision that might imply; this in turn led to speculation about whether it would be feasible to dispense with state welfare and its association with dependency. In his introduction to an important collection of essays on Liberal policy, George Watson argued that: 'in a Liberal society we should look increasingly to the release and stimulation of private endeavour and voluntary agencies of service and mutual aid to diminish the role of the State' (Watson 1957:19). The Institute of Economic Affairs (IEA) began a long sequence of inquiries into the funding of services and the possibility of introducing alternative means of paying for welfare that would be simultaneously more cost-effective and better reflect consumer preferences (IEA 1964).

But the main conclusion reached as a result of the debate about the adequacy of the post-war Welfare State was that the institutions that had originally been created to manage the public services were deficient. A succession of official inquiries — Royal Commissions and departmental committees — examined in turn the civil service, local government (first in London, then nationally), the social services, higher education. London housing, and finally the health service. The conclusions all pointed in the same direction: the institutions needed modernizing (which was to say new standards of efficiency and cost-effectiveness were needed) and professionalizing (improved standards of recruitment and training were required). This led inexorably towards the creation of larger units, with more numerous staff performing a wider range of functions. Nevertheless, both main parties pressed ahead with reforms, presented as an inevitable part of the process of modernization.

Before long, criticisms began to be heard to the effect that this new utilitarianism was producing a new nonsense-on-stilts: a series of bureaucracies setting their own objectives with a vested interest in their own expansion, costly to run and maintain, and diminishingly responsive to the needs of those they were intended to serve.

As it happened, this line of criticism first developed on the left, as part of the work done for the Community Development Projects initiative established by the Labour government of Harold Wilson to deal with the persistence of poverty. But a very similar line of argument was emerging simultaneously on the right, where the IEA had chipped persistently away at the economic foundations of the post-war settlement. All that was needed was for those economic foundations to fall away and expose the structures of welfare to the full effects of recession. In 1973, under the impact of the quadrupling of oil prices, and the consequent shock waves that ran throughout the international economy, that event duly occurred.

Welfare without Growth

The years of the oil price crisis and beyond open a period of welfare without growth. Deprived of the protection of additional resources, politicians entered a world where priorities meant choices made between programmes not for expansion but for cuts. However, this was not yet a universe in which cuts were accepted outside government as a fact of life. The institutional pressures generated by the creation and expansion of the great welfare bureaucracies still persisted. The pressure groups that had played such a notable role in identifying new social problems for action still continued their activities. In Ernest Gellner's brutal phrase, the 'social bribery fund had run out'; but the expectation of continued expansion of provision had not.

In these new circumstances the Conservative Party underwent its own counter-revolution. Two successive election defeats (February and October 1974) put paid to Edward Heath's term as their leader; the choice of those who masterminded his departure fell, after some hesitation, on Margaret Thatcher. She herself had expected the leadership to go to Sir Keith Joseph, but he forfeited his chance by some injudicious speeches on population policy. None the less, she turned to him for new ideas; and he served as the conduit through which the ideas of the New Right on economic and social policy flowed into the Conservative Party. Milton Friedman's monetarism had already penetrated British political discourse, and was shortly to be adopted, in modified form, by the Labour Chancellor, Denis Healey. But despite the early endeavours of the IEA, the New Right lacked an equivalent social policy.

The gap was filled in two rather different ways. First, by a return to first principles in the form of a twentieth-century adaptation of classical liberalism. The key figure here was Hayek, who had moved from theorizing about economics to an elaborate restatement of Liberal theory about the limits of the role of the state. In his model, the individual is restored to the centre of the social universe, and the market regulates where necessary his relationship with other individuals and with the (much diminished) institutions of the state, local and national. In this universe, the function of the constitution is to entrench individual rights, and of the law to provide remedies for grievances. Neither law nor constitution should recognize collective interests, which are artifacts unknown to either — Hayek attributes much misery to the malign operation of pressure groups purporting to represent such interests. A residual welfare system is admissible, *in extremis*, to prevent actual starvation; but of state-run and state-financed social policy scarcely a trace remains. Thus one solution to the problems of redefining social policy was, by adopting Hayekian individualism, to define it away altogether.

A second, and altogether different level of tactic was to draw attention to the abuses that a state welfare system was said to harbour. At the rather grander level of abstraction this drew upon the American public choice school of economists and their theories of bureaucratic self-aggrandisement, by which all public sector agencies unconstrained by market disciplines inevitably deteriorate into vehicles for serving the self-interest of those that run them. On a different plane, exposure of abuses of the benefits system by individual claimants served to undermine the persistent popularity of Welfare State institutions with the general public and make an alternative package of tax cuts and enhanced consumer choice in the market appear increasingly attractive.

Over the course of the late 1970s these views, energetically propagated by the Conservative Opposition and their increasingly confident leader, gradually gained the intellectual ascendancy. In this process a group of journalists, previously closely associated with the popularization of Keynesian ideas on economic management, played a significant part. One of them, Sam Brittan, coined the phrase 'the Wenceslaus myth', to describe the situation that he perceived as having arisen: one in which ample flesh, wine and pinelogs were assumed to be available indefinitely, on demand. Although the economy staged a modest recovery under the semi-monetarist policies adopted by Labour, initially under pressure from the International Monetary Fund, the accord with the trades unions that had helped to bring inflation sharply down eventually collapsed in the so-called 'Winter of Discontent' (1978-9). By then the notion of a resumption of sustained economic growth, even at the comparatively modest level (by international standards) that Britain had enjoyed in the 1950s and 1960s, no longer seemed a realistic proposition. In the circumstances, a 'crisis of welfare' seemed a real possibility.

The drastic cuts that Denis Healey made in public expenditure in response to this situation came under heavy criticism from Labour supporters, especially those on the left of the party, who argued that they demonstrated a lack of commitment to Welfare State objectives. But at the same time, left critics had their own difficulties. A purist analysis of welfare programmes held that they were indeed a sophisticated form of bribery, designed to deflect working-class demands and supply capitalists with a docile and physically efficient workforce. It had long been anticipated that some form of crisis might arise when capitalism could no longer afford to sustain welfare expenditure at the level to which working-class political pressure had pushed it. This was the so-called 'fiscal crisis of the State' (O'Connor 1973). But now that it had arrived, what were left-wing critics to do? Their criticisms of the functioning of welfare bureaucracies and the way in which they served the class interests of those who ran them had been as vigorous as those of the right, which they so strikingly resembled (Offe 1984:153). In addition, a new and energetic school of feminist critics had arisen, arguing that the Welfare State had been fundamentally flawed from the outset by the assumptions of men like Beveridge about the role of women and their place in society. Should such imperfect institutions be defended at all? Reluctantly, the general answer seemed to be that they should. As Louis

MacNeice had once put it, their duty was to 'defend the bad against the worse' (Gough 1979).

In practice, such agonizing had little or no effect on the outcome of events. The Conservatives came to power in May 1979 and immediately proclaimed their intention of subordinating all other policies to the implementation of their economic priorities — in particular, the reduction of inflation. And at the centre of the economic policy debate the government set the problem of public expenditure and the paramount necessity of bringing it under control (HM Treasury 1980). From this moment dates the reintroduction of what one former Conservative minister has called 'Treasury-driven social policy'.

Welfare under the Thatcher Government

At the time of writing, the Conservatives under Mrs Thatcher have been in power for a little over eight years. Long period though this is by the standards of post-war politics, it is still too early to attempt a summary. For present purposes, the best that can be done is to point to some of the fundamental shifts in social policy and practice that have taken place over that period.

Very crudely, the government's basic approach has passed through two stages: the first, in which the concern was principally with management of the economy, and a second phase of 'social Thatcherism', which opened in earnest after the election victory of June 1987, with a few preparatory essays before that event. The first phase has been amply covered elsewhere in this volume; the principal concern there was with releasing market forces through trimming back the interventions of government and curbing the power of the trades unions. Privatization of state-owned assets, a device adopted in the second term (1983–7), has been rapidly extended and became something of a trademark for the government. However, with a single exception, the extension of these principles to social policy over the first two terms was extremely cautious and limited. The exception, housing, was a case in which an existing policy (the sale of council houses) was greatly extended and made binding upon local authorities. At the same time, a very substantial cut in public expenditure on provision of housing in the public sector was achieved.

The major impact, in social policy terms, has been in terms of expenditure levels. Although in aggregate the government failed over its first two terms to achieve its proclaimed objective of a reduction in the proportion of Gross Domestic Product (GDP) devoted to public expenditure, spending in detail on a number of social programmes has been contained or reduced. Local authorities have found themselves sharply constrained in their spending both through a general reduction in the proportion of their budgets met from the Exchequer, and by specific restrictions placed on authorities judged to be unreasonably profligate in their expenditure.

These restrictions aside, Conservative social policy was until 1987 pragmatic and cautious. The Prime Minister went out of her way to repudiate radical options on health and education put to the Cabinet by the Central Policy Review Staff (CPRS) in 1982, proclaiming that the Health Service would be safe for the future with the Conservatives and shortly thereafter abolishing the CPRS itself.

Much talk of Victorian values, both by supporters and critics, found expression chiefly in greatly increased expenditure on law and order (the results of which were not impressive, in terms of crime rates or, indeed, the maintenance of public order) and a strong interest in developing a more active role for the voluntary sector. This has been particularly evident in the field of social care — an emphasis more reminiscent of the National government in the 1930s than of the previous century. The other main reminder of the 1930s has been the castrophe of mass unemployment, which has persisted at a level of over two million since 1980 and as yet shows no convincing signs of falling below that level, if constant definitions are employed. The main onus for dealing with the consequent social problems has fallen on local authorities in the areas affected, at a time when they have been particularly ill equipped to cope with them. A vast increase in the budget of the central government agency designated to provide training and makework schemes (the Manpower Services Commission), and an increase in the cost of unemployment benefit, have together ensured that this is one area where cuts in expenditure have not been feasible. A general review of the whole area of benefits in the summer of 1985, trumpeted as 'The New Beveridge Report', was constrained at the outset by the Treasury to ensure that there would be no further increases in expenditure. Eventually, it shrank to an exercise in 'targetting' of benefits, which produced much individual distress without, critics maintained, adding greatly to the overall coherence or fairness of the system.

Thus the full impact of the present government's change of direction on social policy is yet to be felt. When it is, it is likely to be characterized by the same features that distinguished the new economic policies: primacy for the market, an increased role for the individual, and diminished functions for the state (in this case, primarily local government) produced by contracting out or privatization of as many services as possible. Both in education and housing, the role of local authorities has been greatly reduced through major legislative changes. In this process, the objective of securing greater equality has been explicitly excluded from the agenda.

The government's supporters, with the confidence conferred by three successive electoral successes, are prone to maintain that there has been a permanent shift in values, and that in its new initiatives the government is reflecting, as much as leading these changes. In support of this assertion, they point to the fact that the opposition parties have not been able to persuade the electorate that they have convincing and coherent alternative social policies to offer.

There are, however, some reasons for supposing that matters may not be quite so clear cut. The first is the steady accumulation of evidence from opinion surveys (notably the sequence of studies that make up the British Social Attitudes Survey — Jowell *et al.* 1985:6, 7) to show that the Beveridge version of the Welfare State remains generally popular, with the partial exception of some of the universal benefits (Child Benefit is one example). Moreover, the public seem to view what they see as an alarming deterioration in the quality of health services with deep concern. This concern leads respondents to opt by overwhelming margins, when offered the choice in similar polls, for improved public services rather than for further tax cuts.

The second ground for dissent lies in the existence of at least two separate sets of alternative social policies. The first, centring on local government, seeks solutions to the problems of bureaucratic inflexibility in decentralizing the main agencies of social service delivery and placing them under local democratic control. This change of scale also involves a change of style, drawing on the lessons learnt in local community action and through the women's movement. However, some of the advocates of this position have yet to come to terms with the issue of how far the state should continue to play a central role in social policy, and more particularly the respective rights and duties of the users and providers of public services.

A second alternative approach, associated more with the centre parties, looks to the state to withdraw altogether from many social programme areas, and the substitution of voluntary and community agencies, backed by a more selective benefits system. Neither of these alternatives is fully tested in action, although experiments in decentralization are underway in several Labour- or Alliance-controlled local authorities; but both offer the prospect of producing alternatives based on innovation and consistent with sets of alternative values.

The common characteristic of all these approaches is that they do not fall neatly into slots which can be identified with party labels. The Conservative Party's recent social policies have largely shed the paternalism of their nineteenth-century ancestors; in many ways they have more in common with those of their predecessors' Liberal rivals, like Spencer. But they have retained what their critics would describe as their authoritarian streak, which they would term an attachment to strong government. Labour has begun to move away from its dependence on the state as an instrument for the devising and implementation of social policies, and has greatly moderated its previous suspicion of the voluntary sector. Some cautious exploration of the potentialities of a 'social market' approach is being pursued both within the Labour Party and by the former Alliance partners.

Conclusions

In many senses the wheel has turned full circle in social policy. The state was first feared, but then welcomed to redress the deficiencies of the market. Now, it is in the course of being expelled again for the distortions that it has produced in the market's harmonies. Welfare policies, once seen as little more than a safety net, to be provided only when strictly necessary, eventually achieved autonomy as explicit objectives for government, to the point of submerging anxieties about the level of expenditure required to fund them, only to lose ground again when their size and complexity led them to be regarded as a burden. The individual, once left to cope sturdily with providing welfare for himself and his own family, was first brought into partnership with the state, then found his interests subordinated to collective needs before once again being invited to exercise his own initiative and stand on his own two feet (with the support of his dependent womenfolk). Political parties have at various times either promoted or responded to these currents of opinion.

Nothing in this life is certain, except death and taxes; but the probability — to put it no higher — is that before too long the wheel will spin again and that what now seems fixed and settled for all eternity will in another generation once again be banished or changed out of all recognition.

Further Reading

The historical background is best approached through Derek Fraser, *The Evolution of the British Welfare State* (Macmillan, 1984) or Pat Thane, *The Foundations of the Welfare State* (Longman, 1982).

By far the best general introduction is T.H. Marshall's *Social Policy*, recently republished in a new edition, updated by A.M. Rees (Hutchinson, 1985). There are important discussions of the ideas behind social policy debates in R.A. Pinker, *The Idea of Welfare* (Heinemann, 1979), Ramesh Mishra *The Welfare State in Crisis* (Wheatsheaf, 1984) and Albert Weale, *Political Theory and Social Policy* (Macmillan, 1983). W.A. Robson's *Welfare State and Welfare Society* (Allen & Unwin, 1976) is a bit dated, but still quite useful.

Most debates on social policy still refer back to Richard Titmuss, who is best left to speak for himself, as in *Commitment to Welfare* (Allen & Unwin, 1968) or *Essays on the Welfare State* (Allen & Unwin, 1963). Additional material can be found in *The Philosophy of Welfare*, edited

125

by S.M. Miller (Allen & Unwin, 1987).

Left criticisms of the post-war orthodoxy in social policy are presented in Ian Gough, *The Political Economy of the Welfare State* (Macmillan, 1979). The position of the right is set out in David G. Green, *The New Right* (Wheatsheaf, 1987).

On particular aspects of the vast range of social policy questions, economic questions are covered in Martin Knapp *The Economics of Social Care* (Macmillan, 1984). Howard Glennerster in *Paying for Welfare* (Basil Blackwell, 1985) makes a complex subject as clear as daylight. On political implications of social policy, see David Donnison's *The Politics of Poverty* (Martin Robertson, 1982) or, more generally, Nicholas Deakin, *The Politics of Welfare* (Methuen, 1987). For health policies see *The Politics of Health* (Longman, 1982) by Rudolf Klein. For housing see David Donnison and Clare Ungerson, *Housing Policy* (Penguin, 1982). Finally, on the (alas!) perennial topic of poverty, Muriel Brown and Nicola Madge have a great deal of helpful material in *Despite the Welfare State* (Heinemann, 1982).

Bibliography (published in London unless otherwise stated)

Abel-Smith, B. (1957) 'Whose Welfare State?', in N. MacKenzie (ed.) *Conviction*, Macgibbon & Kee.
Abel-Smith, B. (1966) *Labour's Social Plans*, Fabian Society.
Ashford, D. (1986) *The Emergence of the Welfare States*, Oxford: Basil Blackwell.
Barnett, C. (1986) *The Audit of War*, Macmillan.
Beveridge, Sir W. (1942) *Social Insurance and Allied Services* Cmd 6404, HMSO.
Beveridge, Sir W. (1948) *Voluntary Action*, Allen & Unwin.
Butler, R.A. (1971) *The Art of the Possible*, Harmondsworth: Penguin Books.
Calder, A. (1969) *The People's War*, Jonathan Cape.
Crosland, C.A.R. (1956) *The Future of Socialism*, Jonathan Cape.
Crossman, R. (1966) *Socialism and Planning*, Fabian Society.
Deakin, N. (1987) *The Politics of Welfare*, Methuen.
George, V. and Wilding, P. (1980) *Ideology and Social Welfare*, Routledge and Kegan Paul.
Gough, I. (1979) *The Political Economy of the Welfare State*, Macmillan.
Harvey, A. (1960) *Casualties of the Welfare State*, Fabian Society.
Hayek, F.A. (1944) *The Road to Serfdom*, Routledge & Kegan Paul.
Institute of Economic Affairs (1964) *The Rebirth of Britain*, Pan Books.
Jowell, R. *et al.* (1985, 1986, 1987) *British Social Attitudes Surveys*, Aldershot: Gower.
Keynes, J.M. (1931) *Essays in Persuasion*, Macmillan.
Macleod, I. and Powell, E. (1954) *The Social Services: Needs and Means*, Conservative Political Centre.

Macmillan, H. (1938) *The Middle Way*, Macmillan.
Marshall, T.H. (1965) *Social Policy*, Hutchinson.
Masterman, C.F.G. (1909) *The Condition of England*, Methuen.
O'Connor, J. (1973) *The Fiscal Crisis of the State*, New York: St James' Press.
Offe, C. (1984) *Contradictions of the Welfare State*, Hutchinson.
Seldon, A. (1971) *Churchill's Indian Summer*, Sevenoaks: Hodder & Stoughton.
Spencer, H. (1969) *The Man versus The State*, ed D.G. Macrae, Harmondsworth: Penguin Books.
Thane, P. (1982) *The Foundations of the Welfare State*, Longman.
Titmuss, R. (1962) *Income Distribution and Social Change*, Allen & Unwin.
HM Treasury (1980) *The Government's Expenditure Plans, 1980–1* Cmd 7746, HMSO.
Watson, G. (ed.) (1957) *The Unservile State*, Allen & Unwin.
Webb, S. (1916) *Towards Social Democracy?*, Allen & Unwin.

Chapter six

Economic and Industrial Policy

Leonard Tivey

The cluster of ideas which were of most influence in British economic policy in the post-1945 period took shape in the inter-war years. Such ideas, of course, developed from previous traditions and controversies (Checkland 1983), and they were given particular form by the events of the Second World War. All policies tend to suffer from the problem of time-lapse — they are put into effect by politicians who have been deeply moved by the critical affairs of earlier decades. What is current is seen as some sort of revival of what occurred before, and is seen in terms of rival party ideologies. The task of this chapter is to weave the story of the actual policies pursued around the development of partisan ideologies.

The events which had these formative effects in Britain and in most of the western world were those of the Great Depression of 1929–32. The previous traditions and controversies which provided the basis for new ideas and developments were those of *laissez-faire*, of piecemeal regulation, of tariff protection, and of Fabian socialism. They constituted the stock-in-trade of most politicians in the earlier part of the century. The Great Depression followed the unstable prosperity of the 1920s, and occurred at a time when expectations were high — having been raised politically by the widening of the franchise from 1867 onwards, and by the acceptance during the First World War that people deserved better lives. So the Depression was a shock to the system. For those of left-wing disposition it was yet another lesson, and an opportunity to urge the claims of socialism, of communism, or even revolution. For those without such inclinations, however, it was at least a warning — if they were to retain the allegiance and sympathies of the majority of people, then some way must be found of recovering from the shock, and avoiding future repetition. Economic ideas were, therefore, on the move, and there was a political market for change.

Economic ideas were also much influenced in the pre-1945 period by the image of the Soviet Union, and the Communist regime there. It is hardly necessary to say that impressions, let alone information, were at a considerable remove as far as the British were concerned. Yet there were episodes — in the early 1920s, in the 1930s, and after 1941 in the war — when the Russian example purported to offer something better than the British. The desire to copy, or more often to provide an attractive alternative, was a motivating factor in the evolution of ideas; and again the need was to attract or retain popular sympathies.

The Second World War brought some disturbance to this evolution. The war economy was highly controlled, partly because the First World War had provided lessons in that direction. Many foods and other household goods were rationed, and the supplies of others were minimal. Raw materials and capital equipment were also supplied through a system of administrative controls. The use of factory and storage space was fully controlled. Price controls were very widespread. Manpower was tightly controlled, beginning of course, with conscription for the armed forces, but also extended to other occupations, and included women. Strikes were prohibited (but some took place nevertheless). There was thus a complex web of economic control, with a large administrative apparatus very rapidly created, over the greater part of the economy. The central management too was new. From 1941 budgets attempted to reduce inflationary pressure on prices by taxing for a surplus, and by encouraging savings through special campaigns. The government became a great employer, and a vast purchaser of supplies for military and other purposes, and the competitive process scarcely operated — indeed, many contracts were made on cost-plus principles, so ensuring a return regardless of efficiency. The ending of the war meant that all needed to be unwound and disbanded, but it provided an experience and an example (of good and bad) much in the minds of post-war politicians, civil servants, and people (Hancock and Gowing 1949).

One thing that was not changed was the situation of organized labour. The war had been conducted by a Coalition government, with strong Labour influence, and with trade union advice and consultation. The concept of 'two sides' of industry gained official acceptance and tripartite committees (with the government) became common form.

The thesis of this chapter will be that the *partisan* ideologies were used to interpret and if possible, to capture economic ambitions and problems that emerged from other sources. Two of the party ideologies explained in earlier chapters will be analysed in terms of actual practice in office at different times. This procedure is not possible for the Liberals, and their ideas will be discussed separately.

The Labour Party

In one sense the period of demobilization and readjustment after 1945 was short, in that by 1947 other severe economic problems had taken precedence. However, in a broader sense the 'post-war' period lasted until the middle of the 1950s when the last controls were dismantled.

The Labour Party achieved power in 1945 and its ideas, for long matured in opposition, were brought to face responsibility at last. It was affected by two particular emotions — a desire not to 'let down' the people, as they allegedly had been betrayed in the aftermath of the First World War; and a determination not to flinch from socialist principles, as had supposedly happened in 1931.

A facile analysis would suggest that the Labour government's economic policies were derived from non-party sources, principally the economic theory of J.M. Keynes; and its industrial policies (including nationalization of basic industries) from party ideology. In fact it was not so simple by any means.

To take the economic policies first. The socialist tradition of the party was primarily collectivist and state-oriented; and it was distrustful of competition and contemptuous of *laissez-faire*. Many on the left of the party believed that Soviet planning provided a model from which much might be learned. In office in 1929–31 the party had failed to promote Keynesian policies. Since then much had changed. Keynes's *General Theory* had been published in 1936 and had extended the influence of his ideas (Keynes 1936). During the war he had half-converted the Treasury, and the Coalition government had published a White Paper on *Employment Policy* (1944, Cmd 6527). Moreover, Sir William Beveridge had published *Full Employment in a Free Society* in 1944 and (whatever its faults) the title itself epitomized a programme for a future which resolved the political dilemma which had threatened in the 1920s and 1930s — the need to provide mass prosperity while retaining liberal freedoms (Beveridge 1944).

For some in the Labour Party, however, this approach was suspect, as weak and inadequate. They believed that only control by means of ownership would suffice; and some form of central planning would determine the operation of the economy. In this context it is important to emphasize that Keynes and Beveridge were Liberals — the solution they offered required central management of the economy by relatively remote and indirect means. Its liberal merit was that it made detailed control and direction unnecessary while removing the fear of mass unemployment which, politically, threatened to destabilize the system.

This political attraction was decisive: it was acceptable to the bulk of Labour Party opinion, and it pervaded the Civil Service, the Liberal Party and the majority of Conservatives. It would be fallacious to suppose that many of these converts really understood the macroeconomics involved in any sophisticated way. Indeed, the Labour government made poor attempts to cope with the policies required; and it worked with a complex amalgam of old controls, and crude planning calculations.

What this movement did was to put full employment (or 'high and stable levels of employment') as such, in the forefront of economic policy requirements. It was not to be a mere by-product of general prosperity, nor of a socially owned economy. The need to sustain it was joined rapidly by other economic objectives, but it retained its political priority until the late 1970s.

The actual policies pursued in the 1940s may be briefly recounted. At first the Labour government operated through an ordinary Cabinet committee (chaired by Herbert Morrison, a senior non-departmental minister). The problems of demobilization were overcome, but overseas payments created crisis from the beginning. A loan from the United States was obtained, but ran out quickly. One of its conditions was that sterling (that is, British currency) was to be made convertible into dollars (American currency) on request by 1947. When this condition became operative, holders of sterling began to convert rapidly so that British reserves began to disappear: and the condition had to be abandoned. This crisis and other difficulties led to a shift in the arrangements. A new economic planning staff was created, and eventually this was brought into the Treasury. From 1947 an annual *Economic Survey* was published, which at first attempted to provide quantitative forecasts of economic developments during the year. So an element of 'planning' appeared. Such a notion had become central to Labour ideology; and the crisis had provided an opportunity to deploy it. However, the inaccuracy of the predictions, and the consequent reduction in quantitative content year by year, discouraged enthusiasm. From 1948 a new inflow helped to sustain the economy — Marshall Aid from the United States. This undoubtedly saved western Europe from serious economic crisis. In 1949, however, Britain was obliged to devalue the pound, an action of some resonance through the years, well beyond its immediate effects.

It will be noticed that these events were largely international in their causes. It had become clear by this stage that a second objective of economic policy had, perforce, to take its place alongside full employment — the maintenance of a sound balance of payments. Moreover, it brought into play the factor of wider ideology than the British. At the close of the war attempts had been made to create a world order which would favour the expansion of trade. There was little doubt that in general terms such a regime would be favourable to Britain — a country abnormally dependent on imports, and hence on exports. But in the circumstances of Britain's domestic economy open trading and — more significantly — open financial movements, were liable to create difficulties. This problem has never departed: it lives in the 1980s as it did in the 1940. At all stages it has put strain on Labour's economic ideas.

But what did Labour do about its leading doctrine — state socialism, the common ownership of the means of production? It had a programme, the nationalization of basic industries, and it carried it out. The specific programme was worked out in the 1930s, and the prototypes of the chosen form, the public corporation, had been launched in that period.

The ideas behind the programme were fundamentally political, though other factors shaped priorities. The widening of the franchise had given working people the chance to dominate the political system. To make this power effective a means of economic power was needed — the rights of ownership should not obstruct the democratic power of popular majorities. The means had been controversial. By the 1940s it was clear that for each industry there would be a single corporation with a management board appointed by the government. Governments being elected, that ensured ultimate public power. There can be little doubt that ideological preference was the key factor in determining the policy approach to the industries. However, the nature of the ideas needs stressing — political (democratic) control, a public interest orientation, and a gradual programme were the essentials. There was no mention of the recovery of surplus value appropriated by the capitalist owners, and little reference to property rights, compensation being paid. Nor was much regard paid to workers' control, though recognition of trade unions was guaranteed (Tivey 1966,1973).

The industries on the list were generally described as 'basic', and this gave some plausibility to the claim that they would be the means of sustaining, and potentially steering, the rest of the economy. Coal was in a very depressed and inefficient condition, with a long history of internal conflict. Electricity and gas were in need of rationalization. The railways had been taken over and directed by the Ministry of War Transport, and needed much restoration and modernization. New airlines were set up. Road transport was allegedly in need of co-ordination. The steel industry had been rationalized under government protection in the pre-war years. Its place on the nationalization programme was controversial, both in 1945 and in 1949 when the Act was passed.

There was a practical case for doing something about all these industries — indeed, many of them had been subject to official investigation in the previous decade. Whether a non-socialist government would have nationalized is doubtful: probably there would have been a search for other solutions. But the Labour government was able to claim practical grounds, as well as ideological, in all cases. What was ideological was the driving impulse to the actual solution, and the form it took. The new corporations covered whole industries, not the existing firms. Internal competition was eliminated: and here ideology was relevant. Competition was regarded as wasteful, encouraging unnecessary duplication, and conducive to bad human relations, for each person was set against each other. Efficiency in these industries would be brought about by large-scale organization, elimination of waste and conflict, and by far-seeing strategic direction (Chester 1975).

However, as indicated above, things were not simple. The bulk of the economy was not to be nationalized, or even controlled. That old staple of socialism, land nationalization, was abandoned. Instead, a system of compulsory purchase and other planning regulations was introduced. In agriculture the wartime system of support was remodelled in the Agriculture Act 1947, which besides providing specific grants for farmers, contrived a system whereby the government made up the difference between the amount the farmers could get in the market for specific products and an annually negotiated standard price. Thus agriculture was subsidized without raising food prices.

There was then (as now) one pervasive problem about the British economy: its efficiency. The general measures already mentioned were believed to be relevant — they were all targeted towards modernization. Whether the means were well chosen is a matter of controversy. But the impulse was there; and the various crises of the period convinced anyone who doubted the need. There were other measures. In 1946, the President of the Board of Trade, Sir Stafford Cripps, despatched a series of working parties to the United States to study the productivity of industries there. The wide disparity between Britain and America was already common knowledge. The reports of these working parties were the beginning of long efforts, over many decades, to provide advice, expertise, and pressure to improve industrial productivity. There was also, in 1948, the establishment of the first Monopolies Commission, an investigatory body, to examine particular cases. Again it was the beginning of a long and persistent attempt to limit monopoly. It was created by the Labour government, for private industry of course. The slogan 'where there is monopoly there should be public ownership, but where there is not public ownership there ought to be competition' in the interests of the consumer, explains (or rationalizes) the attitude.

The period thus saw the start of many problems, many policies, and many institutions which have had long careers (Morgan 1984). It also saw one more arrival, perhaps the greatest problem of the contemporary economy. The attempts to keep full employment, the efficiency problem, and its implications for the balance of payments, all contributed to the inflationary spiral. Thus the restraint of inflation — holding prices down — became a third general objective of economic policy.

For the Labour Party the problem has brought strain and stress; for its ideology, it has exposed confusion. In February 1948 the Prime Minister, Attlee, issued a *Statement on Personal Incomes, Costs and Prices* (Cmd 7321) which became the foundation of a wage freeze, endorsed by the Trades Union Congress in March. It was the first of a long series of attempts to establish an incomes policy (Dorfman 1973). Like all such attempts it succeeded in restraining inflation, and like all such attempts it failed to become permanent. The tensions that it brought about reflected the ambiguity inherent in the very conception of the Labour Party: was it 'socialist' in the sense that it should promote the values and interests of society as a whole, or was it essentially a wing of the Labour movement? The dilemma proved insoluble.

In the post-1945 period most countries in the western political sphere had centre-left governments or had undergone a period of response to popular pressures which bequeathed considerable state services of one sort or another. In these circumstances there arose the ideology of the mixed economy. What constituted the mixture was never entirely clear, but what was certain was that such an economy was neither completely state owned, as in eastern Europe, nor was it allowed to run on *laissez-faire* lines. In Britain and other western European countries there was a publicly owned set of industries as well as a larger privately owned range of firms. Hence the terminology of the 'public sector' and the 'private sector' became fashionable.

Conservative Adaptation

For six years the Conservative Party was out of office. It had played its part, of course, in the reconstruction plans of the Churchill coalition. In its time of opposition it needed to reconsider its post-war stance in economic, as in other matters. The result was foreshadowed in the *Industrial Charter* (1947) which advocated 'a system of free enterprise, which is on terms with authority, and which reconciles the need for central direction with encouragement of individual effort' (p. 3). It re-endorsed the coalition paper on *Employment Policy* (1944); and it opposed nationalization 'in principle', though in practice it discussed how best to run the existing nationalized concerns.

The realities became apparent when British politics returned to normality with a Conservative government in office in 1951.

Conservatism was an ideology of adaptation, and the tasks of each generation of leaders was to adapt the party to changing circumstances. It was certainly non-socialist or even anti-socialist in that no one believed in equality or in the further expansion of collectivism. But what had been done was accomplished fact, part of historical evolution. It was the role of Conservatives to curtail socialist excesses, to abandon foolish dreams, and to run the system in a sensible businesslike fashion.

The election campaigns of 1950 and 1951 were run with the slogan 'set the people free'. In fact the system of controls had been partly dismantled by the Labour government, but the Conservatives were able to end consumer rationing, and by the mid-1950s industrial controls had gone too. Within the Treasury there was a plan to launch a 'dash for freedom' (codenamed ROBOT) which would have floated the pound and made other major (and sudden) changes. Though the Cabinet was divided for a time, ministers stopped this initiative, and it was never made public at the time (Cairncross 1985). Conservative freedom was checked by Conservative caution in this as other matters.

The first two Conservative Prime Ministers, Churchill and Eden, were not deeply concerned with economic matters. The two important economic policy-makers were R.A. Butler and Harold Macmillan, and both were confirmed Keynesians in matters of macroeconomic policy. It was in this period that the managed economy took what has come to be regarded as its classical British form. The resemblance between late Labour economic management and early Conservative methods led the *Economist* magazine to coin the work 'Butskellism' to describe it (*Economist* 13 February 1954). The main weapons were fiscal, and the key instrument was the annual Budget. In the 1930s and 1940s Keynesians had advocated public works programmes, financed by borrowing, in deep depressions. The ambition of the 1950s was to use tax changes — principally the size of a deficit — to regulate the expansion of the economy. Other measures, such as the variation of hire purchase rules, might assist. Thus, if there were signs of recession in economic activity, the deficit would be increased, and aggregate demand would stimulate the economy. And vice versa. This ambition has been stigmatized as 'fine tuning'; at the time it seemed a reasonable step to improve on the crude plans of the 1940s. In practice it involved not only stimulus to recession but checks when overactivity encouraged inflation and, characteristically, rises in imports. Emergency measures or 'autumn budgets' thus created problems for industry instead of smoothing out development; and the system was in the end condemned as a 'stop-go' process.

Nevertheless, progress in British terms was good, and the period saw the rise to prominence of the fourth major target of economic policy: growth. Of course, growth had always been an implicit aim of economic actions by government since the Middle Ages. It was obvious to policy-makers in the 1940s that growth was the ultimate purpose. In the 1950s, however, it achieved new importance. For one thing, the Conservatives did not have other targets, in terms of social justice or structural reform. So bettering the standard of living was a necessary future for them. In 1954 R.A. Butler, as Chancellor of the Exchequer, suggested that there was reasonable hope that the standard of living could be doubled in twenty-five years. That sounded good to generations who had grown up with the Depression, wartime shortages and rationing still in vivid memory. Growth was usually measured in terms of an average well-being — 'national income per head' — and the availability of statistics led to the possibility of comparison. Here lay political trouble. These comparisons revealed that in the main, the rate of growth in Britain was not so fast as that in other similar countries. There began a search for explanations and for remedies which has continued unabated into the 1980s, and which has come to dominate political debate in various guises.

Thus politics of growth became part of the politics of nationalism. At this time other developments in the international arena, in Europe, and the continuing process of granting independence to colonies, made the old sources of power and prestige for Britain less significant. Thus the dismay at the realization that the relative rate of growth was chronically slow was all the greater. The roseate glow of everyone becoming better off, so attractive in the early 1950s, was clouded over by the prospect that not only the Americans, but the French, the Germans, the Japanese, and even the Italians would be fairly soon more prosperous than the British.

There was also an evanescent challenge from the Soviet Union. In October 1957 the world's first spacecraft, Sputnik, was launched by the Soviet Union. The prospect of technological rivalry from this source caused reaction over the whole western alliance, and the fact that the Soviet Union had more trained engineers and scientists per head of population than others was yet another source of worry and concern. In time, of course, the rate of Soviet progress in terms of standard of living (or of space exploration) did not match that of the world leaders, but in this period it added to British self-doubts.

It should not be thought that there was no dissent about the techniques of economic management. Indeed, it may be asked what was Conservative about the Keynesian policy mode? In the 1980s such queries have become fashionable. But there was no mystery. The exercise of a *central* state power was always acceptable to Tories, and a means of remedying a manifest evil (unemployment) which could destabilize the existing order, without threatening actual business enterprise, was an obvious opportunity. But actual techniques could vary. In 1957 Peter Thorneycroft, the Conservative Chancellor of the Exchequer, began a policy of 'refusing to finance inflation' (which had risen to over 3 per cent per annum), and in consequence relied more on monetary weapons, such as raising interest rates, than hitherto. His other strategy, that of limiting public expenditure, led to his resignation in January 1958 when the Prime Minister and Cabinet failed to support all his proposals. Thus, in historical terms, this policy was a mere episode, and the real Conservative initiatives came in the early 1960s in a very different direction, discussed below.

Conservative industrial policy in the 1950s showed an obvious change of emphasis. The process of nationalization was stopped, and even reversed in two cases, steel and road transport. Nevertheless there was no direct challenge to the great nationalizations (coal, electricity, gas, railways, airlines) of the Attlee government — they were to be run on business lines. In the event not all the programme was carried out —

British Road Services remained nationalized, and one large steel firm (Richard Thomas and Baldwins) was never sold. Such restraint can be justified in terms of Conservative caution — do not push things too far or too soon.

The main industrial move lay in the matter of competition. The processes of the original Monopolies Commisssion of 1948 were slow and piecemeal. The Board of Trade (under Thorneycroft) in 1956 recast the system and all restrictive practices in private industry and commerce had to be registered, and a process of elimination was put in train. The practices so removed were largely the product of the 1930s when industrial collaboration was encouraged (in the face of falling markets) and marked the beginnings of a direct change in Conservative attitudes in these matters, somewhat ahead of industrial opinion at the time. Later, in 1964 Edward Heath at the Board of Trade pushed through the abolition of resale price maintenance — a system whereby suppliers had been able to fix the price at which goods were to be resold — normally by retailers — to the public.

In industrial relations the policy was one of quietism. The long-term hope of the Conservatives was (as always) that the trade unions would settle down to industrial representation, and take less concern in labour politics and socialism. The tactics were to avoid, if possible, major confrontations. There were plenty of appeals for wage restraint, but no major initiatives in this period.

The Conservatives won the election of 1959 on a tide of economic prosperity. Nevertheless their policies in the succeeding years underwent change which illustrated the flexibility inherent within their ideology. Two major new moves were made by Harold Macmillan. They were carefully and cautiously developed so as not to shock with their suddenness, but they made considerable breaks with the 1950s. The first was to apply for full membership of the European Economic Community (EEC), the Common Market. Macmillan had always favoured European connections, and the danger of diplomatic isolation was probably the prime motive in the application. However, there was also the belief that the superior performance of the West European economies was due to the competitive vigour forced on them by the big 'home' market created by the EEC. Such opportunities and such salutary competition would revitalize sluggish Britain. In the event, the application was vetoed by President de Gaulle of France.

The second major project was the introduction of a form of indicative planning (Leruez 1975).

Such a move by a British Conservative government required a certain amount of ideological legerdemain. The party was nothing if not adaptable in respect of policy matters, but it had come to regard state control as a wartime and socialist burden from which the country had been freed.

Moreover, legislation enforcing competition had recently been enacted. However, both politicians and businessmen were acutely aware of the comparative growth problem, and had come to dislike the stop parts of the alleged stop-go tactics of the 1950s. Anything that would encourage uninterrupted progress would help.

The proximate cause of change was a new balance-of-payments crisis in the summer of 1961, which led to investment cuts and a compulsory 'pay pause'. The idea of planning had been infiltrated into business circles through the Federation of British Industries, in particular at a conference at Brighton in November 1960 (Middlemas 1983). A book published in 1960 by Political and Economic Planning, *Growth in the British Economy*, helped. The model for the new system was France, and visits from French planners were organized. Perhaps the crucial factor, however, was ideological — the new planning was to be voluntary. No controls (or only a few) would be needed. The concept was one of *indicative* planning, as distinct from an *imperative* system. In the latter, compulsory rules or allocations might be made. The indicative arrangements merely drew up a plan which showed the prospects for the next few years. The plan would be drawn up by consent and by collaboration with industry — in Britain, 'both sides' of industry, that is, employers and trade unions. It would thus command confidence. Given this assurance that nothing was being imposed on them, firms would follow the plan because it was in their interest to do so — after all, it would be an agreed forecast of what was about to happen.

This was, of course, an ideal model. It was never suggested that no government measures were possible — indeed tax changes, raising the pressure of demand, special supports, favourable contracts, even physical controls were all mooted (NEDC 1963). The vital political necessity for this model was, however, collaboration. The instrument chosen was a tripartite body — the National Economic Development Council (NEDC). It supposedly copied a similar body in France, and followed a tradition of such bodies started during the Second World War and never given up. On the original NEDC of 1962 there were six employer members, six trade unionists, two nationalized industry chairmen, three members of the government including the Chancellor of the Exchequer in the chair, the Director-General, and two independents. Considerable concessions had to be made to secure the co-operation of the Trades Union Congress.

The reasons for trade union suspicion lay in the belief that some form of incomes or pay planning that would interfere with free bargaining would emerge on the agenda. There was in existence a government-imposed pay pause, and the unions did not want to be seen as collaborators in any such venture. Their suspicions were well founded — the government (and most others) did believe that levels of pay had to be involved in any rational attempt at comprehensive planning. But it had to fall back on a separate body, the National Incomes Commission, for this task, and it had no trade union collaboration.

The NEDC has, over time, been much modified. Indeed, its full glory did not survive the arrival of the Labour government of 1964. But it stands as the supreme example in Britain of a particular approach. If successful it would have taken a major sector of national policy out of government hands — for it was supposed to determine, and plan for, the future growth of the whole economy. Moreover, it was nationalistic in that for success it had to assume that the various interests would sacrifice social conflict, political differences, and industrial disharmony, to the greater good of the national interest.

Labour's Crisis

So Conservative policy developed within its ideology, but Labour found its own path to change much more difficult. The Conservatives won the 1959 general election with an increased majority, and the defeated Labour Party had already gone through a period of some disarray; and, as always, doctrine had counted for more with them than with the Conservatives. The split of 1951 between the Bevanites and the rest turned into a contest for the party leadership. When Gaitskell became leader in 1955 there ensued a period of controversy in which economic and industrial ideas played some part.

The 'fundamentalists' wanted essentially to continue the gradual public ownership of industry, perhaps in some other institutional form. The 'revisionists' adopted the slogan 'socialism is about equality' and wanted policies of a different type. The rise in prosperity and the continual full employment were, for them, crucial historical developments, and the old attitudes formed in depression should be revised. Two documents were crucial in this respect: Anthony Crosland's *Future of Socialism* (1956), and a pamphlet by Hugh Gaitskell *Socialism and Nationalisation* (1956). They wished to remove the collectivization of industry from its central place in socialist advance — not that the possibility of more nationalization should be entirely abandoned, but that it should lose priority to social change in education and tax reform. On the other hand, Aneurin Bevan argued in *In Place of Fear* (1952) that 'one type of property ownership should predominate' (that is, public property) in order to give a lead to the rest.

It would be untrue to suggest that the Labour Party was completely nonplussed by the new affluence, but something had to change. They may have needed new policies: they certainly needed new arguments. They were not slow to take up the issue of international comparisons, and so added to the pressure for new developments which emerged in the 1960s.

139

The new attention to planning proved convenient for Labour. After the death of Gaitskell, the new leader, Harold Wilson, was able to turn away from divisive nationalization, and present the Labour ideology in terms of modernization and dynamic planning.

The NEDC was, it was emphasized, an independent body, a quango. The Labour government of Harold Wilson, when it came into power in 1964, declared that this was not strong enough. A plan was needed that had the full authority of an elected government behind it. So a new Department of Economic Affairs (DEA) was created, the NEDC was sidelined to give industrial advice, and a great new National Plan (Cmnd 2764) was published in September 1965. Like the Conservatives, the Labour government was obliged to set up a separate institution to deal with pay, and so created a National Board for Prices and Incomes.

Meanwhile, back at the Treasury, other issues prevailed. There existed an immediate balance-of-payments crisis when the government took office. It declined to devalue the pound, on political grounds (it would show that Labour could not govern with a strong pound, an instant confession of failure). This policy proved controversial but persisted until 1968. Instead, the goverment created an Import Surcharge, a sort of tariff protection to limit the flood of imports, necessarily temporary owing to hostile international reaction.

The Labour government won a large majority at the election of 1966 but balance-of-payments problems soon re-emerged. A strike by the Seamen's Union aggravated the situation, and investment cuts had to be made. The National Plan had to be abandoned — the production relied on would not be there. And in 1968 the pound was devalued.

So there was further disillusion. There were many explanations of this failure, and it is not necessary to analyse them all. The crucial factor was perhaps political. Planning was introduced as a means of inducing faster growth. There was no point in it otherwise. The plans of the NEDC and the DEA were therefore optimistic. They both forecast a growth rate of 4 per cent per annum. Whether this optimism carried confidence is doubtful: and confidence was the key to indicative planning.

Planning did not disappear; indeed in some form it survived into the 1970s and then it faded way. But something needs to be said about industrial policy.

The Labour government did not forget nationalization. In 1967 the steel industry was renationalized, and fundamentally restructured at the same time. More interesting ideologically was the move to change the party's style to that of a radical modernizing party, principally by associating it with the idea of high technology. Technology is the science which tries to explain how things work, and has no inherent political content. Nevertheless, the image it creates has become a valuable political property, and in the 1960s the Labour Party made its bid. A Ministry of Technology was established in 1964 with promotional and co-ordinating functions, and survived until 1970. This is not to say that the party did not retain its traditional egalitarian values and its collectivist preferences: there were plenty of particular actions to show their survival. Nevertheless, there were always other considerations.

One of these was the state of industrial relations. The Labour Party was the party of the trade unions. At all stages the unions were involved in its policy-making. Yet in the 1960s it found itself in deep conflict with the movement. As suggested above, there is a deep ideological issue at stake. The Labour government believed that there were too many industrial disputes, and that piecemeal bargaining in cash terms led to inflationary rises. But a further cause of its impatience lay in the belief that many union actions, particularly in disputes, but also in 'restrictive practices', were bad for its electoral prospects. It tried to use its strength as a government to remedy these perceived failings. The consequences were bitter arguments, and eventual defeats of government policies at party conferences. A commission was set up under Lord Donovan to investigate industrial relations. Its findings were complex, but a bill was eventually introduced to make reforms, including a compulsory 'cooling-off' period, strike ballots, and if conciliation failed, a way of imposing decisions in inter-union disputes. In the event there was insufficient parliamentary support for this measure and it was withdrawn.

Industrial policy also adopted more flexible tactics. An Industrial Expansion Act in 1968 allowed the government to support firms by owning shares in them, and thus promote key enterprises. Since this allowed public ownership to be created by executive (as distinct from legislative) action, it was fiercely controversial.

At the end of the decade unemployment was running at about 2.5 per cent; inflation had slowed briefly but was over 5 per cent per annum; public expenditure had been very decisively controlled; growth had slackened (from 4.5 per cent in 1968) to about 2 per cent per annum; and the balance of payments was moving into surplus. The Labour government lost the election.

Ideologies and Policies in 1970

As explained, the policies of the governing parties had moved considerably in the 1950s and 1960s. Perhaps the policies had moved faster than the ideologies: or to put it more exactly, leaders like Butler, Macmillan, Gaitskell, and Wilson had tried to select aspects of their parties' traditional ideologies which they perceived as relevant to the concerns of the time, and build policy initiatives from them. But the 1960s had been a decade of disillusion, when great ambitions had fallen short. The beginnings of real ideological change can perhaps be traced to the 1960s, in the reconstruction of Conservative policy in opposition. The Conservative Party in Britain is above all a party of government; out of office in previous times it had behaved more like a government-in-exile than an opposition. In the 1960s, however, it set up a thorough re-examination of policy, culminating in a meeting at the Selsdon Park Hotel, Croydon, in January 1970. It issued a statement which reversed many of the trends of Conservative governments, in favour of free competition and particularly of low government intervention. In a White Paper issued shortly after they came to office in 1970 it was stated that government 'had been attempting to do too much'. There would be a review of government organization. The product of this review would be less government, and better government, carried out by fewer people.

This policy was pursued for some time. The first two Budgets included considerable tax cuts. In 1971 the Bank of England promoted a policy called 'competition and credit control' which in effect made credit much easier to obtain. Entry to the EEC was secured at last, and gradually exposed the economy to competition within the Common Market. It involved the abandonment of the 1947 system of agricultural support for a system of import levies and stockpiling, in order to keep prices at remunerative levels. Much effort was spent on industrial relations legislation, eventually enacted but eventually unsuccessful in operation (Moran 1977). In June 1972 it was decided to 'float' the pound. In the past a fixed rate at which the pound would exchange for other currencies had been maintained by buying and selling pounds (through the Bank of England) to compensate for fluctuations in demand. In 1972, allowing the pound to float meant allowing it to sink. There were limits to this freedom, but in principle the market was to be allowed to operate. In view of the long beliefs in stable rates and the attempts to maintain them, this marked a crucial policy switch. A new doctrine of 'fair trading' with a new institution, the Office of Fair Trading, was created to promote competition and consumerism. The Conservatives did not discover competition in the 1980s as is sometimes suggested — they consistently made efforts to promote it in the post-1945 period.

The most remarkable feature of this period, however, was the 'dash for growth'. It deserves an excursion into policy description. Previous growth strategies had been to smooth its path (in the 1950s) and to plan for it (in the 1960s). These had been frustrated by balance-of-payments problems. If a free exchange rate allowed the pound to find its own price, then perhaps an expanding economy could proceed unchecked. The government also had an incomes policy, eventually made statutory so that it was legally enforceable. Measures to control prices were added. With these weapons in place, it hoped to raise the rate of economic growth to 5 per cent per annum.

It was plagued with crises on all fronts. Entry to the EEC was opposed by the Labour Party, which demanded a referendum. Inflation continued to rise and the economic expansion did not match — 'stagflation' was the word for it. House prices rose dramatically. Trade unions refused to register under the new laws, and resisted their effective operation. Though invited to co-operate in economic management, they were in no mood to do so. Unemployment fell, and employers complained about shortages of skilled labour.

All these problems set the scene for what later critics called a U-turn. Particular elements lay in industrial policy. There had been some denationalization — Cook's travel agency, Carlisle and district breweries, and brickworks owned by the Coal Board were sold. However, the collapse of Rolls Royce Ltd, the famous maker of aero-engines, led to a rescue in which the firm was nationalized. Similar action was necessary for Upper Clyde shipbuilders. In 1973 the Industry Act gave the government wider powers of intervention than any since the wartime controls were abandoned.

In the winter of 1972 there was a strike in the coal industry, in which new tactics (such as flying pickets) were deployed by the miners; and the government (after an enquiry) had to concede. The strike had naturally immense publicity, and the result had immense political consequences. It gave the miners and other militants confidence — they could defeat governments and break pay codes. It undermined the moderate leadership of the Conservatives, since they lost. It further reduced the degree of public sympathy with the trade unions, mainly in consequence of the tactics used rather than the issue. Greater events followed, but a precedent had been set.

It is sometimes implied that, especially after the U-turn, the government of Edward Heath turned to socialist-type policies. This is misleading. The ambition was to break out of stagnation, in the national interest (a Conservative value) and do it by creating a situation openly favourable to business expansion. Public expenditure was limited (but grew) and taxes were adjusted, access to the European market was opened, credit was eased, pay and hence labour costs were held down, so were energy prices, and demand was kept high. These were all intended to suit commerce and industry. Growth reached nearly 8 per cent in 1973. But it was not enough to take up cost pressures and monetary expansion, and inflation continued to rise, to over 9 per cent in 1973 (Browning 1986).

The crisis came at the end of 1973. The miners began an overtime ban (designed to reduce coal stocks), and again claimed pay beyond the statutory limit, since the value of the 1972 settlement had been eroded. The government refused — the pay code was statutory and they would have had to legislate to provide an exception. In December the Organization of Petroleum Exporting Countries (OPEC) announced a world fourfold increase in the price of oil. All oil prices, and the prices dependent on oil were bound to rise dramatically, and the blow to the anti-inflationary cause could scarcely have been greater. In the same month there was a 'secondary banking' crisis in the City of London — some institutions which had taken on banking roles under the post-1971 credit arrangements got into difficulties and had to be rescued (Moran 1984). In January 1974 the government announced that in order to conserve coal stocks through the winter, industry would only work three days a week. Negotiations between government and the miners' union failed to make progress, though attempts to find a 'special case' way out were continually pursued, and might have succeeded. Instead the Prime Minister decided to call a premature general election in February 1974, in effect asking 'Who Governs?' The miners then went on full strike. The Conservatives failed to win the election (though they did better than they had done at by-elections in 1973) (Dorfman 1979).

The Labour Party did not have a majority but it was the largest single party and took office. It conceded the miners' claim and repealed the statutory pay system, and the economy absorbed the oil price shock as best it could. So ended the dash for growth.

It may seem out of the way to detail these events in a book on ideology. However, they are surely relevant, for they presaged the massive shift in economic ideology that took place in the 1970s. The big rise in inflation (to 16 per cent in 1974 and over 24 per cent in 1975) was associated with two successful anti-government coal strikes, and with indecisive election results as well as the oil price rise. The Labour Party had developed a more left-wing programme than in the 1960s, and though the Labour government had little interest in it, it heightened the sense of alarm on the right. There were other non-economic factors at work in the crisis: and to an extent the ideological shift spread over many western countries. In Britain it turned out to be specially acute, but before its effects became operative there was a period of Labour government.

Social Democracy under Strain

These governments (of Wilson and Callaghan) tried to salvage and stabilize the situation. A referendum confirmed the membership of the EEC. Like other countries, an attempt was made to spread out the effect of the price shock over time. Gradually a sort of incomes policy was put together. It involved close discussion with the Trades Union Congress, through a liaison committee. This political arrangement, only possible for the Labour Party, had some success. There was a so-called 'social contract' by which the government promoted certain measures in return for union co-operation. In 1975 a policy giving a flat rate increase of £6 per week (up to a limit of £8,500 a year) was agreed, and there were other agreements in later years. There were other policies — expenditure cuts, removal of subsidies, and interest rate changes — but the bilateral deal with the unions constituted the most significant political operation. It was, of course, highly suspect to other parties.

In 1976 a loan from the International Monetary Fund was negotiated, which made clear the limitation on public borrowing. The social contract was renewed on terms, and the TUC was given the task of vetting wage claims by individual unions.

Industrial relations legislation was part of the social contract deal. The legislation of the Heath government was, of course, repealed, and new laws on health and safety, and on procedures for redundancy were passed. A quango, the Advisory Conciliation and Arbitration Service, was given independent existence. Proposals for industrial policy appeared in *The Regeneration of British Industry* (Cmnd 5710, 1974), and included 'planning contracts' between government and large firms, and a state holding company. Only the latter emerged in the form of the National Enterprise Board.

An unexpected sign of salvation appeared on the horizon, nothing to do with anybody's ideology. This was the discovery of considerable supplies of oil and gas under the North Sea. Strategies for exploitation were prepared, construction began of the essential structures, and a public corporation (British North Sea Oil Corporation, later Britoil) was set up to gather the financial benefits. But the real flows only came to help in the 1980s.

What happened to the socialist ideology in this period? The Labour Party had embraced the philosophy of economic growth long ago — indeed, it was perhaps inherent. It is absurd to suggest that in the period it could have done otherwise — there was a world-wide surge that it could not ignore. There did emerge in the 1960s an environmental and 'green' movement (Schumacher 1973), but it lacked electoral impact. Moreover, to be against growth was to leave Britain behind in the international race, and socialists were no less nationalist than others in this matter. There was certainly a preference for working with trade unions, not against them, but the inherent contradiction between socially oriented macro-management, and labour-oriented bargaining eventually broke out, with ruinous results. The left wing of the party promoted an 'alternative economic strategy' (Holland 1975) which depended on import controls and other restrictions, again highly nationalist in implication. But it was defeated in Cabinet argument in July 1976, and illustrated vividly yet again the non-viability of any domestically centred economic policy. By this time, of course, any admiration for the Soviet economic (or technological) model had disappeared. Perhaps those writers who suggest that socialist values can only be infiltrated in times of rising prosperity were right.

The decade saw the emergence of two other ideas which turned out to have great influence. One was the 'overload' concept. It was argued that the British government had taken on so many tasks that it could no longer cope — the decision-making process could not make the necessary co-ordinations (King 1976). Others suggested that there was a fiscal crisis — too large a proportion of the national income was taken for public purposes. Hence the remedy was to make large permanent cuts in government functions. The other idea was that of cultural weakness. The British had (it was said) a preference for a relaxed, non-acquisitive way of life which disparaged enterprise and industrial activity. So there had to be a very fundamental change of national character (Wiener 1981).

There are three main elements in the new economic strategy of the 1980s in Britain: monetarism, reduction of public expenditure, and privatization. They are, of course, interconnected (Holmes 1985b).

Monetarism re-appeared in professional economic circles in the 1970s, partly as a result of econometric studies of the American economy by Milton Friedman of Chicago. Its political importance was that it provided an intellectual challenge to what had become a Keynesian orthodoxy; and it described an alternative set of operational rules for the management of the economy. In Britain it had a sort of half-life from 1976 onwards, partly as a result of the influence of the International Monetary Fund and international opinion generally. It was vigorously and openly advocated as a creed by members of the Thatcher government from 1979 onwards. Its proposition, at its simplest, is that the cause of inflation lies entirely with the supply of money in an economy, and restraint of inflation (a primary objective) can be achieved by (and only by) regulating that supply. The quantity of money should only be allowed to rise as economic activity rises: it cannot induce such activity. Government borrowing creates money because its credit is always acceptable, and therefore should always be held down to what the economy already requires.

It followed from this that all attempts at 'fine tuning' as in the 1950s and stimulation of growth by easy credit as in the early 1970s were fallacious. The government in 1979 announced a Medium Term Financial Strategy which would keep pace with prospective development.

In fact this aspect of the new philosophy has become its weakest link. By the mid-1980s the problems of finding the appropriate measure had become apparent, and only one of the various criteria was in use (Smith 1987). Borrowing was still in disfavour, however.

Curtailment of public expenditure met with early problems. Perhaps the most striking affirmation of monetarist beliefs was the recasting of expenditure plans in cash terms only, dropping the previous attempts to present them in 'volume' or 'real resource' terms. If the money was right, the economy would follow, instead of the other way round. At first, attempts to reduce total expenditure were frustrated by the rise in social benefits made necessary by unemployment. Nevertheless, very tight and persistent policies were pursued year by year, designed to secure actual reductions as well as to check inflation. This powerful central control was extended to embrace local government, quangos and grant-aided bodies.

The third aspect of policy, privatization, grew rather than diminished in importance. Tentative steps at the beginning of the decade widened into a major programme later, and thoroughgoing prospects were envisaged. Moreover, political angles were developed. The main industries concerned were British Aerospace, Cable and Wireless, Britoil (North Sea Oil), British Telecom, British Gas, the water industry, and electricity generation and distribution, but there were many other smaller and ancillary industries involved. New regulatory bodies were created for telecommunications and gas. The National Freight Corporation was sold to its employees, under the existing management (McLachlan 1983). In other cases great efforts were made to sell shares either to employees or to the public at large. By the mid-1980s 'wider shareholding' became one of the main political justifications of the process. If a larger section of society owned shares, it was argued, understanding of business life and of wealth-creation would spread. Moreover, they might vote Conservative, and letters were sent to new shareholders encouraging them to do so in the election of 1987. There was also an extensive campaign to encourage, and eventually enforce, the contracting-out of services by hospitals and local authorities.

The prime objectives of this development were to create competitive conditions and higher commercial motivation, in the general cause of efficiency. There was also the need to reduce the burden of administration on central government, and (eventually) the range of political responsibility — the reduction of overload.

The government also renewed the offensive in the matter of industrial relations. New legislation was passed restricting 'secondary' picketing and 'sympathetic' strike action, and new means of enforcement (such as the sequestration of assets) were devised.

The ideological distance moved was greater than policy changes indicated — as in all circumstances policies were shaped by practicalities, opportunism, and the need to gain votes. But it was not merely a vigorous repudiation of socialist and Keynesian (that is, 'new Liberal') attitudes. There was an atmosphere of radical change which rejected conservatism as it had hitherto been understood in Britain. Both the 'middle way' approach of the 1950s and the expansionism of the early 1960s were rejected. The belief of these periods, that it was politically prudent (for the sake of social harmony) to try to work with trade unions was dropped. They were to be kept without influence. Strikes were to be defeated,

147

not compromised. When the miners struck again in 1985–6 they were outmanoeuvred and disrupted.

Both full employment and growth were given low priority. Indeed the grounds for suggesting 1981 as the turning point lie in the large rise in unemployment in the previous year. The indications are that the Conservatives did not anticipate so great a surge. The refusal to adjust to this development marked a new political attitude. Employment was regarded as a by-product of a healthy market economy not an end in itself. There was negative growth in that year too, but growth also would take place, securely and naturally, when the economy was sound. It could not be forced. The overriding economic priority was reduction of inflation, for that was the foundation of economic progress and social stability. The idea that social and political stability would be retained without full employment would have amazed most people in the 1940s and 1950s, but the shocks of the 1970s had raised other panics. The fourth objective, a sound balance of payments, was not a problem so long as North Sea oil could be sold, and no petroleum imports were needed.

The great political question was how this transformation would satisfy the electorate. Up to the mid-1970s the allegedly insatiable appetite of voters for well-being had been the driving force of change. Could they be satisfied with the new mix? Elections seemed to show that a proportion of them could.

The policies, however, seem to have been divisive. It is true that opposition to privatization was weak, and that the Labour Party (taken somewhat by surprise) only ventured to suggest rather cautious renationalization, and got no applause for that. Shareholding spread more widely but the spread was very thin. However, neo-Keynesian criticism of the monetary policies continued from all opposition sources. An atmosphere of self-help and self-reliance was encouraged, but it did not prevent people from the health services, education, research, the arts, social services, inner cities, and many other activities, continuing their complaints about chronic underfunding.

Gradually the government managed to roll back the frontiers of state activity. Whether it reduced the range of state *responsibility* is another matter. When the economy seemed to be going well, it claimed the credit Could it, politically, shrug its shoulders if things turned sour?

Three Ideologies at Work

The attention to political practice in this chapter has shown two parties trying to translate their ideologies into policy. The general lesson is not that ideologies were abandoned, but that leadership groups chose parts of rich ideologies to fit the electoral and other pressures of the decades. Thus the Conservatives chose Keynesian macroeconomics, the mixed economy, and industrial peace in the early decades, and these could all be reconciled with principles of elite rule, adaptation, gradualism and 'one nation'. Economic growth and membership of the EEC were all attempts to achieve national success, a long Conservative value. In the 1970s and 1980s policies changed, and other fragments of Conservative ideology were called in to justify the radical shifts. The new policies made much use of the Tory belief in firm authority, particularly in fiscal matters; resistance to pressures was held to embody a true use of central power, distanced from the interplay of faction. Privatization returned to individuals their proper area of activities. Radicalism might seem hard to reconcile with Conservative gradualism — but nevertheless the change of tack could be seen as a proper adaptation to national needs, inflation having become a worse evil than unemployment. Keynesianism and monetarism were relatively technical doctrines, and no more to be regarded as inherent to conservatism than, say, an argument between air power and naval power in defence matters.

Then most obvious congruence between Labour ideology and Labour policy in the economic sphere lay in the nationalization of basic industries in the first period of power. Later, there was an attempt to emphasize the egalitarian and social aspects of the creed, and to minimize the collectivist drive. But it was collectivism in the form of economic planning rather than public ownership that ran up against the issue of incomes policy. Here no means was found of permanently reconciling ideology, policy, and internal party politics. Keynesianism for the Labour Party was a version of state collectivism; free wage bargaining was, however, also 'collective' in that it was carried out by trade unions, not individuals. The tragedy of the Labour Party was that, out of office and eventually in it, no aspect of its broad ideology could secure dominance for long. In the 1980s when there was again a need for new party policies, there were conspicuous attempts to search the ideological stock (of decentralized, localized socialisms, for example) for aspects to re-emphasize.

The Liberal Party's policies appeared in manifestos and pamphlets; they were never put to the test of national action. It is true that many liberal ideas, including Liberal Party ideas, were of enormous influence in this period. Keynes and Beveridge were Liberals; and most post-war policy could be traced to the *Yellow Book* of 1928. The world trend to freer international trade fitted well with traditional Liberal beliefs, and the Liberal Party was the first in Britain to advocate full membership of the EEC. In the 1980s Thatcherism revived 'classical' liberalism in economic matters.

The Liberal Party's attitude to nationalization indicated something of both its ideological policy stances. It accepted the early nationalizations as political and technological necessities. Nevertheless, it was always suspicious of what it saw as over-centralized management. In later years it advocated a standstill — the quarrel over nationalization was irrelevant — nor did it join the drive to privatization. It reiterated its long-standing policies of co-partnership and profit-sharing. In this light it made much of its independence, as the creature of neither capital nor labour. A similar position was taken in industrial relations policy — the Liberals were nobody's client, and would therefore pursue the national interest. In the 1970s it became an advocate, for a time, of a statutory incomes policy.

When the Liberals were joined in the Alliance by the Social Democratic Party, some of these tendencies were strengthened. There was an attempt to reconstruct a neo-Keynesian economy, reinforced by a permanent incomes policy; and monetarism was firmly rejected. On the other hand, the trade union legislation promoted by the Thatcher government was generally supported. In economic matters, as elsewhere, the Alliance produced careful and distinctive policies. What was distinctive about them, however, lay in the difference from one or other of the large parties. The ideological sources were harder to discern.

Looking Back

Perhaps future historians will be somewhat puzzled by all the excitements, policy changes and ideological switches. It should be strongly emphasized that the standard of living of the British people improved vastly over the whole period. There were severe but temporary checks; there was relatively weak performance compared with other countries; there was big inflation in 1975–6, and there was a drastic slump in 1981; there was persistent poverty for some. But by and large there was appreciable betterment, not year by year but decade by decade.

It is possible to relate the actual policies and objectives recounted above to more general ideological positions. The immediate post-war actions, fumbling as they may seem, derived from Fabian gradualism — bit-by-bit progress to a collectivized society — and from 'new liberalism', the view that liberty might be maximized by judicious state intervention rather than *laissez-faire*, because people could better appreciate and enjoy freedoms if social conditions were improved. The conservatism of the 1950s fitted traditional paternalism and caution — the idea that government should respond to social change, neither forcing it back, nor forward into a preconceived future. But there were less partisan ideological factors. The tripartite structures and (to a lesser extent) the social contract acknowledged, at least, pluralist notions that interest groups and intermediate institutions had legitimate roles in society — they had a power-balancing function similar to other institutions in the eighteenth-century mixed constitution. More radically, they could be seen as vehicles for participative democracy, though in practice their lack of empathy with their own followers broke the functional chain. 'Planning by consent' in the 1960s more obviously echoed the ideal of government by consent — the principle that people ought to accept the legitimacy of the way they are ruled. The practices of the 1980s reject a great deal of these philosophies. Government by conviction does not look for pluralist policy-making, still less active participation. Not only are the collectivist trends reversed, but conservatism itself — in the sense of caution and adaptation — is rejected in favour of an attempt to change social values (to an 'enterprise culture') from the top.

There is therefore a striking difference in the ideologies dominating the first part of this account and those of the latest decade. The turning point is debatable — perhaps 1976, or 1979, or most decisively in 1981. In general the changes in the national mood did not coincide with government changes at elections. Dismantling of detailed control began in 1948, the impulse to faster growth in the 1950s, the move to planning in 1961, and the preference for stability in the mid-1970s — and so on.

The original intention of the full employment ideal was to save the liberal-capitalist system from unmanageable social discontent. It can also be seen as an essentially democratic ideal, in the sense that it aimed to secure for all a place in the economy that meant a place in society. There was never any 'right to work' installed, but when all had employment then in one sense at least all were participating in the life of the community. It was increasing international awareness as much as internal pressures that led to the scramble for growth in the 1960s. In any event, the outcome has been an increasing stress on material well-being as the key value in social and economic policy. In part this may be because what is material is measurable, but there is little reason to doubt that most people have found satisfaction and contentment to be associated with prosperity. This has led to a weakening of those economic and industrial ideas which looked to distributional ideas ('fair shares') or to productive organization (democratic control, or industrial democracy). The demand for an even faster growth declined, it is true, in the 1970s, in the face of a perceived crisis and anxiety about social stability. The materialism hardened, and there was a desire for improved order in the economic system, and less conflict. Hence an attempt has been made to restore managerial authority. It combines with the perennial appeal to the national interest to make 'managerial nationalism' a convenient description of much recent economic thinking. The value of authority is certainly a Tory principle, and to argue that the economic policies of the 1980s are not Conservative does not mean that they are not Tory.

The record of economic and industrial policies pursued by parties since 1945 shows that each party tried to use strands from its ideological resources to cope with perceived situations. In policy terms the common targets were faster growth, full employment, a sound balance of payments, and low inflation. In other words, there were non-partisan requirements to be met, and some of these were ultimately ideological too — ideas of national power and prestige, of modernization and of Europeanism, for example. Nevertheless, the party ideologies were significant and led to important differences at all stages, and in the early 1980s these differences widened dramatically.

Further Reading

Some reading on these matters requires a good knowledge of economics, but fortunately there are some very lucid expositions. A classic among these on the early period is Sir Alec Cairncross, *Years of Recovery — British Economic Policy 1945–5* (Methuen, 1985). A longer period is covered in Jim Tomlinson, *British Macroeconomic Policy since 1940* (Croom Helm, 1985), with a full list of useful references. Michael Stewart, *Politics and Economic Policy since 1964 — the Jekyll and Hyde Years* (Dent, 1978) carries the story to 1978. A graphic description of events in the later period can be found in Peter Browning, *The Treasury and Economic Policy 1964–1985* (Longman, 1986) with an appendix of relevant statistics. David Smith describes *The Rise and Fall of Monetarism* (Penguin, 1987). In *The Economic Decline of Modern Britain — the Debate between Left and Right* (Wheatsheaf, 1986), David Coates and John Hillard have put together a collection of readings which illustrates the full range of economic views, especially those of the later period. See also F. Cairncross (ed.), *Changing Perceptions of Economic Policy* (Methuen, 1981). There is a good text in Wyn Grant and Shiv Nath, *The Politics of Economic Policy* (Blackwell, 1984).

Books on particular topics include D.N. Chester's magisterial *The Nationalisation of British Industry 1945–51* (HMSO, 1975) and Leonard Tivey's out-of-date text, *Nationalisation in British Industry* (Cape, 2nd edn 1973).

On planning, read J. Leruez, *Economic Planning and Politics in Britain* (Martin Robertson, 1975). On incomes policy, G.A. Dorfman's books, *Wage Politics in Britain 1945–1967* (Iowa University Press, 1973) and *Government versus Trade Unionism in British Politics since 1968* (Macmillan, 1979) tell most of the story; and for 1965–79 there is W.H. Fishbein, *Wage Restraint by Consensus 1965–79* (Routledge 1984). Other aspects of industrial policies are discussed by Wyn Grant, *The Political Economy of Industrial Policy*(Butterworth, 1982). On special topics read Brian Hogwood, *Government and Shipbuilding* (Saxon House, 1979) and S.R.M. Wilks, *Industrial Policy and the Motor Industry* (Manchester University Press, 1984).

Economics and Industrial Policy

Bibliography (published in London unless otherwise stated)

Addison, P. (1975) *The Road to 1945*, Cape.
Beckerman, W. (1974) *The Labour Government's Economic Record 1964–1970*, Duckworth.
Bevan, A. (1952) *In Place of Fear*, Heinemann.
Beveridge, W. (1944) *Full Employment in a Free Society*, Allen & Unwin.
Browning, P. (1986) *The Treasury and Economic Policy 1964–1985*, Longman.
Cairncross, Sir A. (1985) *Years of Recovery — British Economic Policy 1945–57*, Methuen.
Cairncross, F. (ed.) (1981) *Changing Perceptions of Economic Policy*, Methuen.
Checkland, S.G. (1983) *British Public Policy 1776–1939*, Cambridge: Cambridge University Press.
Chester, Sir N. (1975) *The Nationalisation of British Industry 1945–51*, HMSO.
Coates, D. and Hillard, J. (eds) (1986) *The Economic Decline of Modern Britain — The Debate between Left and Right*, Brighton: Wheatsheaf.
Crosland, C.A.R. (1956) *The Future of Socialism*, Cape.
Dorfman, G.A. (1973) *Wage Politics in Britain 1945–1967*, Ames, Iowa: Iowa University Press.
Dorfman, G.A. (1979) *Government versus Trade Unionism in British Politics since 1968*, Macmillan.
Fishbein, W.H. (1984) *Wage Restraint by Consensus 1965–79*, Routledge.
Gaitskell, H. (1956) *Socialism and Nationalisation*, Fabian Society.
Gamble, A. (1983) Chapter 9 in V. Bogdanor (ed.) *Liberal Party Politics*, Oxford: Clarendon Press.
Grant, W. (1982) *The Political Economy of Industrial Policy*, Butterworth.
Grant, W. and Nath, S. (1984) *The Politics of Economic Policy*, Oxford: Blackwell.
Hancock, W.K. and Gowing, M.M. (1949 and 1975) *The British War Economy*, HMSO.
Hanson, A.H. (ed.) (1963) *Nationalisation*, Allen & Unwin.
Heald, D. and Steel, D. (eds) (1983) *Privatising Public Enterprises*, Royal Institute of Public Administration.
Hogwood, B. (1979) *Government and Shipbuilding*, Saxon House.
Holland, S. (1975) *The Socialist Challenge*, Quartet Books.
Holmes, M. (1982) *Political Pressure and Economic Policy — British Government 1970–74*, Butterworth.
Holmes, M. (1985a) *The Labour Government 1974–79*, Macmillan.
Holmes, M. (1985b) *The First Thatcher Government*, Westview Press.
Jay, D.P.T. (1962) *Socialism in the New Society*, Longman.
Kay, J., Mayer, C., and Thompson, D. (eds) (1986) *Privatisation and Regulation — the U.K. Experience*, Oxford: Clarendon.
Keynes, J.M. (1931) *Essays in Persuasion*, Macmillan.
Keynes, J.M. (1936) *General Theory of Employment, Interest and Money*, Macmillan.

153

King, A. (ed.) (1976) *Why is Britain becoming Harder to Govern?* BBC Publications.

Leruez, J. (trans. Harrison) (1975) *Economics Planning and Politics in Britain*, Oxford: Martin Robertson.

McLachlan, S. (1983) *The National Freight Buy-out*, Macmillan.

Middlemas, K. (1979) *Politics in Industrial Society: the Experience of the British System since 1911*, Deutsch.

Middlemas, K. (1983) *Industry, Unions and Government: twenty years of the NEDC*, Macmillan.

Moran, M. (1977) *The Politics of Industrial Relations*, Macmillan.

Moran, M. (1984) *The Politics of Banking*, Macmillan.

Morgan, K.O. (1984) *Labour in Power 1945–51*, Oxford: Clarendon Press.

Political and Economic Planning (1960) *Growth in the British Economy*, Allen & Unwin.

Schumacher, E.F. (1973) *Small is Beautiful*, Abacus.

Shanks, M. (1977) *Planning and Politics*, Allen & Unwin.

Skidelsky, R. and Bogdanor, V. (eds) (1970) *The Age of Affluence 1951–64*, Macmillan.

Smith, D. (1987) *The Rise and Fall of Monetarism*, Harmondsworth: Penguin Books.

Smith, T. (1978) *The Politics of the Corporate Economy*, Oxford: Martin Robertson.

Stewart, M. (1978) *Politics and Economic Policy since 1964 — the Jekyll and Hyde Years*, Dent.

Tivey, L. (1966 and 1973) *Nationalisation in British Industry*, Cape.

Wiener, M.J. (1981) *English Culture and the Decline of the Industrial Spirit 1850–1980*, Cambridge: Cambridge University Press

Wilks, S.R.M. (1984) *Industrial Policy and the Motor Industry*, Manchester: Manchester University Press.

Important official publications include:

Employment Policy (May 1944) Cmd. 6527, HMSO.

Statement on Personal Incomes, Costs and Prices (1948) Cmd 7321, HMSO.

Economic Survey (Annual 1947–62), HMSO.

The Financial and Economic Obligations of the Nationalised Industries (1961) Cmnd 1337, HMSO.

Nationalised Industries: a review of economic and financial objectives (1967) Cmnd 3437, HMSO.

The Nationalised Industries (1978) Cmnd 7131, HMSO.

Growth of the UK Economy to 1966 (1963) National Economic Development Council.

Conditions Favourable to Faster Growth (1963) National Economic Development Council.

The National Plan (1965) Cmnd 2764, HMSO.

Royal Commission on Trade Unions and Employers Associations: Report (Donovan) (1968) Cmnd 3623, HMSO.
In Place of Strife (1969) Cmnd 3888, HMSO.
The Reorganisation of Government (1970) Cmnd 4636, HMSO.
A Programme for Controlling Inflation: the first stage(19782) Cmnd 5125, HMSO.
The Programme for Controlling Inflation: the second stage (1973) Cmnd 5205, HMSO.
The Regeneration of British Industry (1974) Cmnd 5710, HMSO.
The Attack on Inflation (1975) Cmnd 6151 (for the 'social contract'), HMSO.

Chapter seven

Foreign and Defence Policy

Edward Johnson

The Background

The record of British foreign and defence policy since 1945 has been largely one of constant readjustment to a changing world over which British policy-makers have had diminished control. One major effect of the Second World War was to bring about the final collapse of the old Euro-centric international system, in which Britain had been a major actor, to be replaced by an international system increasingly dominated by the USA and the Soviet Union as superpowers. The change in power relations was, however, perceived by British policy-makers in a mixed fashion. In some areas British weaknesses and declining capabilities were recognized promptly and policies were designed to offset Britain's reduced power. However, British policy-makers at both the political and administrative levels were wedded to the idea of Britain having a distinctive and global role to play in post-war world politics. Thus, while British governments recognized the power differentials between themselves and the superpowers, they sought to compensate for this difference by maintaining a distinctive set of international relationships: with the United States, with the newly-emerging Commonwealth, and with Europe; and by retaining Britain's traditional foreign and defence policy goals, and where necessary by maintaining or acquiring the symbols of power in the international system.

The goals which British governments sought were broadly traditional. These were: the defence of the United Kingdom and the European continent from domination by other powers; the maintenance of Britain's economic and commercial interests; and the preservation of international order and stability. Yet while British governments repeatedly found they lacked the capabilities to secure these goals, it was not until the late 1960s that British decision-makers accepted that a global role was beyond Britain's declining capabilities.

The defence of Britain and Europe was a policy area which clearly demonstrated Britain's ambivalent attitude towards its reduced status in

156

the post-war world. British governments recognized, after the exertions of the war, that Britain would be unable to secure its own defence or that of Europe without the assistance of the United States, and sought therefore to retain US power and forces in Europe as a balance against the perceived Soviet threat to Britain and Western Europe. This linking of the United States to Britain and Europe was formally achieved through the formation of NATO in 1949, and informally through the British construction of a special relationship with the United States. The British felt that the special relationship would allow them to play a role as a world power independent from the United States, and also bestow on them the responsibility for retaining US power in Europe and the status which went with that position. As part of this relationship British governments developed and maintained a nuclear capability as part of NATO's nuclear deterrent, and undertook a major conventional commitment to the defence of Western Europe through the British Army on the Rhine (BAOR). The British post-war defence commitment to Europe found no immediate political echo in terms of British membership of the European integration movement. While there was an initial British commitment to European recovery through the Marshall Plan and the OEEC, British governments became increasingly wary of the supranationalist tone of the integration movement and believed that British power, while reduced, was not limited to Europe, but still retained global dimensions. Therefore, a political commitment to Europe would have, it was felt, run counter to Britain's perception of itself as a world power.

In seeking to secure Britain's economic well-being, both Labour and Conservative governments recognized that Britain's imperial possessions would have to be renounced, but that Britain's commercial interests in the Empire could best be assured and protected through a programme of decolonization, supported by a defence commitment to a rather ill-defined area east of Suez. This defence role involved the presence of British forces in Aden, the Gulf, Malaysia, Singapore, and Hong Kong, thereby securing the lines of communication from Britain to the Far East, and supporting the British claim for a world role.

The British commitment to international order remained as a traditional goal. As a trade-dependent state, Britain had a long-standing interest in the peaceful resolution of international disputes through traditional bilateral diplomacy, and also the multilateral arrangements of the United Nations and other international organizations. In the immediate post-war period, Britain's status as a world power appeared to be institutionalized through its position as a permanent member of the United Nations Security Council.

In the period after 1945, both Labour and Conservative governments sought for as long as possible to retain Britain's freedom of action, but were unable to do so given the changed international system, the constraints of the economy, and the demands of domestic politics. Governments, however, vainly pursued the symbols of world power status while Britain's decline appeared inexorable. The persistent British defence of sterling, the commitment to a British nuclear deterrent, the Korean rearmament programme of 1950, the British refusal to participate in the European movement, and Britain's commitment in 1954 to maintain the British Army on the Rhine, were all examples of decisions of enormous political and economic significance taken with little reference to Britain's declining position in the world (Blank 1977).

Gradually Britain's relationships were eroded. The special relationship was increasingly limited to nuclear and European security questions: there was, for example, very little that was special about Britain's relations with the United States in the Middle East and the Far East. The Commonwealth connection declined to the point that Commonwealth relations were more of a liability than a source of status to Britain, leading governments, beginning with Macmillan's in 1961, to turn their attention to Europe. The east of Suez defence commitment was wound down between 1967 and 1971 and this jelled with Britain's renewed attempts under Wilson, and later Heath, to join the European Community; the withdrawal of forces from the Gulf and Singapore was forced on Britain by economic circumstances, but could be rationalized as a statement about Britain's increasingly pro-European outlook. Thus the move to Europe by 1973 was a recognition, if long overdue, of Britain's inability to play a global role in world politics. The commitment to Europe was continued, albeit unenthusiastically and not without discord, by the Wilson and Callaghan governments in the mid- and late 1970s. By the end of that decade the long process of readjustment appeared to be complete.

The record of post-war British foreign and defence policy has, therefore, with justification been termed 'the Long Odyssey to Europe' (Goodwin 1972). It was a journey characterized by bipartisanship between the leadership of the political parties and an absence of rigid doctrinal ideas as the basis for government policy. This bipartisan approach removed the issues from the centre stage of British politics; there were few votes and little popular interest in foreign policy, and general elections were fought largely on economic issues and the question of the credibility of each party as a potential government. The consensus was, of course, never complete, the Suez episode in 1956 being a case in point. But the failure or unwillingness of the Labour Party to exploit the Suez débâcle in the 1959 general election is an indication of the limited political and electoral gain to be made from foreign affairs in this period. This contrasts with the period since 1980: foreign and defence policy divisions are now found both within the political parties, and significantly between the parties. The traditional bipartisan or even tripartisan approach to foreign and defence affairs has disappeared. Thus, from playing little part in most elections since 1945, the issues of foreign, and particularly defence, policy have figured large and significantly in the elections of 1983 and 1987.

The reasons for this earlier convergence of policy can be found in the structure of the policy-making community in Britain, in the nature of foreign and defence policy, and in the dominance of domestic issues in elections after 1945. Foreign and defence policy-making has traditionally been elitist, involving Parliament and public opinion only marginally (Richards 1973:246–7), and policy scrutiny, especially in the area of defence, is restricted by the demands of secrecy which has limited discussion not only within Parliament and the parties, but also within government itself. Thus, the absence of a significant democratization of policy-making, in the form of a questioning of the traditional assumptions of policy, assisted the dominant policy consensus after 1945. Any government coming to power was, and remains, faced with the bureaucratic inertia of the Foreign and Commonwealth Office and the Ministry of Defence, so restricting the ability of any government to embark on policies which sought to break the consensus. Moreover, much of foreign and defence policy is set in the long-term, and is thus less susceptible to change by one government over the lifetime of an administration, and it is comprised of international agreements and understandings which further limits the freedom of any government to change or reverse policies it has inherited from its predecessors.

However, by far the major set of factors reinforcing the consensus between the parties has been the constraints exerted by the domestic and external environments. Policy has been framed against a rapidly changing and no longer Eurocentric international environment, at a time when the relative decline in the capabilities available to British governments was accompanied by persistent and heavy demands from the domestic politics of the Welfare State. This affected the Labour Party more than it did the Conservatives, in that the Labour left, which could have threatened, if threat it was, to break out of the traditional type of policy in the post-war period, was deeply committed to the creation and development of the Welfare State. This meant that when Labour was in power its putative, radical role in foreign and defence policy was peacefully diverted.

These compelling factors had the effect of depleting foreign and defence policy of any doctrinally distinct base. British readjustment to the post-war international system has been a record of policy that has often been disjointed, reactive, yet pragmatic and flexible, in which rigid ideas on the role of Britain and its place in the international system have been held at the edges of the parties not at the centres. Thus the divisive effect of ideas in foreign and defence policy in Britain was felt within the parties, between the leadership and those internal sections which demanded either a distinct, even doctrinaire, set of policies, or those who, on specific issues, felt their leadership to be betraying the ideological traditions of the party's thinking on foreign and defence policy. Thus for the period from 1945 to 1980, the role of competing ideas in British foreign and defence policy was largely one that was played out within parties and not between them.

This intraparty dissent was largely manageable and did not erode the interparty consensus. However, since 1980 this consensus has been fragmenting, and with the movement of the Conservative and Labour Parties to their respective right and left wings, the ideas previously contained within the parties have now appeared as distinguishing elements between them. Competing ideas and values about the world and Britain's place in it have now become central features of British politics. In particular, the question of Britain's nuclear defence policy and the Labour Party's commitment to unilateralism, on which it campaigned in the 1983 and 1987 elections, clearly divides the major parties. However, it is not solely the Labour Party that has shifted foreign and defence policy on to the agenda of British politics. The Thatcher government has been eager to reverse much of the drift of policy that it inherited, as part of its general reaction against a traditional consensus. While some of this exercise has been mere declaratory policy, there is no doubt that in its relations with the USA and Europe the Thatcher government has sought to revive British foreign policy and British status. To understand the movement of the 1980s we must first examine the ideas of the parties on foreign and defence policy, and their role in the period after 1945.

Ideas and Policy

The ideas of the British political parties on foreign and defence affairs are often fragmentary, vague, inconsistent and contradictory, with many of the ideas about the world and Britain's position in it being shared by sections of more than one party. For example, the Conservative Party is traditionally associated with nationalism and the defence of British interests, whereas the Labour and Liberal traditions in foreign policy emphasize the promotion of larger moral objectives such as humanitarianism and justice on an international, rather than a merely national, level. However, within this broad division there are opposing tendencies and contradictions. In the Conservative Party there is a strand of economic liberalism which has come to prominence under Heath and Thatcher, but has a long lineage in the party. This injection of economic liberalism into foreign affairs has created a number of complications for the party, particularly on the question of the defence of British economic interests. Here the traditional nationalist orientation of the Conservatives comes under pressure from the free-marketism of liberal ideas within the party. As for the Labour Party, the internationalist spirit has to coexist with the very conservative and nationalistic outlook of much of the membership, especially those in the trades unions. To complicate matters further, it has proved quite easy for those on the extremes of the British political spectrum to be united on important aspects of foreign and defence policy. Thus Enoch Powell and Tony Benn can both advance similar arguments against continued membership of the European Community or British reliance on US nuclear technology as being inimical to British sovereignty (*Guardian*, 13 April 1987). Yet Powell is an economic liberal, who in foreign and defence policy terms supports essentially nationalist views about the goals of policy. This gives some of the flavour of the cross-currents of ideas and the difficulty of easy categorization.

Dominating these ideas since 1945 have been the constraints on foreign and defence policy-making, so much so that these ideas often amounted more to a set of aspirations than to the basis of an operational policy (Frankel 1975:36). In the period after 1945, the bipartisanship over policy was skewed more to the defence of traditional goals, thus requiring more accommodation in its ideas from the Labour Party than from the Conservatives. The Labour Party in particular was divided on a number of foreign and defence policy issues, with the Labour left accusing the leadership, be it Attlee, Gaitskell, Wilson or Callaghan, of compromising on goals and betraying the socialist ideals of the Labour movement in prosecuting or promoting a foreign or defence policy indistinguishable from its Conservative opponents. The Conservative Party too was not without its internal dissent over foreign and defence policy; there were those on the 'gothic wing of the Conservative Party' (Hanning 1964:1) who considered the bipartisan policies to have eroded traditional British interests, especially in the decolonization movement in Africa and the Indian subcontinent, and thereby reduced Britain's already perilous status as a world power.

The Conservatives

Mainstream Conservative Party thinking is firmly based on what is essentially a 'power politics' view of the world. Besides recognizing the value and utility of force in international relations, this has meant subscribing to the idea of a balance of power, recognizing a hierarchy of states in world politics, and supporting an active foreign policy established on capabilities which typically have been military, economic and technological. The Conservatives have also been a pragmatic party, generally suspicious of theories and systems as guides for action, and this has been a useful asset in the face of the changes forced on all British governments operating foreign and defence policy since 1945. The persistent demands of the external and domestic environments have eroded the ability of all British governments to act with very much freedom in foreign and defence affairs. This reduced freedom of manoeuvre, while not easily accepted by the Conservative Party, has at least been recognized on pragmatic grounds, and has limited the volume of dissent in the party, even when policy has been inconsistent or incoherent.

The party has for long built a tradition as the patriotic party, committed to a defence of national interests as the priority of foreign and defence policy. This canon of policy has required a long-standing commitment to defence spending and support for the armed forces on the premiss that to defend one's interests requires force, if necessary, in the last resort. In the pre-1945 period, the Conservatives exploited their tradition of patriotism by proclaiming themselves as the only sound defenders of Britain's interests. However, the advent of the Attlee government's foreign and defence policies not only made it difficult to attack the Labour Party as unpatriotic, but laid down the basis of a tradition of consensus which emasculated the previous claims of the Conservatives. Since 1980 however, when the Labour Party adopted unilateralism as party policy, the Conservatives have been prepared and able to reassert this claim, and accuse the Labour Party as untrustworthy in the defence of Britain's interests (*The Times*, 6 June 1987).

The party has also acquired an imperialist strand, largely due to the efforts of Disraeli in the nineteenth century. The creation of the Empire promoted Britain's commercial and economic interests, which were formalized through the policy of imperial preference, and which associated the party with protectionism. However, the Empire also appealed to the paternalistic Conservative sentiments of loyalty and kinship, emphasized through the white Dominion connections, and symbolized Britain's responsibilities in the form of national obligations to the colonies and the international system. The creation and maintenance of the Empire was thus an extension of Disraeli's paternalistic tradition of 'One Nation' projected overseas.

Thus strong and traditional attachments to the nation state as the focus of political loyalty reside within the Conservative Party. The defence of national interests must, for the Conservative, lie primarily through national efforts; emphasis on retention of British independence is important and there is a suspicion towards, and wariness of, foreign alliances, except as specific, goal-oriented arrangements to defend British interests. This suspicion of general alliances is extended to an unease with international organizations which might seek to limit Britain's sovereignty and independence, and which set themselves vague and, to the Conservative, unrealistic and ahistorical goals. The party is also status-orientated; it has been in power for much of the period of British dominance of the international system, and has become used to exercising the apparatus of power. For those of the paternalist tradition, Britain must give a lead in the world, not only to secure British economic and political interests, but also to establish civilizing values and to ensure the defence of those values. It has therefore been difficult for the Conservative to accept easily a reduced status in world politics, a position which the post-war declining economy has allocated to Britain. These ideas of status, defence of national interests, and power politics, are particularly representative of the paternalistic wing of the party, which through the era of Churchill, Eden, Macmillan and Home dominated the articulation of foreign and defence attitudes for the first two decades of the post-war period.

The neo-liberal strand of the party has introduced a number of apparently contrasting ideas into the foreign and defence policy arena. This wing has more of an economic internationalist sentiment, which has meant that they have been more zealous supporters of free trade than imperial preference, and thus the bonds of Empire have not been felt so strongly. However, for most of this century the neo-liberal influence in the party's foreign policy has been minor and has not diluted the party's imperial claims. At the same time, the neo-liberal strand has demonstrated some of the foreign policy contradictions in the party, particularly over the question of the balance between the defence of the free market and support for Britain's economic interests and the pound sterling. While the party as a whole is a supporter of capitalism as the basis for economic and political activity, the neo-liberals have a greater devotion to the mechanisms of the free market yet have inherited a tradition of support for sterling as an indicator of British status. This is a division which has created dilemmas for policy during the Thatcher leadership.

In the post-war period, policy has been broadly accepted by the party as a result of loyalty to the leadership and the pragmatic, if tardy, recognition of post-war realities as limiters of British action. Moreover, traditional Conservative ideas about foreign and defence policy could be equated with the policies operated by successive governments, both Labour and Conservative. The British Commonwealth was supported as a surrogate Empire and as a means of maintaining global and distinctive influence, until — in the late 1960s — it became a source of embarrassment, even a burden, for the British. Similarly, the Anglo-American special relationship invoked tangible and intangible links with both American administrations and the American people, and presumed a further element of distinctiveness in British policy, especially in relation to Europe. The European Community aroused Conservative suspicions as its goals of political integration constituted an unpalatable burden of membership for most of the party, but given its apparent early success, which threatened to leave Britain, as then not a member, trailing as a power of any economic and political weight, the Macmillan government was pressed to apply for membership. However, British motives were guided by aspirations of playing a leading role in the Community, both as a source of status, and as a way of diverting the EEC from its integrative goal.

Under Heath, the move to Europe was more positive and undertaken with more commitment than under Macmillan. This arose as a result of Heath's Europeanism and his attachment to the EEC as an institution which could regenerate British industry. Heath's commitment to Europe was reinforced by his lack of interest in the Commonwealth and his interpretation of the special relationship with the United States as, by 1970, a natural one (Frankel 1975:212). While Heath's ideas on foreign policy seemed out of line with the paternalistic, great power traditions of the Conservative Party, his support for Europe was undertaken with a view to seeing the Community — with Britain as its leading member — challenge the USA and the Soviet Union as a third superpower (ibid.: 168–73). Heath's nationalism was rooted, not in fading symbols, but in the desire to see an efficient Britain operating as the leading power in Europe. Thus his policies, while having a rather different motivation, merely speeded up the process begun under Macmillan.

The withdrawal from Empire and the move to Europe triggered the major element of dissent from those sections of the party who saw the Conservatives moving away from the traditional basis of policy as a world power. The British evacuation of Egypt in 1954 crystallized these opinions within the party around the 'Suez group' of MPs, who feared British withdrawal from the Middle East would destroy any claims Britain might have to lead the Commonwealth and retain global status. They were notable in opposing Britain's withdrawal from the strategic base in Egypt in 1954, and not surprisingly felt Eden should have continued with the Suez invasion of 1956 (Epstein 1964:41–60). This attachment to the imperial idea is something that decolonization has not fully expunged from the party as a whole. It has found expression through sympathy towards, and even support for, the Smith regime in Rhodesia, and a less than committed opposition to the South African regime, either by individual MPs, fringe groups, or even from the party as a whole. The dissent over decolonization was echoed — although not necessarily from the same quarters — over the move to Europe, with a number of Conservatives failing to share Heath's vision of Britain's place in the EEC. The anti-marketeers were vocal and prominent both in Parliament and outside. Some, like Neil Marten, feared the effects membership would have on British agriculture, while others such as Powell and John Biffen based their opposition on grounds of loss of sovereignty. This episode of EEC membership revealed the contradictory nature of ideas on policy in that Powell, who shared an outlook of economic liberalism with Heath, saw the Community as a threat to

British sovereignty and power and not a forum for its expansion.

In defence policy, British nuclear weapons remained a symbol of great power status, and their retention was supported by all Conservative governments. In fact the 1957 Defence White Paper indicated that Britain's credible defence would in future depend on the development of an independent nuclear deterrent. This decision not only allowed Britain to abolish conscription and move towards the creation of smaller, more professional and mobile conventional forces, it also permitted Britain to claim an independent status from the United States. In practice, this independence has been questioned by critics of British policy, especially since the 1962 Polaris agreement, although Macmillan was able to gain broad Conservative support for the agreement by the inclusion of the national interest clause, whereby British governments retain the right to use Polaris outside NATO when supreme national interests dictate. Britain's defence commitment east of Suez represented an active and global role in defence of the Commonwealth links until economic circumstances forced a reappraisal by the Wilson government in 1968. This was opposed by the Conservatives in opposition, but confirmed when in power under Heath from 1970 to 1974. However, Britain's defence commitment to Europe, of four divisions and a tactical airforce, under the 1954 Paris Treaty, and the continuing support for NATO, jelled with Conservative ideas on the nature of alliances as representing limited and specific commitments which defend British interests yet do not presume any broader political goals, nor any promise of integration.

In brief then, the Conservative Party has been associated with the defence of British interests and has been traditionally a vociferous proponent of Britain's world power status. Yet it has also been pragmatic and sensitive to *realpolitik*, attributes which have been essential for British governments managing policy in the twentieth century. While the neo-liberal strand in the party has held somewhat different priorities in foreign and defence policy, these were not readily articulated until Heath's leadership, whose policies, though having rather different motivation, happened to coincide anyway with continuing practice. During the 1940s and 1950s criticism of the party leadership came largely from those of the same paternalist tradition as the leadership, from the die-hard imperialists and those who had misgivings about the loss of British sovereignty through membership of the EEC. When compared to the record of the Labour Party's ideas on foreign and defence policy, Conservative ideas have been less rigid and have permitted trimming by the leadership without too much internal disruption.

The Labour Party

The ideas of the Labour Party on foreign and defence policy come closest

165

to endowing a British political party with a comprehensive doctrine of thought. The Labour Party's ideas on foreign and defence policy have a number of origins, including the basic Christian, socialist, and radical traditions which influenced the party in its early days and which still find expression within it. The party has endorsed the socialist view that social tensions within states are the source of international frictions (Northedge 1960:642). This distinguishes the assumptions held by the Labour Party about the rightful goal of foreign policy, and the nature of conflict in the international system, from those of the Conservatives. Whereas the latter see the potential for conflict lying with intrinsic human fallibility, the Labour Party has a more optimistic view, seeing instead conflict caused by the underlying extrinsic relationships between human beings and the structures and institutions which support those relationships. The Labour Party, particularly its left-wing, has a commitment to reject a traditional foreign policy based on power politics and the defence of purely national interests for a socialist foreign policy (Attlee 1937:211). Thus the Labour Party has identified the goals of a socialist foreign policy as the creation of a world free from poverty, inequality, and war, and one liberated from political and economic oppression (Labour Party 1982:238).

However, these goals have yet to be translated into the foreign policy of a Labour government. The centre-right of the party — which has traditionally provided the leadership — might not reject the long-term aspirations of a socialist foreign policy, but its actual policy stance invites the conclusion that it has seen a socialist foreign policy as irrelevant to British needs since the end of the war. The party leadership has been closer to the traditions of British policy and has accommodated to the 'realism' of the internal and external constraints on policy-makers when in power. The policies and attitudes of both Bevin, as Attlee's first post-war Foreign Secretary, and Denis Healey, as Defence Secretary between 1964 and 1970, were examples of this process of accommodation to *realpolitik* at times of persistent readjustment for Britain. However, to those on the left of the party, this process of accommodation, abundantly evident in the post-1945 period when Labour governments have had working majorities, has been considered a betrayal of socialism and been used as a weapon in internal party struggles. It has been portrayed as a refusal of the leadership to challenge the bureaucratic, political and economic constraints which have moulded policy options in traditional casts for post-war British governments, and represented as indicative of the leadership's 'fudging' over the implementation of socialism when in power, and provides much of the substance of intraparty disputes during this period.

A number of distinctive ideas form the components of a socialist foreign policy which the left has been advocating, as a break from traditional policies, since the end of the First World War. Michael Gordon (1969:13–44) has identified four broad themes, these being: anti-capitalism, international working-class solidarity, internationalism, and pacifism. The socialist element of the party has given to it an opposition to capitalism, and those policies, both domestic and foreign, which support the maintenance of capitalist interests and the relationships based on capitalism. Traditional foreign policy is seen as supporting these interests and therefore the Labour Party should adopt policies aimed at dismantling them. In its attack upon traditional foreign policy, the party has adopted old radical positions in support of the democratization of policy-making through opening up the process to greater accountability and the ending of secret diplomacy. The anti-capitalism of the party has also generated an anti-Americanism, which regards the United States as the citadel of world capitalism and, therefore, a state of which British socialist governments should be wary.

The obverse of this anti-capitalism has been a fascination with, and support for, the Soviet revolution. In the 1920s and 1930s, the Soviet state was seen as a potential model for socialism and one which should be supported on the basis of international working-class solidarity. The excesses of Stalinism in the late 1930s did much to erode this attachment to the Soviet Union, but the heroic exertions of the Soviet people during the Second World War restored the Labour Party's perception of the Soviet state. In the immediate months following the end of the war, the Labour Party held high expectations about the future relations between the Attlee government and the Soviet Union. It was felt that 'left should be able to speak to left', so ensuring a degree of harmony and co-operation in Anglo-Soviet relations. When, after the Soviet expansion in Eastern Europe, Ernest Bevin, the Labour Foreign Secretary, sought a United States commitment to European defence he had to endure the odium of those on the left of the party, some of them 'fellow-travellers', who retained their support for, and faith in, the Soviet system. The later suppression of the 1956 Hungarian uprising and the 1968 Czechoslovakian reform movement by Stalin's successors did, however, erode much of the remaining emotional attachment to the Soviet Union even on the left of the party. Yet even if the admiration for the Soviet revolution has disappeared, the party as a whole still finds solidarity with revolutionary movements, especially in areas dominated by capitalist interests and those operating against right-wing dictator-ships supported by US administrations.

The anti-capitalism of the left has also nourished an anti-colonialism which has been shared generally by the whole party. The anti-colonial idea not only derives from a Leninist identification of imperialism as the highest form of capitalism, but also because imperialism conflicted with the party's attachment to the liberal notion of self-determination and its basic internationalism. There have, however, been apparent discontinuities in its attitude to imperialism. First, there is a clear paradox in that the liberal attachment to self-determination is an attachment to the basic principle of nationalism which should find no room in the Labour Party's ideological portfolio. Second, in the heyday of the British Empire at the end of the nineteenth century, some of the Fabians — part founders of the party — defended the imperial idea as a way of improving the welfare of the dependent territories and their subjects and spreading the advantages that they perceived British culture and education would bestow. This attachment to 'social imperialism' was supported by some on the far left of the party such as Hyndman and Blatchford, and one can even detect in the party's approach to the post-war Commonwealth, as a multiracial focus and centre-piece of British power and status, shades of this old attitude.

The internationalism of the party rejects nationalism as a focus for political loyalty and sees in the preservation of national sovereignty and national interests the road to competitive international tensions and anarchy. National security can only be fully achieved through world security, which entails submerging sovereignty to loyalty to international organizations and the creation of universal economic development and global peace. This has led to the League of Nations and the United Nations occupying a central place in the declaratory foreign policies of the Labour Party. The ultimate goal of a socialist foreign policy is the establishment of a world government presiding over people united by socialism, not divided by nationalism. However, the internationalism of the party has been strained by the hostility of some of the left towards the EEC and NATO, and their promotion of neutrality as a basis for British foreign and defence policy. The suspicion of these two organizations arises from their capitalist foundations and also from a protective attitude towards British sovereignty and independence which are perceived as threatened by them (Benn 1980:17). This attitude would appear to be the very antithesis of internationalism, but as the left considers both the EEC and NATO to be neither democratic nor representative of true internationalism, no discontinuity of thought arises. While those on the centre and right tend to moderate their criticism of the EEC to specific Community policies and are firm supporters of NATO, they too can display a national attachment to British sovereignty even if the threat to it is not specifically identified as coming from particular institutions or relationships. Thus Benn and Foot from the left can share this protective attitude towards British democratic institutions with those such as Gaitskell from the right and many labourist trade union leaders from the centre of the party.

Pacifism is also a component of a socialist foreign policy. The origins for this are numerous. The founders of the party and many of the

Liberals who joined had a strong pacifist commitment which has remained to this day. Thus the use of force was regarded as morally wrong and contrary to the basic tenets of Christianity by the Christian pacifist elements within the Independent Labour Party (ILP) founders of the party. For others, the experiences of the Great War reinforced the view that war and conflict were the product of imperialist rivalries, and worked against the international socialism and class solidarity of the Labour movement (Naylor 1969:8). The Labour Party has also inherited a radical anti-militarism, a traditional English opposition to the creation of standing armies and conscription as threats to civil liberties (Attlee 1937:201), while the Liberals who joined the party after the First World War reinforced this hostility to the use of force in international relations. For them, all states had an interest in the avoidance of war, which ran counter to the economic development of all states. In the post-Second World War period the pacifist strand of the party has been manifested through an uneasy stance in relation to British and American nuclear weapons and the promotion of British unilateral nuclear disarmament by those on the left of the party. Opposition has also been directed to conventional arms and spending on conventional weapons; specifically towards the retention of peace-time conscription and the Korean rearmament programme, both instituted by the Attlee government.

Much of the basis for post-war British foreign and defence policy was laid by the Attlee governments between 1945 and 1951. The commitment to decolonization exemplified by the grant of independence to the Indian subcontinent in 1947 reflected the party's anti-colonialism, but the aligning of US power to Europe through NATO following the identification of the Soviet Union as a potential adversary, the maintenance of conscription, the unwillingness to lead Europe's integrative efforts, and the decision to construct Britain's own nuclear weapons in secret without any democratization of policy-making, were perhaps less like the actions that might have been expected of a Labour government. Such policies in the traditional mould stimulated dissent from the left, which rejected the direction of British policy under Bevin and Attlee. For example, NATO's creation appeared to relegate the status of the UN in Britain's foreign and defence policy and thereby offended the internationalism of the left, who in some cases went to the extent of abstaining on the Commons' vote which approved British membership of NATO (Bullock 1983:688). The 'Keep Left' group of Crossman, Foot, Mikardo, and others was concerned that British policy reflected a 'dangerous dependence on the USA' (ibid.:395) and called instead for Britain to become the standard bearer of a 'third force' in international politics, distanced from the superpowers and the developing tensions of the Cold War. Hence some on the left, in the internationalist tradition, initially supported a British involvement in European co-operation, although this attitude was to change when, in 1948, the Council of Europe was seen to be dominated by Christian Democratic, rather than Socialist, forces.

The left was to be further critical of the Attlee government's hasty termination of the Palestine Mandate in 1948, without any guarantee for the creation of an Israeli state, even though it signalled a withdrawal from imperial responsibilities. The Bevanites such as Crossman, Wilson, and Mikardo, and those from other parts of the party such as Dalton, Morrison, Shinwell, Silkin, and Strachey had a sympathy for Zionism which was not shared by Bevin or the Foreign Office. It is interesting to note that by the 1970s the left had shifted its ideological ground through a sympathetic approach to the Palestine Liberation Organization and the Arab cause. This movement reflected the left's perception of Zionism as a movement that now runs counter to the internationalism of the Labour Party and has been a factor in the denial of self-determination for the Palestinians.

The explanation for the Attlee government's rejection of a distinctively socialist foreign policy lay in the realism which came with office, something both Attlee and Bevin had experienced in the wartime coalition, and in the demands of the international situation after 1945. Moreover, Bevin did not subscribe to the left's attachment to the Soviet Union, while Attlee was concerned to eradicate the perception that the Labour Party was not responsible in the defence of the nation and its interests (Frankel 1975:35). This refusal to adopt a blanket left stance on foreign affairs was continued into the 1950s and 1960s, during which time the party displayed a range of ideological positions both in and out of power, while the party leadership maintained the policy consensus with the Conservatives. The Suez episode, however, constituted a major area of disagreement between the front benches in the 1950s, but even then the party's position was complicated, with Gaitskell's suspicions of Eden's intentions being matched by his hostility to Nasser, while some Jewish and left-wing Labour MPs opposed the government's intervention but retained considerable sympathy for Israel (Epstein 1964:173–98).

Generally, through the 1950s, dissent over foreign and defence policy characterized the relationship between the leadership and the left, with the question of nuclear weapons creating the major conflict within the party when unilateralism was adopted, albeit for one year only, as party policy in 1960. Unilateralism brought together a number of strands in Labour's ideological tradition: rejection of British nuclear weapons and US nuclear bases in Britain at the Scarborough conference was an expression of the pacifist, anti-militarist, and anti-US features of a socialist foreign policy. Significantly, however, the party did not vote to leave NATO, thereby revealing a paradox in policy: that Britain should reject its own nuclear weapons yet accept membership of an alliance committed to their use if necessary. It was a contradiction which was to return to the party in the 1980s. The party's acceptance of unilateralism was largely assisted by temporary support from those sections of the party opposed to Gaitskell's attempts to reform the party constitution who used the defence issue to indicate their displeasure with his leadership (Taylor 1970:235).

Over Europe the party leadership has wavered between suspicion towards the Community and acceptance of membership as a basis for the regeneration of British power. Gaitskell feared that membership of the Community would entail the ending of one thousand years of history, but Wilson's application in 1967 indicated a continuity with Macmillan's earlier attempts. Wilson, though intrinsically hostile to the EEC, justified seeking membership in 1967 and supported retention of membership in the 1975 referendum on the status argument that Britain's influence would be greater within Europe than outside. However, the goal of supranationalism was firmly rejected, the emphasis being placed on the protection of British interests through the veto in the Council of Ministers (Labour Party 1975:3–8). While the British people voted to remain in Europe, the Labour Party has never been fully reconciled to membership. This opposition to the EEC can be traced to a number of sources: the EEC is a capitalist organization whose ethos is hostile to socialist economic planning, and hence to the creation of democratic socialism; the European Commission is seen as overly bureaucratic, an eroder of sovereignty, and largely unaccoutable, and therefore a challenge to democracy. Moreover, some of the Community's common policies have been seen as devices to protect the entrenched national interests of particular member states, something which, paradoxically, the Wilson and Callaghan governments sought themselves.

Labour under Wilson, who had resigned from Attlee's government over the Korean rearmament programme, thus pursued a foreign and defence policy which showed a marked continuity with its Conservative predecessors, including the belief in Britain's great power status. Wilson claimed a world role for Britain by maintaining the nuclear deterrent, seeking a mediatory role in the Vietnam War, defending the status of sterling, and promoting Britain as an international peacekeeper. Thus, until the election of Foot as leader in 1980, the Labour leadership clearly subscribed to the view of Britain's great power status and consequently was the target of criticism from the left. However, the latter's promotion of a socialist foreign policy has also been based on an inflated view of British influence. The 'third force' concept of Crossman and others assumed that Britain's role in a European grouping would be the equal of the superpowers, and much of the unilateralist argument in the 1950s was based on the premiss that British renunciation of nuclear weapons would provide a moral lead for the other nuclear powers to emulate.

The Liberal Tradition

The influence of liberal ideas in British politics has been extensive, so extensive that they have found expression in the foreign and defence policies of more than one party. Thus the decline of the Liberal Party in the inter-war period did not herald the decline of liberal thinking about international affairs. The neo-liberal strand of the Conservative Party has carried some of the economic canons of classical liberalism into the 1980s, while the Labour Party inherited some of the liberal assumptions about the nature and origins of war. However, like the other parties, the Liberal Party has been saddled with contradictions in its thinking about foreign and defence policy, and these still haunt the party to the present day. Classical liberal theory, associated with minimal intervention by the state in domestic politics and sound money in the economy, assumes in international affairs that peace is in the interests of all states. Peace can best be assured through the creation of commercial relations between states, which in turn supports the liberal attachment to free trade. Extensions of this aspect of liberalism are a minimalist foreign policy and an anti-militarism. There were aspects of this part of liberalism which motivated Gladstone's foreign policy in the nineteenth century, particularly in liberal opposition to Conservative imperial policies, which were seen as jingoistic, extending the powers of the state and increasing the levels of public expenditure.

However, while one part of the radical liberal tradition has supported a minimalist foreign policy, another part has had a pronounced internationalism which is founded upon the promotion of individual rights, liberty and justice as universal (Butt Philip 1983:217). This aspect of liberalism, highlighting humanitarianism and justice, identified Britain, and British power, as the protector of liberties in other states, and found support from Galdstone, particularly in relation to the Bulgarian atrocities of 1876. Thus the anti-militarist and minimalist side of liberalism coexisted, but not always easily, with those liberal sentiments which were supportive of the use of force to defend the interests of the powerless.

The Liberal Party's decline in the period after the First World War reduced its role as a vehicle for the expression of many liberal sentiments on international affairs, from which the Labour Party profited in both numbers and ideas. The Liberal Party's aversion to war, which was aggravated by the memories of the Somme, stimulated the interventionist sentiments in the inter-war years to support a collective security system to ensure that war did not blight European relations ever again. Yet, the contradictions remained (the party retained pacifist elements) and increasingly lacked anything distinctive to say in foreign and defence policy that was not said, for the most part, by the Labour Party. This problem of avoiding the squeeze effect of the two major parties and having someting distinctive to say has recurred since 1945. In response to this the party has been receptive to new ideas in advance of the other parties: for example, its early advocacy of British membership of Europe. This support for a supranational Europe was rooted in the internationalist sentiment of the party, while the goal of a united Europe, devoid of national boundaries, could find support from the party's free trade tradition. The Liberals no doubt also perceived a united Europe as a means of avoiding a future war in Europe. However, support for Europe has revealed some of the contradictions within the tradition, especially as the centralizing nature of decision-making within the Community is contrary to the liberal tradition of decentralization. Although support for the Community remains solid with the Liberals, the Community appears in the 1980s to be moving further away from the party's original aspirations.

Other contradictions in foreign and defence policy have arisen from the interpretation of liberalism made by the Young Liberals. The 1960s saw the younger wing of the party adopt a radical stance on many foreign and defence issues, such as the demand for British withdrawal from NATO, and the entry of the Warsaw Pact states into the ETC (Sked and Cook 1984:251); ideas which went further than much of the left wing of the Labour Party. In the 1970s this radicalism led to the development of an extra-parliamentary style by the Young Liberals, at variance with the party leadership, one clear expression of which was the organization of the 'Stop the 1970 Tour' against the touring South African cricket team. The more recent problem for the leadership of the Liberal Party has been the revival of the pacifist, anti-militarist tradition within the party, which has manifested itself as a rejection of a nuclear defence policy, thereby causing the major policy tension during the period of the Liberal-SDP Alliance, as the SDP was firmly committed to maintaining a British nuclear capability. Thus the SDP, whose founder members left the Labour Party because of its drift to the left, of which one manifestation was its endorsement of unilateralism at the 1980 party conference, have re-encountered similar ideas from the anti-militarist tradition within the Liberal Party.

The Revival of Ideas in the 1980s

The formation of the Social Democratic Party in 1981 had as its stimulus the evacuation of the centre ground of British politics. The shift of the leadership and ideological centre of gravity of the Conservative and Labour Parties introduced competing values and ideas about policy on to the agenda of British politics, thereby fragmenting the earlier consensus. The nature of this fragmentation in relation to economic and social policy is discussed elsewhere, with the Thatcherite revolution committed to rolling back the state's role and responsibilities, but both foreign and defence policies have similarly, though to a less noticeable extent, revealed the divergent ideas now distinguishing and dividing the political parties. Thus the Thatcher government has refused to accept all of the trends of policy under previous governments, and has emphasized a restored status to Britain. This process of restoration has required the creation of 'solutions' to some foreign policy problems that beleaguered its predecessors, while maintaining continuity for those policies which have bestowed status on Britain.

In this process, the Thatcher government has exhibited a mixture of ideological influences. The dominant idea behind its foreign and defence policy positions has been a crude if effective identification of Britain's interests. However, the neo-liberal sentiments associated with Thatcherism have coexisted with traditional pragmatism and compromise as the Conservative government has sought to re-create British influence in international politics. This intermeshing of ideas and attitudes has produced contradictions and repeated discontinuities which thus remain a feature of present Conservative policy. For example, the Thatcher approach to Europe has been motivated by traditional Conservative nationalist sentiments as well as by a neo-liberal antipathy towards what the Community had become by the 1980s (and towards the 'social' Europe that threatened further ahead). The overall approach of the Thatcher government to the Community has been in marked contrast to that of the Heath administration. The Thatcher government's relations with Europe have been dominated by the question of Britain's payments to the Community budget and the demands for British rebates from it, which has allowed Mrs Thatcher to be portrayed as a traditional defender of British interests against a Community for which she has no special concern. The fact that the contributions to the large and apparently bottomless budget could be depicted as an example of financial profligacy supporting a bureaucratic base, and running counter to the neo-liberal sentiments of efficiency, low taxation, and reduced expenditure, served merely to confirm Thatcher's unease with the Europeans. However, Britain's membership is not in any doubt under the Conservatives. Britain under Thatcher has been prepared to hector the Commission and EEC governments for the return of 'our money', and this position found more support from the electorate than Labour's desire up to the mid-1980s to withdraw from the Community. Yet relations with the Community have still not been fully normalized in that Britain has, again as the result of the personal opposition of Mrs Thatcher, refused fully to join the European Monetary System, and put a very restrictive interpretation on the 1986 Single European Act, both of which come too close to economic and potential political union for the traditional Conservative in Thatcher.

Over Rhodesia, another major foreign policy issue of the 1970s which

the Thatcher government inherited, it can be assumed that Mrs Thatcher had little feeling for the Commonwealth's views over the need for
a legitimate and fair transfer of power to the black majority, and wanted
a quick and efficient solution to the problem in order to regularize
Britain's relations with Rhodesia. However, this drive for an easy
settlement was outweighed by the advice from the Foreign Office, and
Carrington, the Foreign Secretary, that Britain would have to come to
terms with the black majority leaders if it was to retain some influence
in Africa and the Third World. In this Mrs Thatcher's policy reversal
is indicative of her pragmatism in defence of Britain's political and
economic interests, overcoming her initial political instincts (Stephenson
1980:82–3). In relation to South Africa, however, Mrs Thatcher's
government has continued traditional British policy where British
opposition to apartheid has been outweighed by South Africa's importance
resulting from its strategic location and mineral wealth, its pronounced
anti-Communist sympathies, and its position as a trading partner for
Britain. The Thatcher government, in line with all previous British
governments, has condemned apartheid, while refusing to institute general
and mandatory sanctions against the Botha government. The problem
of South Africa remains one where questions of *realpolitik* and the morality of policy clash and, as a result, Conservative governments have been
far more comfortable in dealing with it than have Labour.

Britain's relations with the United States during the Thatcher years
have seen the interweaving of traditional pragmatism and liberal
sentiments as motivators of policy. Under Thatcher, Britain's relations
with the USA have moved closer to the concept of a special relationship
than they had been for some time. The neo-liberalism of Mrs Thatcher
found easy support for the US as the leader of world capitalism, especially
under Reagan, and the Thatcher government has been at pains to portray
itself as a good ally of the US in return for seeking to re-establish Britain
as the vehicle for the expression of US power in Europe and restore its
place as a political confidant to US governments. However, this has meant
that the concept of the special relationship has been extended beyond
traditional European security relations to include co-operation in areas
now outside those associated with British interests. Thus besides fully
supporting the US administrations of Carter and Reagan in nuclear affairs,
through the NATO twin-track decision of 1979, and taking the final decision for Britain to remain a nuclear power through the Trident purchase,
the Thatcher government has also allowed Britain to play a role in some
conventional US security commitments in the Middle East through a force
contribution to the US-sponsored multinational forces in the Sinai and
Beirut, and by allowing the US to make use of its NATO bases in Britain
in the 1986 raid on Libya. In return the Thatcher government sought,
and received, political and military support from the Reagan government

during the Falklands War in an area traditionally within the US sphere of influence. And, while the Thatcher government has sought to re-cement the special relationship, there have been notable areas of discord: the Grenada intervention, and the US embargo on the Soviet gas-pipeline contracts would be examples.

In its relationship with the Soviet Union the Thatcher government has again reflected the contrasting ideological traditions. Mrs Thatcher herself has been prepared to exploit the sobriquet 'Iron Lady' in her early deal-ings with the Soviet Union, and the neo-liberal, avowed anti-collectivist in her political character would endorse this stand. However, this has not been allowed to obstruct a subsequent improvement in relations under Gorbachev: a leader with whom Mrs Thatcher thinks, in the pragmatic tradition, Britain can do business.

In defence policy, the Thatcher governments have retained and expanded Britain's nuclear status and, under the 1981 Defence White Paper, began to define a greater European commitment for Britain, which entailed a reduction in the Royal Navy's forces and a seeming rejection of British security commitments outside the North Atlantic and home waters. However, this articulation of priorities was abruptly disrupted by the Falklands War in 1982. The claim that Britain has, under That-cher, restored some lost pride and status has been most clearly nourished by the South Atlantic campaign, although the commitment by the Thatcher government to the Falklands has created tensions within the Conservative Party. For the neo-liberal wing of the party, Britain has little to gain from the Falklands and this approach would correspond with the realism of the Foreign and Commonwealth Office in seeing no long-term future for the Falklands as a British dependency, and seeking some solution, possibly in the form of lease-back, for some time prior to hostilities. However, the claims of the Falklanders appealed to Mrs Thatcher's tradi-tional Conservative, patriotic and populist sentiments and, in the way that the EEC rebate was 'our money', these were 'our people' to be defended against the Argentinian regime and way of life (and also against what Thatcher might see as the spinelessness of the Foreign Office). The success of the war provided Mrs Thatcher with the means to claim firm leadership in defence of British interests and the British public with a replay, probably the last, of the type of military action that appeared to have died with the loss of Empire.

Thus, under the Thatcher government, policy has been pulled in opposing directions. While some remaining dependency problems appear to have been solved (Rhodesia and Hong Kong being cases in point), the Falklands commitment has revived debate about Britain's extra-European commitments and at a time when there appeared to be a recognition that Britain's security role lay in Europe. Furthermore, Thatcher has reversed the political and economic movement towards

Europe, not by threatened withdrawal, but rather by a fierce defence of British interests and by the amplification of Anglo-US relations.

While the Conservatives have embarked on a revival of British power and influence in the 1980s, the Labour Party has moved closer to a foreign and defence policy more in keeping with the basic tenets of the left of the party. Much of the motivation for this has come as a result of a process of introspection and the seeming failure of the party to introduce socialist policies when in power under Wilson and Callaghan. The main pillars of this policy since 1980 have been a continued hostility to the European Community, as anathema to the promotion of international socialism (Labour Party, 1980:131–2), and the adoption of a non-nuclear policy as the basis of British defence policy in line with the party's pacifist and anti-American traditions. In 1983 the Labour Party fought the election on a manifesto which included withdrawal from the EEC, the cancellation of Trident, the removal of American Cruise missiles from British bases, and the commitment to place Polaris into future arms negotiations. Thus, although the party was committed to a non-nuclear defence policy, it recognized the potential value of British nuclear weapons in any future arms negotiations. By 1987 the party had dropped the pledge to withdraw from the European Community, but moved further along the unilateralist course by proposing the cancellation of the Trident programme and the immediate decommissioning of Britain's Polaris force, thus foreclosing the possibility of using it to gain concessions from the Soviet Union in any disarmament process. The party further indicated an intention, though without being specific about the time scale, to remove all US nuclear bases from Britain.

As a form of quid pro quo Labour has affirmed its conventional commitment to NATO and its intention to direct savings made from a renunciation of the deterrent to conventional forces. In this latter proposal the Labour Party of the 1980s has again indicated its desire to be seen as responsible in its version of the credible defence of the realm, even though breaking with the tradition of the party since 1945 which, while it has never been comfortable with the possession of British nuclear weapons, has been committed to multilateral disarmament rather than to unilateralism. The party has refused to go as far as withdrawing from NATO, as some parts of the left would like, but it has adopted a stance whereby both superpowers are held equally responsible for the arms race (*The Times*, 8 August 1984). Moreover, it has resurrected a moral argument on the wickedness of nuclear weapons as a reason for Britain not to possess them, yet been prepared to recognize the nature of a deterrent relationship existing between NATO and the Warsaw Pact, from which Britain could, under a future Labour government, enjoy the benefits. There is no doubt that there has been a conflict of thinking within the party over nuclear issues in the 1980s; for example, the 1980 party conference approved both multilateralist and unilateralist resolutions (Labour Party 1980:159–62), and even managed a resolution which espoused both in the same text (ibid.:163).

While unilateralism has been the major focus of the leftward movement of the party's foreign and defence policy objectives, ideological purity has been further sustained through a commitment to the work of the Brandt Commission on the North-South divide in the international system (largely ignored by the Conservative government) and to foreign aid, along with support for popular struggles in South Africa and Chile. Where the Labour Party has chosen to identify the erosion of human rights, its targets have been those Central and South American regimes supported by the Reagan administration. Here, the Falklands War was a source of some discomfort to the left, in that its reflex opposition to the British use of force to regain the islands was tempered by a desire not to be seen to be giving moral support to aggression by the Argentinian military junta, which had a disgraceful record in human rights. The Conservatives, by contrast, have focused their attention almost exclusively on the absence of human rights in the Soviet Union.

As the Conservative and Labour Parties departed from the consensual tradition of 1945, the Liberal-SDP Alliance sought to occupy the space made vacant. However, the major problem for the Alliance was that the SDP was a multilateralist party whereas the Liberals, while being in general multilateralist, have — through their pacifist tradition — a tendency towards unilateralism. From the inception of the Alliance, the nuclear question proved a major irritant in relationships between the parties. There was a clear difference over the question of American Cruise missiles, with the Liberals being opposed to their deployment (Liberal Party 1982:16), while the SDP was in favour, providing a dual-key arrangement could be concluded between the US and British governments (Social Democratic Party, n.d.[1985]:5–10). There was agreement within the Alliance that Trident, the nuclear force that will replace Polaris in the early 1990s, should be cancelled, but disagreement over what should stand in its place. The SDP was committed to retaining some British nuclear capability, while the Liberal Party was opposed to a British nuclear force as an example of the worst form of nationalism. Yet the Liberal leadership has at the same time been critical of the unilateralist argument, found in its own party, that renunciation would give a lead to other states, a position — with more than a whiff of nationalism about it — that somehow British renunciation is best (Liberal Party 1982:16). Thus the Liberals have been intent upon phasing out Polaris as soon as possible, but as part of multilateral negotiations, in contrast to Labour's unilateralism, while the SDP remained committed to maintaining a British nuclear capability, holding simply that Trident should not be it.

The issue came to a head in 1986, when the Liberal Assembly, reflecting the old anti-militarist tradition in the party, rejected the need to retain the British deterrent. Consequently the 1987 election was fought on a mere semblance of unity in the Alliance, through the adoption of mainly SDP policies, and it was not surprising therefore that the nuclear issue loomed large in the subsequent merger negotiations between the parties after the disappointment of the election result. With the resulting split of the Owenite SDP from the merged SLDP, the centre was, by 1988, showing a range of positions on nuclear defence, with the SDP by then supporting Trident, the SLDP being led by the Liberal Paddy Ashdown, a convert to multilateralism during the 1986 Liberal Party conference, and the radical Liberals still broadly unilateralist in persuasion.

Defence policy has therefore been a critical factor in the politics and general elections of the 1980s, as sharply competing ideas about Britain's role and responsibilities have been displayed before the electorate for the first time in post-war British politics. These issues now divide both the parties and the nation, and even the Alliance found it difficult to be convincingly united on a nuclear defence policy. The Labour Party's commitment to unilateralism signifies a triumph for the left of the party and an attempt to convince the British public that a fundamental re-think of Britain's role in the world is necessary, one which escapes from many of the orthodox views about British foreign and defence policy which the party leadership has shared since 1945. However, in the period immediately before the 1987 general election, opinion polls were showing that a clear majority of the British people were in favour of retaining the British independent nuclear deterrent (*The Times*, 25 April 1987), and in the light of the 1987 general election result, it appears that the electorate are not ready for such a re-think, or at least remain to be convinced of the Labour Party's position. Since the election defeat, the Labour Party has begun a process of reviewing its policy through a series of policy committees which expect to produce ideas on reform by 1990 (*The Times*, 29 September 1987). However, when Kinnock sought to short-circuit the review process and move away from the rigid unilateralism of the 1987 campaign, as in his 'something for something' rather 'something for nothing' statement of 5 June 1988, the dissent created in the party (including the resignation of Denzil Davies, the Labour defence spokesman) was such that Kinnock was forced to reassert the orthodox unilateralist position, but at the cost of further confusion on the issue.

It is not clear what the party's position on nuclear weapons will be in the approach to 1992 (the earliest date that Labour can expect to be returned to power). Certainly the apparent improvement in superpower relations will have some effect on how the Labour Party chooses to present its defence policy in the period; and by then the momentum for arms control, which appears to have been created by the 1987 agreement between the superpowers to ban all intermediate nuclear forces (INF) may be such that a non-nuclear defence policy may no longer appear as a political liability but rather as an example of the party's political sagacity and foresight. But the removal of Cruise missiles under the INF treaty has been exploited by the Conservative government as a victory for initial deployment and negotiation from strength, and already removed a part of Labour's unilateralist package. By 1992 Trident will be coming into service, leaving few options open for the Labour leadership: either acceptance of the deterrent as a *fait accompli*, with its attendant risks of internal bloodletting, or maintaining the unilateralist platform and again risking electoral rejection. Kinnock has indicated that by 1992 it might be possible to include the Trident force in some multilateral arms negotiations (*Guardian*, 2 October 1987), and this may prove to be a workable compromise, although why the Soviet leadership should be interested in reducing their strategic nuclear forces in return for renunciation of a missile which the Labour leadership has committed itself never to use may prove to be a weakness in the argument.

While nuclear defence issues have divided the parties in the 1980s, there is still some common ground in the support, although variable, for Britain's membership of the UN and the continuation of Britain's NATO obligations, while the Labour Party now recognizes that Britain is a member of the EEC and that withdrawal is no longer a realistic option. For the time being, however, a high proportion of the electorate still appears to find more comfort from the ideas of the Conservatives in foreign and defence policy — ideas which have themselves reversed some of the direction of policy under previous Conservative and Labour governments. There can be little doubt that the Thatcher government, which has been impatient with the canons of consensus, identified as responsible for Britain's failure to break out of the spiral of post-war decline, has similarly not been content with an acceptance of Britain's reduced status in world politics. Whether the long-term result will be a restoration and redirection of British influence, or whether the stewardship of Thatcher will be seen as yet another period during which the rhetoric of greatness was mouthed while Britain's influence further declined, and necessary adjustments were not made, or made too slowly, will be for the successors of Thatcherism to decide. Competing ideas may have forced foreign and defence policy on to the centre stage of politics, but the persistent effects of the domestic and external environments, which have determined much of British policy since 1945, will remain as constant restraints on future British governments of whatever ideological complexion.

Further Reading

There is no fully adequate text which deals with the range of ideas found in British foreign and defence policy, and the reader will be forced to refer to works related to individual parties instead. There is no specific work on the Conservative Party's ideas on the subject, although Gamble (1974) is useful for the post-war period, while Gordon (1969) provides the best explanation of the Labour Party's ideas. The radical tradition is dealt with in part by Taylor's (1957) classic text, and there are useful chapters by Brock (1983) and Butt Philip (1983) on the liberal tradition and the Liberals and Europe respectively. The substance of policy is thoroughly examined in Northedge (1974), and Spence (1984) provides a well-written review of policy adjustments since 1945, while the process of policy-making is dealt with by Wallace (1976). Smith *et al.* (1988) is a recent text which looks at both the substance and making of policy, as does Frankel's (1975) earlier classic work. Kitzinger (1973) deals with British official and party positions on British entry to the EEC, while Britain's experience with nuclear weapons is examined in the excellent texts of Pierre (1972), Freedman (1980) and Groom (1974), the latter being a comprehensive study of official, party and public attitudes. A standard text on defence policy up to the 1980s is Baylis (1977), while Roper (1985) is a useful collection of papers on future options for defence. Kaldor *et al.* (1979) and Smith (1980) provide an indication of more recent left-wing thoughts on defence, while the Alternative Defence Commission (1987) contains ideas shared by the left and radical traditions. Coker (1986) deals with the defence splits within the parties, while the Thatcher government's approach to foreign and defence policy forms part of the general and excellent review by Riddell (1985).

Bibliography (published in London unless otherwise stated)

Alternative Defence Commission (1987) *The politics of alternative defence*, Paladin.

Ashford, N. (1980) 'The European Economic Community', in Z. Layton-Henry (ed.), *Conservative Party politics*, Macmillan, pp. 95-125.

Attlee, C.R. (1937) *The Labour Party in perspective*, Victor Gollancz.

Baylis, J. (ed.) (1977) *British defence policy in a changing world*, Croom Helm.

Benn, T. (1980) *Arguments for socialism*, Harmondsworth: Penguin.

Blank, S. (1977) 'Britain: the politics of foreign economic policy, the domestic economy and the problem of pluralistic stagnation', *International Organization* 31, 4:673-721.

Brock, M. (1983) 'The Liberal tradition', in V. Bogdanor (ed.) *Liberal Party politics*, Oxford: Clarendon Press, pp. 15-26.

Bullock, A. (1983) *Ernest Bevin: foreign secretary 1945-51*, Heinemann.

Butler, D. and Kavanagh, D. (1980) *The British general election of 1979*, Macmillan.
Butler, D. and Kavanagh, D. (1984) *The British general election of 1983*, Macmillan.
Butt, Philip, A. (1983) 'The Liberals and Europe' in V. Bogdanor (ed.) *Liberal Party politics*, Oxford: Clarendon Press, pp. 217–40.
Chichester, M. and Wilkinson, J. (1982) *The uncertain ally: British defence policy 1960–1990*, Aldershot: Gower.
Coker, C. (1986) *A nation in retreat? Britain's defence commitment*, Brasseys Defence Publishing.
Craig, F.W.S. (ed.) (1982) *Conservative and Labour Party conference decisions 1945–1981*, Chichester: Parliamentary Research Services.
Epstein, L.D. (1964) *British politics in the Suez crisis*, Pall Mall Press.
Frankel, J. (1975) *British foreign policy 1945–1973*, Oxford University Press.
Freedman, L. (1980) *Britain and nuclear weapons*, Macmillan.
Gamble, A. (1974) *The Conservative nation*, Routledge & Kegan Paul.
Goodwin, G. (1972) 'British foreign policy since 1945: the long odyssey to Europe', in M. Leifer (ed.), *Constraints and adjustments in British foreign policy*, Allen and Unwin, pp. 35–52.
Gordon, M.R. (1969) *Conflict and consensus in Labour's foreign policy 1914–1965*, Stanford: Stanford University Press.
Grimond, J. (1963) *The Liberal challenge*, Hollis and Carter.
Groom, A.J.R. (1974) *British thinking about nuclear weapons*, Frances Pinter.
Hanning, H. (1964) *Britain and the United Nations: proposals for peacekeeping including a Commonwealth force*, Bow publications.
Kaldor, M., Smith, D., and Vines, S. (eds) (1979) *Democratic socialism and the cost of defence*, Croom Helm.
Kennedy, P. (1981) *The realities behind diplomacy: background influences on British external policy 1865–1980*, Allen and Unwin.
Kitzinger, U. (1973) *Diplomacy and persuasion*, Thames and Hudson.
Labour Party (1975) *Labour and the common market*, Labour Party.
Labour Party (1977) *The EEC and Britain: A socialist perspective*, Labour Party.
Labour Party (1980) *Report of the 1980 annual conference*, Labour Party.
Labour Party (1982) *Labour's programme 1982*, Labour Party.
Labour Party (1983) *Report of the 1983 annual conference*, Labour Party.
Liberal Party (1982) *The Liberal programme*, Liberal Party.
Morgan, K.O. (1984) *Labour in Power 1945–51*, Oxford: Clarendon Press.
Naylor, J.F. (1969) *Labour's international policy: the Labour Party in the 1930s*, Weidenfeld and Nicholson.
Northedge. F.S. (1960) 'British foreign policy and the party system', *American Political Science Review*, 54, 3:635–46.
Northedge, F.S. (1974) *Descent from power: British foreign policy 1945–1973*, Allen and Unwin.
Norton, P. (1978) *Conservative dissidents: dissent within the Conservative Party 1970–74*, Temple Smith.

Pierre, A.J. (1972) *Nuclear politics: the British experience with an independent strategic force, 1939–1970*, Oxford: Oxford University Press.

Richards, P.G. (1973) 'Parliament and the parties', in R. Boardman and A.J.R. Groom (eds) *The management of Britain's external relations*, Macmillan, pp. 245–61.

Riddell, P. (1985) *The Thatcher government*, 2nd edn, Oxford: Blackwell.

Roper, J. (ed.) (1985) *The future of British defence policy*, Aldershot: Gower.

SDP/Liberal Alliance (1983) *Working together for Britain: a programme for government*, SDP/Liberal Alliance.

Sked, A. and Cook,C. (1984) *Post-war Britain: a political history*, 2nd edn. Harmondsworth: Penguin.

Smith, D. (1980) *Defence of the realm in the 1980s*, Croom Helm.

Smith, M., Smith, S. and White, B. (eds) (1988) *British foreign policy: tradition, change and transformation*, Unwin Hyman.

Snyder, W. (1964) *The politics of British defence policy, 1945–1962*, Columbus: Ohio State University Press.

Social Democratic Party, n.d. [1985] *Defence and disarmament: peace and security*, SDP Policy Document no. 9.

Spence, J.E. (1984) 'British foreign policy, tradition and change', in R.L. Borthwick and J.E. Spence (eds), *British politics in perspective*, Leicester: Leicester University Press, pp. 195–229.

Stephenson, H. (1980) *Mrs Thatcher's first year*, Jill Norman.

Taylor, A.J.P. (1957) *The troublemakers, dissent over foreign policy 1792–1939*, Hamish Hamilton.

Taylor, R. (1970) 'The campaign for nuclear disarmament', in V. Bogdanor and R. Skidelsky (eds) *The age of affluence 1951–1964*, Macmillan, pp. 221–53.

Wallace, W. (1976) *The foreign policy process in Britain*, Allen and Unwin.

Waltz, K.N. (1968) *Foreign policy and democratic politics*, Longman.

Chapter eight

The Constitution

Anthony Wright

'We Englishmen are Very Proud of our Constitution, Sir. It Was
Bestowed Upon Us By Providence. No Other Country is so Favoured
as This Country.'
'And *other* countries', said the Foreign gentleman. 'They do how?'
'They do, Sir', returned Mr. Podsnap, gravely shaking his head; 'they
do — I am sorry to be obliged to say it — *as* they do'.

(Charles Dickens, *Our Mutual Friend*)

It would come as a disagreeable surprise to Dickens' Mr Podsnap to
find a chapter devoted to constitutional matters here. Indeed, Podsnappery
may still be sufficiently alive and well in some quarters that an equivalent
surprise is capable of being occasioned even today. We have, perhaps,
grown so accustomed to regarding (often with a smug and self-
congratulatory eye) the constitutional framework of British politics as
a fixed and familiar landscape, outside and beyond the arenas of party
strife and ideological battle, that it is easy to miss the political significance
of this custom; though less easy, surely, to miss the fact that, during
the 1970s and 1980s, constitutional issues have increasingly forced their
way on to the political agenda. There is now, conspicuously, a politics
of the Constitution, involving something very different from a traditional
counting of providential blessings.

The purpose of this chapter is to offer a description, an interpretation, and an argument. The description is of the general character of
constitutional politics in the period since 1945, from the complacent consensus of the post-war years, through the turbulent pockets of the 1970s
(on issues like devolution and the referendum) to the more generalized
and comprehensive assaults of the 1980s. The interpretation is of the
approaches which the political parties have brought to bear on these
matters; and the relation between these approaches and larger ideological
positions. The argument is that a politics of containment has been practised hitherto, across ideological boundaries, by parties in defence of
the constitutional status quo; that this status quo can no longer be

defended; and that the constitution — in its widest sense as 'the system of laws, customs and conventions which define the composition and powers of organs of the state, and regulate the relations of the various state organs to one another and to the private citizen' (Hood Phillips 1978:5) — is therefore likely to remain a matter of lively political controversy in the period ahead.

Post-war Settlement

It might have been expected that the election of a majority Labour government in 1945 would have inaugurated, or precipitated, an era of radical constitutional change. The charge that Labour was 'unsound' on the constitution had long formed part of the stock-in-trade of Conservative propaganda and was again deployed during the 1945 election campaign. It surfaced in Churchill's infamous 'Gestapo' broadcast, in the allegations that Labour's internal constitutional structure implied the dictation of parliament by party, and in the identification of Professor Harold Laski (then chairman of the party) as a Jewish-Marxist bogey man who preached revolution. This last charge issued in a celebrated libel action which has become one of the footnotes of the period. However, beyond this kind of unsavoury bluff and bluster (which, anyway, came oddly from the party which, in its stand on Ulster earlier in the century, had come closest to condoning political violence and constitutional illegality), there were other reasons why a period of constitutional politics might have been expected.

Perhaps two in particular should be mentioned. There was, first, the fact that sections of the Labour Party (with Stafford Cripps, Labour's post-war Chancellor, prominent among them) had constructed an argument in the early 1930s, as one of the 'lessons' of 1931 (Eatwell and Wright 1978), that a future Labour government would need to adopt a series of radical constitutional measures to enable its socialist programme to be implemented and to overcome the strenuous — and unconstitutional — resistance which could be expected. The second, less dramatic, reason for thinking that a majority Labour government would bring with it significant constitutional consequences turned on the institutional implications of its whole domestic programme. It was likely that a massive extension of collective provision and state action would require major modifications to the machinery of government and raise many questions about the adequacy of existing constitutional arrangements in relation to an enlarged state.

In the event, none of these expectations proved correct. The 1945 'revolution' was accomplished without any equivalent constitutional revolution, a fact which produced much relief and satisfaction all round. Labour's programme met no serious resistance from the institutional framework, even the Lords 'took their medicine like sportsmen and gentlemen', while Labour's conservatism in relation to the institutional landscape exhibited 'almost a reverence for the constitution' (Morgan 1984:84, 494). The fact that the House of Lords survived with its composition intact, suffering nothing more serious than a reduction in its delaying power in the 1949 Parliament Act, is sufficient testimony to Labour's lack of constitutional radicalism. The Conservatives made half-hearted attempts to conjure up a spectre of a bureaucratic state tyranny as the future destination of a socialist Britain, but this was hard to reconcile with the prim propriety of Mr Attlee and his colleagues on constitutional matters. Indeed, it soon became the new orthodoxy on the left, replacing the darker forebodings of the 1930s, that the experience of 1945–51 had shown that the institutions of British parliamentary democracy could be pressed into service as the vehicle for socialist advance if there was sufficient will and vigour. Aneurin Bevan, for example, was a consistent advocate and exponent of this version of parliamentary socialism (Bevan 1952). What the experience of 1945–51 also revealed was that Labour's collectivism, at its confident high-water mark, was centralizing and nationalizing in its institutional implications. It had a job to do, asserting national priorities and imposing national structures. One casualty of this was local government and municipal socialism, the victim of 'a relentless drive towards centralisation and bureaucracy sweeping everything else out of the way' (Robson 1953). The National Health Service was one example of the prevailing tendency, but there were many others. Whatever else this revealed, it could be taken as evidence that the British constitution offered few institutional blockages to the reforming ambitions of a parliamentary majority which knew its mind.

It is not surprising, then, that the consensus which formed around the post-war 'settlement' was also a constitutional consensus. Conservatives might quibble about some of Labour's tidying up (for example, the abolition of university seats and business votes) and present themselves as the unique guardians of a non-party view of the constitution (in the words of their 1950 election manifesto: 'Conservatives believe in the Constitution as a safeguard of liberty, Socialists believe that it should be used for Party ends'), but rhetorical flourishes could not conceal the lack of a real issue. Even at the time of the 1945 election, with the Conservative manifesto warning of 'a permanent system of bureaucratic control, reeking of totalitarianism', a group of Conservatives had produced *Some Proposals for Constitutional Reform* (Group of Conservatives 1946) which, in their espousal of a strong executive combined with greater adminstrative efficiency, reflected the wide area of political agreement. Labour, of course, had found that here was a constitution it could use, and that it was no longer necessary to flirt with electoral reform (as in the 1920s) or with dangerous constitutional radicalism (as in the 1930s). The post-war rump of liberalism continued to voice its distinctive constitutional concerns about such matters as devolution and a fairer voting system, but in the world of two-party politics which established itself after 1945, there was no need for anyone to listen.

Reflection without Debate

Perhaps the clearest illustration not merely of the post-war constitutional consensus, but also of the *kind* of consensus it was, comes from a comparison of two works of constitutional reflection from opposite ends of the political spectrum. Both appeared in the immediate post-1945 period; and both attempted to take stock of the constitution in twentieth-century terms. The Tory approach was given robust statement by Leo Amery in his *Thoughts on the Constitution* (1947). The essence of the British constitution was that it had always been government-centred, with the executive as the 'active and originating element' and the elector's role confined to that of passive approval or disapproval. It was only the errors of nineteenth-century liberals and radicals which had 'grievously misled' opinion on this essential historical truth that the British system was one of 'government of the people, for the people, with, but not by, the people'. There was a natural congruence between this basic characteristic of the British constitutional system and a system of two-party politics:

> The two-party system is the natural concomitant of a political tradition in which government, as such, is the first consideration, and in which the views and preferences of voters or of members of Parliament are continuously limited to the simple alternative of 'for' or 'against'.
>
> (Amery 1947:15–21)

Both Amery's warnings and proposals flowed from his central proposition. The chief contemporary danger was held to be a view of party which threatened this constitutional tradition. The Labour Party was the culprit here, of course, although Amery's tentative verdict was that it had now settled down on 'normal constitutional lines' (ibid.:48). His proposals (for example, for a super-Cabinet) were designed to enable government to be conducted more efficiently in a situation where, irrespective of which party was in power, its range of responsibilities would necessarily continue to expand. So here was the constitutional pedigree for a Tory collectivism, which it is illuminating to set alongside the stance adopted by the socialist Harold Laski in his *Reflections on the Constitution* (1951). Having spent much of the 1930s arguing that British political arrangements could not accommodate the fundamental challenge which socialism represented, Laski now emerged as a staunch defender of the

187

constitutional status quo against its critics and putative reformers (amongst whom he included Amery).

However, what united the socialist Laski and the conservative Amery was a government-centred interpretation of the constitution and an antipathy to proposals which threatened a stable and powerful executive. It was important to understand that 'the first and most vital function of the electorate is to choose a House of Commons the membership of which makes possible the creation of a Government which can govern'. This constitutional axiom meant that Laski was hostile to all proposals which might weaken executive power. Thus proportional representation was judged to be 'a continuous threat to the stability of executive power', while the kind of administrative devolution symbolized by the Secretary of State for Scotland lay 'at the very margins of what we can attempt with either wisdom or safety'. Existing constitutional arrangements should be celebrated, not criticized. The critics had a 'distorted historical perspective' and should remember that the alternative to the House of Commons was the concentration camp. The greatness and supremacy of the House of Commons was undiminished, while the British electorate was the most mature in the world. There was, Laski concluded, no threat to 'the historic traditions of our constitution' (Laski 1951:16, 47, 54, 55, 93).

Taken together, the books by Amery and Laski can be seen as representing the constitutional underpinnings of the post-war settlement. From left and right there was agreement that a strong executive was the efficient secret of the British constitution and that a system of two-party politics was its natural expression. There might well be scope for procedural and administrative reforms in the machinery of government to improve its efficiency in line with its enlarged responsibilities, but no radical constitutional surgery was required. Indeed, Laski's institutional conservatism was a more accurate reflection of the prevailing mood than Amery's Tory reformism with its proposals not merely for a reorganized Cabinet but for an economic sub-Parliament organized on functional lines and a stronger regionalism. Such ideas were not new, of course, but they found little resonance in the post-war political world. A similar fate was suffered by Churchill's proposal in 1950 for a select committee on electoral reform in view of what he described (in the Debate on the Address following the electon of that year) as the 'constitutional injustice' perpetrated by the election results. The Conservative Party as a whole was not interested and nothing came of it. There were inconsequential Liberal-Conservative talks on electoral reform in 1953, and in 1958 some Conservatives again flirted with the alternative vote as a way of preventing a rise in Liberal support from splitting what they saw as the anti-socialist vote, but these were no more than noises off.

It was the golden age of two-party politics, and it was easy to elevate this political circumstance into a constitutional truism. The two parties which dominated the political system also dominated thinking about the constitution. Both judged existing arrangements to be essentially satisfactory, though for somewhat different ideological reasons, and vied with each other only to win majority power. In Conservative terms, it was a Tory constitution which enshrined the need for strong executive power and contained adequate protection against pressure from without. In Labour terms, it was a collectivist constitution which enabled a class party to practise a solidaristic politics of class representation, reflecting Labour's role as 'the principal means by which a new theory of representation has been propagated' (Birch 1964:83–92; Beer 1965:69). On both views there was no place for radical or liberal constitutional politics which elevated the status of individual electors, citizens, or parliamentarians, and mischievously sought to reorganize the polity in line with this false elevation. The politics of the period ensured that there was, literally, no place for such aberrations from the now conventional constitutional wisdom.

There were, of course, constitutional skirmishes during the two decades after 1945, including that provoked by Lord Stansgate in the process of remaining Mr Anthony Wedgwood Benn (a facility confirmed by the 1963 Peerage Act). There was even a measure like the 1958 Life Peerages Act, initially opposed by the Labour Party, but this measure was entirely typical of the period in reflecting an evasion of any more fundamental institutional reform. The Labour Party had by this time (it had not always been so, nor was it necessarily so) identified itself firmly with the centralized British state and its institutions. The Conservative Party was, usually, in power. Against this background, it is scarcely surprising that a survey of constitutional reform proposals over the thirty years up to 1960 (Hansard Society 1961) could confidently report that constitutional radicalism could safely be regarded as a faded phenomenon of the early part of the period under review. The change in the public standing of parliamentary institutions was judged to have been 'one of the happiest features of our public life' (ibid:143).

Happy it may have been, but it was also illusory. What had really been happening during the course of the twentieth century, reaching its peak in the 1940s and 1950s, was the development of an 'extended political system' (Middlemas 1986:8) in which the major corporate institutions of business and labour had taken a share in running the state 'in ways not dreamt of when Dicey in the late nineteenth century canonised the doctrine of parliamentary sovereignty' (ibid:1). Indeed, the effect of that doctrine was to provide an ideological cloak behind which this development could take place. Thus the post-war settlement had been constructed through traditional machinery, there was no interest in the kind of corporate models (involving industrial parliaments, or functional representation) which had surfaced earlier, no recognition that a new system of informal power had come into existence which required constitutionalizing but, instead, a turning away from any serious constitutional argument. It was not until much later, when the moment of high corporatism had passed, that the fundamental questions began to be asked, if not answered.

Back to the Constitution

Long before then, though, a revival of interest in the machinery of government and constitutional matters had taken place. This began gently and confidently in the 1960s, but became much rougher and messier in the 1970s. It started with a drive for institutional modernization, but ended with lamentations about the whole condition and nature of government in Britain. In terms of constitutional ideas, this period revealed how unprepared and ill equipped was the British political tradition to respond to the issues that were raised. The arrival of constitutional issues on the political agenda encountered a political tradition distinguished by its 'lack of familiarity with the language of constitutional debate' (Norton 1982:261). There were notable exceptions (such as John Mackintosh, the scholar-politician Labour Member of Parliament) but these were generally confined to a maverick existence in the political margin. In the absence of a secure framework of debate, it is not surprising that what prevailed was a politics of expediency and containment informed by familiar ideological reflexes and a predisposition to avoid constitutional fundamentals.

This may, at first glance, seem a curious judgement on a period which even established a Royal Commission on the Constitution. Yet that Commission (appointed in 1968 and reporting in 1973) took its cue from the political circumstances — the rising support for Scottish and Welsh nationalism — which prompted its establishment, confined its attention to the political matter in hand, and was happy to impose a self-denying ordinance as far as any larger constitutional inquiry was concerned. A similar verdict, though the self-denial was imposed from without, may be recorded on the other reports and inquiries into aspects of the machinery of government which decorated the landscape of British politics in the late 1960s and early 1970s. For example, the Fulton Committee on the Civil Service (which reported in 1968) was constrained by its narrow terms of reference from exploring such crucial matters as ministerial responsibility which would necessarily have opened up wider avenues of constitutional inquiry. Likewise the Redcliffe-Maud Commission on local government (reporting in 1969), which was hemmed in by terms of reference which excluded anything beyond a consideration of how the existing functions and structures of local government might be reorganized. Even then its proposals were mutilated by the incoming Conservative government after 1970 on no better grounds than those of partisan political expediency.

The general point here, then, is that the separate inquiries which were initiated into aspects of British government were intended to be just that — separate. They were not seen by those who initiated or received them, whether Labour or Conservative, as connected elements in a larger review of constitutional fundamentals. There was no new theory of the constitution struggling to get out. This was true even of the parliamentary reform movement which had generated an impressive head of steam in the early 1960s and is best represented by Bernard Crick's *The Reform of Parliament* (1963). The reform argument claimed only to be concerned with enabling Parliament (through such devices as a select committee system, of which more was to be heard later) more effectively to perform those functions, especially that of scrutiny, which were firmly rooted in existing constitutional theory but thwarted by current institutional practice. It was an argument for reform within the terms of traditional constitutional orthodoxy, not a challenge to that orthodoxy (except to live up to its own best self).

Issues and Ideology

What did connect this argument with the subsequent institutional reform initiatives — and these with each other — was a rapidly developing ideology of modernization. It was an ideology which confounded the familiar demarcation lines of left and right. If it was first taken up by the reforming left, with the assault on antique establishment institutions forming part of the general indictment against British backwardness which was the background to Labour's election in 1964, it was soon echoed by the modernizing right. In prime ministerial terms, it was the link between Wilson and Heath. Thus Labour's election manifesto in 1966 spoke of the party being engaged in 'the radical reorganisation of the whole machinery of the state', while in 1970 the Conservatives promised to undertake a sweeping institutional rationalization in order to establish a whole new style of government. What united the assorted reform initiatives of these years — whether directed towards Parliament or the civil service, local government or the health service, or the restructuring of government departments — were the watchwords of efficiency and modernization. It was constitutional reform with the politics left out (which may, incidentally, explain why so much of it came to grief).

There was, though, a sub-theme during this period too, which also defies any neat ideological classification. In significant respects it was at odds with the thrust of the major theme, although this was not generally recognized or its implications explored. It did, moreover, carry within it the potential to effect radical changes in the nature of the polity, although this never really seemed likely. The watchwords of this movement were participation and protection: more participation by people in the business of government and more protection for people against the bureaucratic excesses of government. The first was the flavour of the month for a while, and left its monuments (like the Community Development Projects in the inner cities). Labour's 1964 manifesto had declared its objective as that of 'an active democracy' and its rejection of the view that democracy was 'a five-yearly visit to the polling booth that changes little but the men at the top'. This theme continued to have a rhetorical resonance for the next decade, though its practical fruits were meagre, and in October 1974 both major parties were still promising to extend citizen participation in a range of public services and institutions. They were also promising to extend the protection of the citizen against the state, a reminder of the second watchword of the period. Here the main monument was the creation of the Ombudsman in 1967 to investigate complaints of maladministration. However, what is significant about this for present purposes is that the form of its establishment was as conservative as possible, carefully grafted on to traditional doctrine about executive accountability to Parliament, lest there was any suggestion that this doctrine now harboured a constitutional fiction.

On none of these issues was there any real ideological divide between the two major parties. The Conservatives might continue to present their opponents as the purveyors of a bureaucratic statism, but it was a Labour government which introduced the Ombudsman and a Conservative government which, in the early 1970s, established a massive apparatus of state intervention to buttress its economic and industrial policies. Conversely, it was a Labour government which, after the 1974 election, was thrown into 'absolute panic' by a parliamentary attempt to reform official secrecy and exhibited 'more hostility to the idea of a Freedom of Information Act than to almost any other measure, because it really touched the centre of power' (Benn 1982:54). On Northern Ireland, of course, which by any test represented the constitutional issue above all others in contemporary British politics, the cross-party consensus came to be formally sanctified by the doctrine of 'bi-partisanship'. Both parties flew the consensual flag of modernization and efficiency in their approach to institutional reform, and neither of them seriously sought to engineer a democratic revolution in the machinery of British government (which is why parliamentary reform was destined to remain, like the weather, much talked about but little acted upon). The broad constitutional agreement which underpinned the post-war settlement at its inception was, like the two-party system which presided over it, still largely intact three decades later.

The most telling illustration of this was provided, paradoxically, by this period's most radical constitutional innovation. When a referendum was held in 1975 on British entry to the Common Market, this was not the result of a process of constitutional reflection but of the desperate need for a divided Labour Party to find a political life raft of some kind. It did provoke a bout of constitutional argument (and was deployed again in 1979 over the devolution proposals), but what was interesting about this argument was that it was at least as much intraparty as interparty. The referendum idea had originated with Mr Benn on Labour's left, but was soon flirted with by Conservatives, who saw it as a device for trumping the left (as with Michael Heseltine's attempt in 1981 to deploy it in his battle against local authorities, until his party told him to drop the idea). In this respect the referendum debate was similar to a number of other constitutional issues in forging alliances and identifying affinities across the ideological frontiers of normal party politics.

Beyond Left and Right

Significantly, such alliances were not infrequently between those on the Labour left and the Conservative right. In personal terms, a Foot-Powell axis was established against constitutional reform. This swung into action in the late 1960s on two fronts to block reform initiatives. On one side, it set its face against the establishment of a system of select committees (and succeeded in preventing the establishment of an effective system) on the grounds that it would dilute and divert what Michael Foot called 'the clash between the parties' on the floor of the House which was the hallmark of British adversarial politics. On another side, this same unholy alliance of Labour left and Conservative right successfully filibustered an agreed reform package for the House of Lords: the left because it would make the Lords stronger and its abolition harder, the right because it would make the Lords weaker and its abolition easier. However, it was in the 1970s, on the issue of the Common Market, that the alliance was most fully consummated, if not most successful. Both left and right identified the constitutional issue as the fundamental one, and both rallied to the defence of the British state and its sovereign Parliament against a move which would 'mean the end of Britain as a completely self-governing nation' (Benn 1979:95).

Thus left and right frequently emerged as the staunchest defenders of the constitutional status quo and, in doing so, threw a revealing shaft of light on to their larger ideological positions. More generally, though, the impact of constitutional politics was to reveal how ideologically unprepared were the political parties to receive this unwelcome intrusion. This explains why their response was generally so confused; why normal political alignments were prone to break down; and why a politics of containment was practised in the face of issues which it was hoped would eventually go away. The devolution issue, which kept the constitution near the top of the political agenda for much of the 1970s, was the paradigm case in all these respects.

The issue had been forced by the surge in support for the nationalist parties in Scotland and Wales. However, it failed to evoke a coherent and principled response from majority opinion in either the Conservative or Labour Parties. What it did reveal was the extent to which centralism and statism had become the common constitutional orthodoxy of opposed political traditions, tempered only by a large dose of expediency. On the Conservative side, Mr Heath had signalled a commitment to a directly elected Scottish assembly in his Perth 'declaration' of 1968, but the subsequent story is of the progressive abandonment of his commitment by the Conservative Party. Mrs Thatcher's leadership was a factor in this, but the truth was that the commitment to devolution had 'never really entered the party's bloodstream' (Smith 1977). On the grounds of good Conservative principle, the party could either have responded to the devolution issue by a resolute defence of the union, or (as with Heath) by integrating it with wider beliefs about the importance for Conservatives of diffused power. For a Conservative of the latter persuasion 'the strong antipathy to devolution of many Conservatives is not easy to understand' (Gilmour 1978:221). In fact, neither course was adopted. The antipathy prevailed, but it was visceral rather than principled. The party 'preferred to adopt a policy of ambiguity, supporting devolution in theory while opposing it in practice' (Bogdanor 1980:93).

On the Labour side, the devolution issue threw the party into wholesale ideological confusion. It did not fit easily into the left-right divide, but if this enabled the issue to escape from the ideological struggle which was being waged within the party it also made a coherent and consistent response more difficult. Yet a response was required, not merely because Labour was in office when the issue pressed hardest but because of the critical importance of Scotland and Wales in the party's electoral base. In ideological terms, what the prolonged, painful and shabby response to devolution convincingly demonstrated, glimpsed also in relation to other institutional matters, was the 'underlying ambivalence in Labour's attitude to the state' (Jones and Keating 1985:vi). Faced with the renewed demands from the periphery for devolution, Labour could have summoned up its own decentralist and home rule traditions and integrated this demand with a wider commitment to devolved power of both territorial and functional kinds. Although there were some attempts to do this, they did not amount to very much in political terms. Instead, other ideological traditions were generally called upon, reducing territorial issues to economic ones, refusing to regard devolution as a 'real' issue, denouncing nationalism as a distraction from class politics, emphasizing the importance of central state planning and working-class unity in the achievement of socialist objectives. However, most of the party was simply bored by the whole issue and wanted it to go away. They were prepared to accept the leadership's view that political necessity required some action, but even political necessity could not sustain the fragile coalition put together in support of devolution when it came under combined attack from threatened interests and ideological reflexes. In the final death by referendum in 1979, Labour's authentic voice seemed to be the one warning of the disintegrative dangers to the central British state.

Argument on Fundamentals

By this time, though, at the end of the 1970s, constitutional argument in Britain had already entered a new phase. The devolution bubble may, once again, have been burst, to much relief and satisfaction all round, but the removal of this particular issue was overshadowed by the extent to which constitutional argument had now entered the bloodstream of British politics as a whole. Moreover, what was new was that this argument was no longer conducted in terms of a number of discrete issues but addressed itself, for the first time in the post-war period, to constitutional fundamentals. What was also new was the tone of the argument. Gone was the complacent affirmation of orthodoxy of the immediate post-1945 years; in its place had come an urgent and alarmed questioning of existing arrangements coupled with prescriptions for radical constitutional engineering. This was true of the academic political science of British politics as well as of the protagonists of party. The background to both was the collapsing post-war settlement of the late 1970s, which precipitated the search for constitutional causes, consequences, and remedies. It also brought the collapse of the two-party system, which had dominated and sustained a particular model of British politics for thirty years, but which (from 1974) could no longer be reconciled with electoral reality. Not only did this create a space in which constitutional argument could re-emerge, but it also created a new constituency for such argument.

The concern here is with the party arguments. These came from right, left, and centre, and were often strikingly similar in what they attacked if not in what they recommended. One of the significant features of British politics in the late 1970s was the way in which leading Conservatives abandoned a traditional role as the self-proclaimed guardians of the British constitution and instead became its scourge. As it was remarked at the time, 'the Conservative party today finds itself in the somewhat unusual role of protagonist of constitutional reform' (Johnson 1980:126). The political context is, of course, crucial. Labour had been in power for most of the 1960s and 1970s and the prospects for the Conservatives could seem bleak. Moreover, Labour could be seen as moving leftwards, but able to exercise majority power for its ideological purposes notwithstanding its minority electoral support. This unappetising prospect had the effect of turning Conservative minds towards the constitution.

The representative figure here is Lord Hailsham, veteran Conservative politician who became Lord Chancellor in the Thatcher government after 1979. The extent of the change in Conservative thinking can be measured by the distance between *The Case for Conservatism* (1946), the post-war testament he had produced in his earlier incarnation as Quintin Hogg, and *The Dilemma of Democracy* (1978), in which he attempted to 'rethink (his) own political philosophy' (Hailsham 1978:9). The former book said little about the constitution (except to warn that Labour was unsound on it): the latter said little about anything else. Hailsham's central theme, expounded with ferocious bluster, was that Britain was rapidly abandoning a theory and practice of limited government and was 'moving more and more in the direction of an elective dictatorship' (ibid:21). Although contemporary political circumstances had exposed and accelerated this baneful trend, the real culpability lay with the nature of British government itself, since:

> the political apparatus consists of an omnipotent Parliament virtually consisting of a single chamber, dominated by a vastly powerful executive, and controlling a centralised bureaucracy, and completely uncontrolled by an effective judicial machinery.
>
> (Hailsham 1978:68)

In case even this description of the despotic nature of British government was too restrained, it could be expressed in a more populist version too:

> We have the most highly centralised administration in the free world. We are in fact governed by a bureaucracy of mandarins and their subordinates imposing on a people partisan policies devised by a government of amateurs who have achieved their position by a minority of votes under an unfair voting system.
>
> (Hailsham 1978:160)

Strong stuff indeed from an imminent Lord Chancellor.

Moreover, the prescription was as radical and comprehensive as the indictment. Nothing less than 'a new constitution' was required, written and entrenched, not merely some '*ad hoc* tinkering' with existing arrangements. The object of this new constitution would be to 'institutionalise the theory of limited government' (Hailsham 1978:203, 226). Limited government would be reflected in a range of specific constitutional reforms (including a reformed second chamber, a bill of rights, regional devolution and electoral reform), but these would all be rooted in the new constitutional settlement. Other Conservatives were, perhaps, less fundamentalist than Hailsham, but were no less inclined to draw constitutional conclusions from their attack on Labour's exercise of office. A moderate Conservative like Ian Gilmour recommended a package of constitutional reforms because the House of Commons had become 'the despised tool of the executive' (Gilmour 1978:197); while an immoderate Conservative like Rhodes Boyson confessed that he had even come to 'envy the checks and balances of the American constitution, 'something I would not have believed twenty years ago' (Boyson 1978:159), and advocated a number of measures which together — for example, a liberal use of referenda *and* a hereditary-only House of Lords — reflected a characteristic mixture of populism and elitism. Meanwhile, Sir Keith Joseph (in many respects the key political figure in the construction of Thatcherism) had decided that a check on 'the unbridled supremacy of Parliament' was needed and espoused a bill of rights as a constitutional protection against 'social injustice' and 'the effects of socialist theory on the climate of opinion' (Joseph 1975).

Yet it was not merely those on the political right, who could be accused of turning to the constitution as an alternative to winning elections, who sought to revive constitutional argument during these years. On Labour's left, and pre-eminently in the person of Tony Benn, there developed a comprehensive indictment of existing constitutional arrangements. Indeed, the terms of this indictment, with its emphasis on the nature of unbridled executive power behind the constitutional fictions, were common to the critics on both left and right. If Hailsham's claim was that the 'real government machine' was 'shrouded in mystery' and concealed by elaborate legal fictions, then Benn's similar claim was that 'the democracy of which we boast is becoming a decorous façade' (Benn 1981:4), behind which irresponsible and partisan power was exercised. Benn's message to the left was that constitutional questions, far from being irrelevant, were 'the key to power in a parliamentary democracy' (ibid:173). One of Benn's followers took up and developed this theme in a sustained attack on the British 'secret Constitution': 'Two things only can be said with certainty about Parliamentary democracy in Britain today. First, effective power does not reside in Parliament. Secondly, there is little that is democratic about the exercise of that power' (Sedgemore 1980:11). Thus constitutional issues were part of the general challenge mounted by the Labour left in the late 1970s and the early 1980s, especially so in the case of the Labour Coordinating Committee, which 'expressed more concern over the location of power within British institutions than any group on Labour's left since the Socialist League in the 1930s' (Seyd 1987:92). Even in 1988, when Benn again entered the lists for the Labour leadership, he still endeavoured to make 'democracy' his distinctive and dominant campaign theme.

However, a number of things should be noticed about this constitutional Bennery. On the one hand, it reflected a radical and popular tradition in pressing the rights of the 'people' against the powerful, although the reforms proposed (for example, constraints on prime ministerial power and patronage, freedom of information, ministerial cabinets, and an effective Select Committee system — with the latter judged as doing 'more to set up countervailing power to the power of the executive than any other single reform' [Benn 1981:40]) were rather more modest than some of the populist rhetoric suggested. On the other hand, though, it reflected an ambivalence — even a 'major contradiction' in Benn's position according to his New Left Review interviewers (Benn/New Left Review, 1982:39) — between an affirmation of the virtues of British parliamentary democracy and an indictment of its democratic deficiencies. Indeed, this points to further tensions in his position, with wider ideological implications. On one side, the task was to enable the people (or people-as-party) to get their way by sweeping aside blockages erected by the system in their path. Here is Bennery as the mirror image of Thatcherism (to which it has paid its respects in this regard), exploiting the political potential of an elected dictatorship for the pursuit of ideological purposes. On the other side, though, the task was to constrain and inhibit government by an assortment of democratic controls. This tension remained unsolved.

It revealed a further characteristic, not just of Mr Benn but of the Labour left as a whole. This was the tendency to approach constitutional matters in collective, class and party terms, rather than in terms of individual citizenship. Hence there was a disinclination to take up measures (for example, electoral reform, devolution, or a Bill of Rights) which could be seen as weakening rather than strengthening the role of party in the political process and elevating the role of others (whether individual electors or judges) through checks and balances which could thwart the popular will as expressed by the existing party system. Such devices were distractions, either dangerous or irrelevant, and ignored the fact that there could be 'no short cut to political decision making through political control' (Sedgemore 1980:46). This may also explain why, in the arguments about Labour Party democracy which provided the real terrain for constitutional debate on the left in this period, the Bennite left found it possible to claim that it would be undemocratic to enfranchise individual party members. Thus the left might echo the right's dissatisfaction with British political arrangements, but was not interested in those proposed remedies which might inhibit majoritarian politics. However, at least Labour's left had taken up the constitutional issue, both within the party and more generally. This contrasted with a Labour leadership whose stance was nicely captured by a leaked Cabinet minute (*New Statesman*, 10 November 1978), which reaffirmed the need to maintain existing cabinet secrecy conventions on the grounds that: 'The present convention is long established and provides a basis on which we can stand. Any departure from it would be more likely to whet appetites than to satisfy them'.

A New Orthodoxy

By the end of the 1970s, then, a chorus of criticism, drawing in significant voices on both left and right, had developed in relation to constitutional arrangements in Britain. An earlier orthodoxy that all was fundamentally well with this department of national life, or required only some sensible modernization, was rapidly being replaced by a new orthodoxy that insisted that there was a fundamental disorder. There was, moreover, abundant evidence of different kinds to suggest that the post-war political system was breaking down. Thus left and right could unite in denouncing a system of government which had lost its democratic legitimacy, even if the tension between ideas of limited government and popular government ensured that there was no similar agreement on either the causes or the remedies for this condition.

However, it was not from right or left but from the parties of the political centre that the most concerted and comprehensive constitutional argument was to be heard in the 1980s. During the period of Alliance politics the case was consistently made for the centrality of constitutional issues to the wider political agenda. If it was to be expected that constitutional reform (and, pivotally, reform of the electoral system) should commend itself to parties which suffered most from the existing arrangements, it was nevertheless the case that the argument became much more ambitious and pressing during the Alliance years of the early and mid-1980s. There was a long Liberal tradition to draw upon, more than half a century of largely ineffectual attempts to arouse interest in such issues as decentralization, devolution and electoral reform, but the new ingredient was not merely the strengthening of the political centre with the arrival of the Social Democrats, but the use of this increased strength to press an argument that constitutional reform was not simply desirable in itself (on grounds of justice or democracy) but was the key to the solution of Britain's other problems and, above all, its economic difficulties. This involved a significant change — from political justice to economic expediency — in the presentation of the case for electoral reform. It also involved an integration of this item into a wider package of constitutional proposals (involving decentralization, a Bill of Rights, and freedom of information) and the elevation of this package into the Ark of the Alliance covenant.

The apotheosis of this process was reached in the run up to the 1987 general election. The need for fundamental change in the nature of the political system, as the prerequisite for everything else, became a relentless Alliance theme. The general thesis was that 'we have to change the way in which we govern ourselves rather than simply change the guard at Westminster' (Holme 1987:5). A 'great' constitutional reform charter was energetically promoted by Shirley Williams and Des Wilson, the two party presidents, as the symbol of what the Alliance stood for. As the election approached, therefore, the Alliance leaders were able to proclaim that: 'The Alliance Parties propose nothing less than a new constitutional settlement. We believe that fundamental political reform is the key to the creation of a more successful economy and a more just society'. It was thus not a 'luxury' but the 'essential foundation stone' for everything else (Owen and Steel 1987:86). Behind the public rhetoric there was much less agreement, with Liberal suspicions that many Social Democrats were really centralizing corporatists, meeting Social Democratic suspicions that many Liberals were really neo-anarchists, as well as tension between those who saw constitutional reform as part of a larger, democratic project, and those who had converted it into an argument about economic modernization. In the event, none of this mattered very much since what the election brought was not a new constitutional settlement engineered by the Alliance parties but the disintegration of the Alliance itself.

Party, Ideology, Constitution

Once again, then, it seemed by the late 1980s that the intrusion of a politics of the constitution had been contained. Several approaches to constitutional thinking have been glimpsed in the foregoing, none corresponding neatly to party labels although all relating in some way to larger ideological positions. There is a Tory approach which emphasizes the importance of strong government and the limited role for popular participation. There is a Socialist approach which emphasizes class representation and the dominant role of party in the political system. There is a Liberal approach which emphasizes the need to place limitations on government in the interests of a pluralistic liberty. There is a Radical approach which emphasizes popular participation and the need to hold government to democratic account. There is, too, a Managerial approach which eschews arguments about values and ideology and emphasizes the need to organize the 'business' of government as efficiently as possible. These approaches are not exhaustive, other terms could be used, and parties have drawn upon more than one. Nevertheless they do offer a useful vantage point from which to survey the post-war experience of constitutional politics and the state of the art at the end of the 1980s.

What this reveals is that the approaches drawn upon by the Conservative and Labour Parties in the post-1945 period issued in remarkably similar conclusions (seen in the earlier discussion of Amery and Laski) about the importance — whether on good Tory or good socialist grounds — of governments being able to do what they wanted to do. Both parties, of course, were infused with enough of the Liberal tradition to acknowledge the framework within which executive-led government should operate (but not with enough to question the basic adequacy of this framework), with sufficiently little of the Radical approach to make them disinclined to explore fundamental issues of power and accountability, and were Managerial enough to make an appropriate response when the modernizing moment seemed to require this, but not enough to embark on a sustained and sweeping modernization of the machinery of state. The result was a constitutional consensus so extensive that the intrusion of constitutional issues was met with a politics of containment, with the Labour left and Conservative right as frequently the staunchest defenders of this consensus. It was only in the second half of the 1970s, with both the two-party system and the system of government itself in trouble and disarray, that there were those in the major parties who sought to give a constitutional dimension to the prevailing discontents.

However, the approaches adopted were not sufficiently coherent (reflecting, perhaps, the lack of a modern tradition of constitutional debate) to be integrated easily into wider political argument, nor did they manage to command an effective political constituency either within their respective parties or more generally. When, in the 1980s, constitutional issues did find a constituency and a carrier, in the shape of the Alliance parties, this promised to inaugurate a sustained period of constitutional politics. When this promise collapsed with the Alliance itself in the wake of the 1987 general election (and notwithstanding the fact that the merged Social and Liberal Democrats will doubtless want to continue running with the constitutional issue), this had the effect of turning constitutional attention firmly back to the two parties whose occupancy of the political system had — at least for the immediate future — become more secure. What this reveals is a political situation in which the constitution has become a prominent and pervasive issue, but where the political response remains ideologically uncertain.

This may seem a curious judgement on the Thatcher years, yet it is significant that the 'new' conservatism in Britain (unlike that in the United States or West Germany) has shown no interest in exploring the constitutional implications of its social and economic arguments. There were some moves in this direction in the period before 1979, and Hayek (1979) had prepared a radical constitutional prospectus for a liberal economy, but Thatcherism in power buried all this dead. Indeed, it is from that earlier period that the dire prospect of a centralized democracy which

> will assert the right of a bare majority in a single chamber assembly,
> possibly elected on a first past the post basis, to assert its will over
> a whole people whatever that will may be . . . will impose uniformity
> on the whole nation . . . will crush local autonomy . . . will dictate
> the structure, form and content of education
>
> (Hailsham 1978:9–10)

unwittingly provides the most telling anticipation of the essential flavour
of Thatcherism in constitutional terms. Little was heard about the perils
of elected dictatorship once the right dictatorship was elected. A Tory
constitution could be deployed, though now cynically and ruthlessly, to
pursue the 'liberal' Conservative mission. On issue after issue, from
institution to institution, even from convention to convention, the
Thatcher years have provided an object lesson in the nature and potential
of concentrated executive power in Britain and the feebleness of the
constitutional inhibitions. Here, literally, was a 'winner takes all' kind
of politics.

However, if this has prompted the Labour Party to take up the charge
of authoritarianism against the Conservatives, it is also significant that
it has not yet converted the party into an engine of constitutional
radicalism. These matters were noticeably absent from the policy reviews
which followed the party's third successive election defeat in 1987, just
as they were absent (for example, see Hattersley 1987) from attempts
to restate the party's general philosophy. There was a flutter of Labour
interest in electoral reform after the 1987 defeat as 'an idea that the
Labour Party is going to have to take seriously' (Robin Cook, *Guardian*,
10 August 1987), but this interest was not shared by the party conference
of that year. The Labour left has either been uninterested in constitutional reform or has wanted to suggest the irrelevance of electoral reform
and the usual shopping list of reform measures when set against its own
'alternative programme of radical political reform' (Hain 1986:6); while
the party as a whole still has difficulty in regarding the constitution as
a 'real' issue beyond the rhetorical needs of the moment. It was significant
that a new movement for constitutional reform, Charter 88, was launched
from within Labour's ranks at the end of 1988, and drew influential
support. However, it was no less significant that prominent among the
voices raised to repudiate this movement and reassert conventional constitutional wisdom was that of the deputy leader of the Labour Party (Roy
Hattersley, *Guardian*, 12 and 19 December 1988). It was clear from
such skirmishing that the real arguments on this front had scarcely begun.

In fact, for a radical party Labour has displayed a marked lack of
radical imagination as far as the constitution is concerned. Sometimes
it has wanted to celebrate it (as in the Attlee verdict on the 1945 period)
as an admirable vehicle for socialist advance, at other times to denounce

it (as in the early 1930s, or the judge-bashing of the 1970s) as an institutional obstacle to such advance. There has been little serious constitutional exploration between these positions. Partly, this is an intellectual failure, the reflection of a long neglect of issues concerning the nature of power and the state. Partly, too, it is the inheritance of a centralizing collectivism, a 'top-down' socialism, which has made it well disposed towards a top-down constitution and unfriendly towards more fissiparous tendencies (a stance reflected in its 'puzzling indifference' (Sharpe 1982:148) to decentralization and the geography of inequality). This may explain why, now, Labour seems divided between a position which hopes to emulate Thatcherism in its ideological drive through the constitution, and a position which senses the need to generalize its assault on Thatcherism into a critique of the constitutional system which underpinned it. The latter position, in which the 'grotesque imbalance' (Smith 1986:46) against democracy in the contemporary constitution became the issue, would require the party to think freshly about questions of power, democracy and citizenship. Whether or not it does so seems, at the end of the 1980s, to be the key to the next phase of constitutional politics in Britain.

Further Reading

Two books, both now a generation old, continue to illuminate the ideological dimension of party attitudes to the political system. These are Samuel Beer's *Modern British Politics* (Faber, 1965) and A.H. Birch's *Representative and Responsible Government* (Allen & Unwin, 1964). More recent constitutional debate, on a range of issues, is usefully surveyed in Philip Norton, *The Constitution in Flux* (Martin Robertson, 1982). An excellent account of the tensions in Labour's approach to these matters is to be found in Barry Jones and Michael Keating, *Labour and the British State* (Oxford University Press, 1985). An elegant Conservative argument on the connection between constitutional issues and wider social and economic positions, and on the consequent need to fill 'the present constitutional vacuum', is offered by Nevil Johnson, *In Search of the Constitution* (Methuen, 1980). Aspects of the contemporary politics of the constitution are discussed in two articles by Anthony Wright: 'The Politics of Constitutional Reform', *Political Quarterly*, October-December 1986, and 'British Decline: Political or Economic?', *Parliamentary Affairs*, January 1987. The centenary of the publication of A.V. Dicey's *The Law of the Constitution* has prompted a flurry of constitutional stocktaking in the mid-1980s, providing a useful point of entry into current issues and concerns. See, in particular, Jeffrey Jowell and Dawn Oliver (eds), *The Changing Constitution* (Oxford University Press, 1985); Patrick McAuslan and John

McEldowney (eds), *Law, Legitimacy and the Constitution* (Sweet & Maxwell, 1985); and Ian Harden and Norman Lewis, *The Noble Lie: The British Constitution and the Rule of Law* (Hutchinson, 1986). The tercentenary of the Glorious Revolution and the Bill of Rights also occasioned rather more constitutional complaints than celebrations: see Richard Holme and Michael Elliott (eds), *1688–1988: Time For a New Constitution* (Macmillan, 1988); and Cosmo Graham and Tony Prosser (eds), Waiving the Rules: The Constitution under Thatcherism (Open University Press, 1988). Essential for understanding the context of many of these themes is Leonard Tivey, *Interpretations of British Politics* (Harvester-Wheatsheaf, 1988).

Bibliography (published in London unless otherwise stated)

Amery, L. (1947) *Thoughts on the Constitution*, Oxford University Press.
Beer, S.H. (1965) *Modern British Politics*, Faber.
Benn, T. (1979) *Arguments for Socialism*, Cape.
Benn, T. (1981) *Arguments for Democracy*, Cape.
Benn, T. (1982) *Parliament, People and Power*, Verso/New Left Review.
Bevan, A. (1952) *In Place of Fear*, Heinemann.
Birch, A.H. (1964) *Representative and Responsible Government*, Allen & Unwin.
Bogdanor, V. (1980) 'Devolution', in Z. Layton-Henry (ed.) *Conservative Party Politics*, Macmillan.
Boyson, R. (1978) *Centre Forward*, Temple Smith.
Crick, B. (1963) *The Reform of Parliament*, Weidenfeld & Nicolson.
Eatwell, R. and Wright, A. (1978) 'Labour and the lessons of 1931', *History*, 63:38–53.
Gilmour, I. (1978) *Inside Right*, Quartet.
Group of Conservatives (1946) *Some Proposals for Constitutional Reform*, Eyre & Spottiswoode.
Hain, P. (1986) *Proportional Misrepresentation*, Aldershot: Wildwood House.
Hailsham, Lord (1978) *The Dilemma of Democracy*, Collins.
Hansard Society (1961) *Parliamentary Reform 1933–1960*, Cassell.
Hattersley, R. (1987) *Choose Freedom: The Future for Democratic Socialism*, Michael Joseph.
Hayek, F.A. (1979) *Law, Legislation and Liberty, vol.3, The Political Order of a Free Society*, Routledge & Kegan Paul.
Holme, R. (1987) *The People's Kingdom*, Bodley Head.
Hood Phillips, O. (1978) *Constitutional and Administrative Law*, 6th edn, Sweet & Maxwell.
Johnson, N. (1980) 'Constitutional reform: some dilemmas for a conservative philosophy', in Z. Layton-Henry (ed.) *Conservative Party Politics*, Macmillan.
Jones, B. and Keating, M. (1985) *Labour and the British State*, Oxford: Clarendon Press.

Joseph, K. *(1975) Freedom under the Law*, Conservative Political Centre.

Laski, H. (1951) *Reflections on the Constitution*, Manchester: Manchester University Press.

Middlemas, K. (1986) *Power, Competition and the State, vol. 1, Britain in Search of Balance 1940-1961*, Macmillan.

Morgan, K.O. (1984) *Labour in Power 1945-51*, Oxford: Clarendon Press.

Norton, P. (1982) *The Constitution in Flux*, Martin Robertson.

Owen, D. and Steel, D. (1987) *The Time Has Come*, Weidenfeld & Nicolson.

Robson, W.A. (1953) 'Labour and local government', *Political Quarterly*, 24, 1:39-55.

Sedgemore, B. (1980) *The Secret Constitution*, Hodder & Stoughton.

Seyd, P. (1987) *The Rise and Fall of the Labour Left*, Macmillan.

Sharpe, L.J. (1982) 'The Labour Party and the geography of inequality: a puzzle', in D. Kavanagh (ed.) *The Politics of the Labour Party*, Allen & Unwin.

Smith, G. (1977) 'The Conservative commitment to devolution', *Spectator*, 19 February.

Smith, T. (1986) 'The British Constitution: unwritten and unravelled', in J. Hayward and P. Norton (eds) *The Political Science of British Politics*, Brighton: Wheatsheaf.

Chapter nine

Endpiece: Ideological Politics Now

Anthony Wright

> Never, never underestimate the importance or the power of the tide
> of ideas. No British government has ever been defeated unless and
> until the tide of ideas has turned against it. And so far from turning,
> the tide of ideas that swept us into office in 1979 is flowing even more
> strongly today.
>
> (Nigel Lawson, Chancellor of the Exchequer, 14 May 1987)

When leading Conservative politicians are to be found celebrating the
power of ideas, there could scarcely be a clearer indication that British
politics have entered a new phase. We have travelled a long way since
Conservatives were happy to endorse Burke's opinion that ideas were
dangerous things and best left alone, an aversion which was elevated
into the hallmark of Conservative politics and used as a stick with which
to attack the 'ideological' politics of their opponents. Likewise, it is not
so very long ago that academic debate (in shorthand, Beer 1965 versus
McKenzie 1964) could be joined on the issue of whether party politics
in Britain could be explained in terms of common organizational and
electoral imperatives, or whether there was also a residual role for distinctive ideological factors, yet these now seem like voices from a different
world. Contemporary British politics are, conspicuously, ideological
politics.

Nowhere was this more evident than in the 1987 general election.
The leaders of the two major parties were more deeply divided than at
any election in the post-war period; and this division went far beyond
policy matters to embrace fundamental issues of social philosophy, social
values, and even of human nature itself. Britain now had a Prime Minister
who believed (as she told a woman's magazine in 1987) that 'there is
no such thing as society'. This was also a Prime Minister who, uniquely
and revealingly, had given her name to an ideological 'ism'. It is
impossible to tell the story of the revival of ideological politics in Britain
unless the the centrality of Thatcherism is emphasized.

When Thatcherism hijacked the Conservative Party in the mid-1970s, there was an ideological vacuum waiting to be filled. From this base it could reach out to occupy the similar vacuum opening up in the wider polity. The post-war settlement, constructed around 'Keynesian social democracy' (Marquand 1988), was visibly collapsing. It was the time for new, or old, alternatives. The post-war tide of ideas seemed to be on the turn and this was seen by Mrs Thatcher (and has continued to be seen) as a unique historical opportunity to roll back social democratic collectivism and reinvigorate market capitalism. It was the moment for a vigorous ideological offensive and a confident cultural project. Addressing the Zurich Economic Society in 1977, Mrs Thatcher warned that previous historical opportunities had been missed and declared that:

> It is up to us to give intellectual content and political direction to these new dissatisfactions with socialism. . . . If we fail, the tide will be lost. But if it is taken, the last quarter of our century can initiate a new Renaissance.
>
> *(Guardian*, 15 March 1977)

Thus Thatchersim had an ideological mission, which went beyond particular policies and single elections. It was culturally confident and historically ambitious. Hence Mrs Thatcher's frequently proclaimed objective not merely to defeat the Labour Party electorally, but to eliminate what she describes as 'socialism' from British politics altogether so that, on the American model, there would be political competition between two parties both committed to 'the free enterprise system'. Some observers even detected a suitable oppositional role for Dr David Owen in this Thatcherite scenario. It is not merely the ideological ambition of this project which is significant, but also the extent of its success. Nor is this merely the fact of three successive election victories, but the way in which it could be seen as having changed the ideological face of British politics. Norman Tebbit, as party chairman, could tell the 1987 Conservative conference that: 'What was seen only a decade ago as outrageous political adventurism has become the orthodoxy, the new realism, within which parties must exist, or be confined to the sidelines'. In similar vein, if more painfully, a leading Labour politician (Michael Meacher, *Guardian*, 25 June 1987) could say in his election post-mortem that 'it has to be accepted that the set of values and ideas described as Thatcherism have established an ideological dominance that still retains a powerful vote-winning resonance throughout large sections of the population'.

It will be necessary to say something more about this 'resonance' shortly, but the evidence is impressive enough. As the broad consensus around the post-war settlement broke down during the 1970s, as that settlement was itself progressively unsettled by economic and governmental failure and finally blown apart by the industrial chaos of 1979, the radical initiative was seized by the Thatcherite right. In the 1979 general election there was a prevailing mood that things could not go on as they were, on a range of fronts, and that a new approach was needed. While the Labour leadership, with Prime Minister Callaghan radiating a Baldwinesque 'safety first' sobriety, posed as the party best able to stitch together the disintegrating fabric of the post-war settlement, and warned of the dangerous radicalism of the Thatcherite Conservatives, the political opening was available to a party that took as its starting point the fact that the post-war period had ended and that something had to be built upon its ruins.

This is the context for the politics of the last decade. The New Right at least offered a coherent political project, whatever its other characteristics. This was not the case with those 'one nation' Conservatives, which may explain why Mrs Thatcher was able to dispose of her 'wets' with such little difficulty. Nor, more significantly, was it the case with the Labour Party, immobilized after 1979 by the intellectual vacuum of its social democratic wing and the political advance of its left wing to fill the space available. This, in turn, prompted the splinter into the Social Democratic Party, but its own lack of ideological identity meant it could never really escape the jibe that it promised 'a better yesterday'. What is remarkable is not that the New Right, with its particular mixture of liberal economics and Tory politics, should have begun to make the ideological running in the late 1970s, but that this was still the case a decade later. In the 1979 general election it was Labour which was the conservative party, still promising to shore up the crumbling framework of the post-1945 social democratic state, while the Conservatives were the radical carriers of a new political agenda. Yet, more striking, was the fact that this was still the position two elections — and two terms of office — later.

The significance of Thatcherism is not merely that it has won elections, but that it seemed to have captured the political agenda and altered the terms of political debate. Its ideology of market capitalism and the 'enterprise culture', with its reworking of conceptions of the state, freedom, and the individual, could be seen as having accomplished an ideological revolution in British politics which left nothing untouched and against which everything else had to be measured. Certainly the response of the opposition parties seemed to confirm this judgement. The organized confusion which was the Labour Party during much of the 1980s could find a semblance of unity only in a negative 'anti-Thatcherism', while David Owen's attempt to equip the Social Democrats (and the Alliance) with a 'social market' philosophy could be regarded as a version of sub-Thatcherism with a human face. These remained responses, more or less inadequate, to a political agenda being set by somebody else, not a coherent ideological project in their own right.

The political commentator, Hugo Young, made the essential point when he identified (*Guardian*, 15 September 1987) the lack of a Big Idea among the opposition forces comparable in scale and scope to Thatcherism and capable of an equivalent ideological offensive.

The main focus of this book has been on the period since 1945 and, so extensive has been the impact of Thatcherite 'conviction' politics, that it is tempting to draw a direct parallel between the 'revolutions' of 1945 and 1979. Perhaps the Thatcher Years will come to be set alongside the Attlee Years, each representing an ideological watershed and establishing a framework of assumptions and beliefs within which politics is conducted for many years afterwards. Just as the Conservatives made a historic adjustment to the Attlee revolution, so Labour may be seen in the late 1980s as making its own historic adjustment, though more painful and protracted, to the Thatcher revolution. In 1945 the foundation was laid for the Keynes-Beveridge-Fabian state which became the structure of policy and belief within which party competition operated for the next thirty years. Even if, in retrospect, it is possible to make too much of the 'consensus' nature of this long period, since the verdict that 'a centre party has in effect been in power for most of the time since the war' (Benn 1981:107) has to be matched against the contrary verdict (for example, Stewart 1977) that it was the ideological reflexes of 'adversary politics' which thwarted coherent and consistent economic and industrial policy-making during these years, the period does nevertheless have a broad unity. In 1979 that period, and that unity, came to an end. The Thatcher revolution was explicitly made against the legacy of the Attlee revolution, unpicking the post-war settlement and rolling back the social democratic state, but it could, perhaps, be seen as resembling its predecessor in its durable reconstruction of the ideological landscape of British politics.

Yet the temptation to erect a neat symmetry between the Attlee and Thatcher years should be resisted. What was significant about the 1945 revolution was that it represented the culmination, and consummation, of a progressive tradition which had already scored important victories and had long been on the march. Indeed, Labour's programme had 'largely been cast in a mould of thought provided by the non-socialist intelligentsia between the wars and during World War II' (Addison 1977:278); and the Attlee government could be seen as implementing the progressive consensus of the time, doing what was widely agreed had to be done, and to which even the Conservatives could adjust without too much pain and soul-searching. By contrast, what was significant about the 1979 revolution was that it was made against the consensus, or the remnants of it, and offered a programme that had long been held to be politically impossible to deliver. It is true that some of its harbingers were to be found in the disoriented and disintegrating social democratic consensus of the 1970s (in the sense that 'monetarism' had already been adopted by the Callaghan government, accompanied by declarations that it was no longer possible for a government to spend its way out of a recession, and that 'the party was over' as far as local government spending was concerned, while on the social policy front a 'great debate' on the quality of education had also been started), but the radical break into market liberalism was nevertheless made against the consensual grain, not with it. It was an audacious rupture from the spirit of the age, not its consummate expression.

This suggests a further reason why the apparent symmetry with 1945 should be avoided. The Attlee revolution was built upon a widespread popular commitment to the idea of the full employment Welfare State, which was why the Conservatives became so anxious to be identified with it. It is worth recalling that Harold Macmillan, as Minister of Housing in the 1950s, built his own political reputation on the basis of the record number of council houses that were built during his tenure. By contrast, while the Thatcher revolution was born out of the assorted discontents of the late 1970s (with high inflation, growing unemployment, and industrial disruption feeding a generalized sense of state failure), which resulted in a swing to the right by public opinion on a range of issues, the survey evidence does not suggest that this swing has been consolidated into a new ideological order as far as popular opinion is concerned. Indeed, the evidence points rather towards a movement of opinion leftwards through the 1980s: 'The 1980s may be the decade of Mrs Thatcher but it has not so far been a decade of popular "Thatcherism" ' (*British Social Attitudes*, 1987:182). A MORI poll in mid-1988 (*Sunday Times*, 12 June 1988), while giving the Conservatives a decisive lead in the popular vote, also revealed the extent to which the New Right had failed to reconstruct hearts and minds. Some 49 per cent of electors favoured a 'mainly socialist' society in which public interests were given priority, against 43 per cent who preferred private interests and free enterprise; while 55 per cent preferred collective welfare, against 40 per cent who wanted self-help. The Conservatives, it seems, have won elections, but not souls. In the wake of the Attlee revolution it was possible to say that 'we are all Butskellites now'. By contrast, after a decade of New Right politics, we are clearly not all Thatcherites now.

So what are we? The short answer would seem to be 'better off', which is also the best answer to the apparent paradox of political success and ideological failure. Mrs Thatcher's cultural revolution may not, yet, have carried all before it, faced with the stubborn resistance of old values, but it has succeeded in winning the politics of the economy. On this key front, and with a mixture of political skill and economic luck, the Conservatives have seized and retained the advantage. They came to power on the claim that Britain's long economic decline was attributable to the post-war social democratic state, and the further claim that only a revitalized market economy, stripped of its social democratic excrescences, could deliver economic renewal. Both claims were plausible (which is not the same as correct); and remain plausible — and politically potent — for as long as the economy grows and (enough) individuals prosper. If the rest of Thatcherism is seen as the price to be paid for economic success, then it may not necessarily be liked but it may well get voted for. Here is the sense in which Thatcherism has managed to keep the advantage, by having a simple prescription based upon a clear diagnosis, by seeming to have all the answers, by insisting that there is 'no alternative'.

This, in turn, points attention to another essential element in the story, and to a further contrast with the post-1945 settlement. Unlike that earlier period, there has developed neither a coherent adjustment to the new order (of the kind that enabled the Conservatives to preside over it uninterrupted for thirteen years after 1951), nor a coherent opposition to it. There is substance in the Thatcherite claim that there is no alternative, in both a narrowly political and a broader ideological sense. The former sense is well understood and need not be rehearsed here. It is enough to record that the political hegemony of conservatism in the 1980s has been founded, not upon massive electoral endorsement (as the merest glance at the electoral arithmetic makes clear), but upon a divided and damaged opposition. In the case of the Labour Party, this damage was enthusiastically self-inflicted and, even after three election defeats, the appetite for self-mutilation remained undiminished in some quarters. The Alliance, of course, having blown a few bubbles, finally exploded into its constituent parts. Having promised to be the era of multi-party politics, the 1980s turned out to be the era of one-party politics, when the opposition parties extended a standing invitation to the Conservatives to govern.

However, this story needs to be told in ideological terms too, if its full significance is to be understood. The lack of effective political opposition reflects the lack of coherent ideological opposition. The pervasive sense of governmental failure which characterized the disintegration of the post-war settlement in the 1970s, the sense in which the collapse of a half-hearted corporatism symbolized the exhaustion of a whole tradition, presented a radical intellectual challenge to all political parties. The fact that this challenge was taken up vigorously by the New Right, on the basis of a series of great simplicities which pulled together the assorted dissatisfactions of the time (from strikes to taxes, inflation to crime) into a comprehensive indictment of the post-1945 social democratic state, and a no less comprehensive alternative in the form of market liberalism, serves only to highlight the other fact that the

211

challenge was not similarly taken up by the left. While Thatcherism promised an economic future for Britain as an open market economy, a political future in which freedom was tied to a free economy, a social future based upon self-reliance and a diminished state, and a moral future grounded in 'Victorian' values, the left seemed unable to offer a plausible alternative prospectus of its own capable of sustaining an equivalent political project.

Hence, while the New Right was both confident and radical, the left was disoriented, defensive and conservative. It knew that it did not like the values of Thatcherism, and grew red in the face in denouncing them, but seemed not to know much more than this. The historic character of the Labour Party as a motley ideological coalition, from sub-Marxism to old labourism and taking in social democracy along the way, made the task of intellectual renewal peculiarly difficult. The party even prided itself (usually with remarks about a 'broad church') on never having defined the kind of party it was with any intellectual seriousness. The rhetorical glue of 'socialism' held together a political practice that was an uneasy mixture of labourism and social democracy. This served well (or ill) enough when the task was to ride the back of the long post-war economic boom which underpinned the post-war political settlement, but when these collapsed simultaneously in the 1970s the Labour Party was soon plunged into factionalism and disarray, a disabling condition which persisted through the 1980s.

It knew what it was against, but what was it for? It plunged leftwards in the direction of an 'alternative' economic strategy, but then drew back from the national autarky that this involved. It demanded more state intervention, but also protested its antipathy to statism and bureaucracy. It defended the Welfare State and public services, but conceded that there were problems with their organization and delivery. It argued for more public spending, but denied that it simply believed in spending more money. It opposed the privatization of public industries, but had lost its faith in nationalization. It attacked the market mechanism for its inequities and deficiencies, but no longer seemed to believe in planning either. These uncertainties were compounded by a brooding sense that the world was changing in ways which were hostile to at least some versions of the traditional socialist project. Technological change was dissolving the old mass production industrial structure. Economic change was globalizing the economy and dissolving national autonomy. Social change was accelerating, and dissolving a traditional class structure. In other words, the world of 1945 — Labour's world — was dead and gone.

There was a curious reversal of ideological roles at work here. The left's historic claim to be riding the tide of history, a claim which had won wide acceptance (for example, Schumpeter 1943) and became the conventional collective wisdom of the post-war world, found itself usurped by the right. In British terms, while the Conservatives of the New Right displayed the kind of political and ideological confidence, even arrogance, which derived from a belief that history was now on their side, Labour looked like the bewildered and demoralized defenders of a disappearing status quo, protecting the past against the future. There can be little doubt that Mrs Thatcher's political success owes much to this sense of being in step with the world as it is, and offering a strategy for British economic renewal consistent with it, just as Labour's political failure reflects a sense that it is afflicted with a protracted crisis of identity and an associated loss of political and economic direction. In crudest terms, at least the Thatcherites seemed to know what they were doing, whereas their opponents (whether Labour, Liberal, or Social Democrat) did not. Labour's decision to wipe clean its policy slate in the aftermath of its third election defeat and start again was an acknowledgement of this. Whether it turns out to have been more than that remains to be seen.

At the end of the 1980s, then, ideology continued to dominate British party politics. Thatcherism, after a decade in power, set its face against 'consolidation', and promised further instalments of its ideological revolution. Labour was meanwhile engaged in its own ideological revolution, as the 'revisionism' of the Kinnock leadership tried to remake the party in its own image. The Social and Liberal Democrats, a new party with a new leader, continued the old search for a clear ideological location and identity. Moreover, an academic revisionism now emphasized the importance of ideology and principles to the electorate, unlike those earlier studies (for example, Butler and Stokes 1969) which treated them as an elite preoccupation without a widespread resonance in the electorate. Thus one study revealed that over half of electors held a political ideology of some kind and observed that 'this is not a picture of electors who have little understanding of the political world in ideological terms' (Scarborough 1984:66). A major study of recent trends in electoral behaviour identified political principles as now the most important single factor influencing voting (Rose and McAllister 1986), although there was not a neat fit between principles and parties: 'The best way to describe the relationship between the principles of the electorate and the parties is to say that no party represents the constellation of principles widespread in the electorate' (ibid.: 125). This last fact might be thought to provide a rich terrain for ideological politics in the future.

It also cautions against mistaking the political fashion of the moment for the historical destiny of the polity. If the most striking feature of British politics in the 1980s has been the ideological offensive of the New Right, destroying the remnants of an old consensus and insisting on its partisan definition of a new one, it remains to be seen whether its real importance will be judged in terms of a durable reconstruction of the terms on which politics in Britain is conducted or as something more modest, symptomatic, and transitional. Are we dealing with the Thatcher settlement or the Thatcher interlude? It may well turn out to be something less than the former but more than the latter. Yesterday's counter-revolution becomes today's orthodoxy and tomorrow's *ancien régime*. It is always useful to recall the leading article in *The Times* at the end of 1945 which announced that there was unlikely to be another Conservative government this century.

Yet it is not just this historical axiom which provides grounds for thinking that the Thatcher settlement may well prove much less durable than the settlement of 1945, and much less complete than its proponents (and even many of its opponents) are inclined to suggest. In historical terms, its significance may lie more in its role in breaking the deadlock into which British politics had fallen by the late 1970s in the face of seemingly intractable economic and industrial problems, overturning old assumptions and opening a space for new initiatives, rather than in its permanent reconstruction of the ideological framework of political life. The political success of the New Right (which, in electoral terms, needs severe qualification anyway) should not be confused with ideological success. If its economic basis was the oil economy of the 1980s (it was widely said at the time that the party that won the 1979 general election might well be in power for a decade on the back of it), the post-oil economy of the 1990s will be a very different place. This will present particular difficulties for a government whose political success has been linked so crucially to its economic claims, and which has not — on the available evidence — succeeded in remaking the polity in its own ideological image. Moreover, while it is not difficult to sell off public assets, or turn a public monopoly into a private one, it is much more difficult (as the Thatcher government's problem with the National Health Service, the antithesis of all it believed, clearly revealed) to deliver instant ideological solutions to services, like education, health, and law and order, on the condition of which governments are judged.

It is even possible to detect the glimmers of an emerging consensus around which a post-Thatcherite politics might be constructed:

> What it is possible to see, albeit still very dimly, is the making of a new consensus, under a variety of slogans: caring capitalism, the social market economy and the Enabling State. All would seem to be groping attempts to seek ways of reconciling the market and the state, economic dynamics and social justice, pluralistic diversity and a central sense of direction.
>
> (*Political Quarterly*, 1986)

Such a consensus would start from the recognition that the post-war era of Keynesian social democracy was over, that new forms of economic management and new forms for the delivery of public services were required, but that market liberalism of the Thatcher variety, with its repudiation of community and citizenship, was a wholly inadequate social vision. Yet the fact that the materials for a new ideological consensus, for a 'popular front of the mind' (*Samizdat*, One, November 1988) which at least enables parties to talk to each other, might be available, does not mean that it will be assembled in a politically effective way. There is a peculiarly British factor here. It was not just in Britain that the New Right prospered as post-war social democracy was thrown on to the defensive in the 1970s, as the economic environment changed, but it has been peculiarly in Britain that this temporary conjuncture has been converted into a prolonged political hegemony. The success of the right is the failure of the left, and this failure is (*pace* Mrs Thatcher) not that of an idea but of its British carrier. Unless that failure is corrected, then the political hegemony of the New Right may well — simply because it has held power for so long — become an ideological hegemony too. That may be the real significance of Mrs Thatcher's seemingly perverse claim, made at the 1988 Conservative conference, that her position now occupied 'the common ground of British politics'. Whatever happens, it is clear that British politics in the period ahead will continue to be a politics of ideas; and it is equally clear that this is what politics ought to be about.

Further Reading

There are many books on contemporary British politics, but not many of them throw much light on the politics of ideas. Among those that do, Samuel Beer's *Britain Against Itself: The Political Contradictions of Collectivism* (Faber, 1982) is worth reading for its interpretation of the disintegrating consensus of the 1970s. A useful account of the recent past is provided by D. Kavanagh, *Thatcherism and British Politics* (Oxford University Press, 1987), and Andrew Gamble's *The Free Economy and the Strong State* (Macmillan, 1988) is essential reading on Thatcherism. Other useful texts are Robert Skidelsky (ed.), *Thatcherism* (Chatto, 1988), and Kenneth Hoover and Raymond Plant , *Conservative Capitalism in Britain and the United States*, (Routledge, 1989). Above all, though, there is David Marquand, *The Unprincipled Society* (Cape, 1988), an ambitious and important exploration of the politics of ideas in modern Britain by a born-again social democrat.

Bibliography (published in London unless otherwise stated)

Addison, P. (1977) *The Road to 1945*, Quartet.
Beer, S. (1965) *Modern British Politics*, Faber.
Benn, T. (1981) *Arguments for Democracy*, Cape.

Butler, D. and Stokes, D. (1969) *Political Change in Britain*, Macmillan.
Jowell, R., Witherspoon, S., and Brook, L. (eds) (1987) *British Social At titudes: The 1987 Report*, Gower: Social and Community Planning Research.
Marquand, D. (1988) *The Unprincipled Society*, Cape.
McKenzie, R.T. (1964) 2nd edn, *British Political Parties*, Heinemann.
Political Quarterly (1986) 'Caring capitalism, the social market economy or the enabling state?' 57, 2:121–3.
Rose, R. and McAllister, I. (1986) *Voters Begin to Choose: From Closed Class to Open Elections in Britain*, Sage.
Scarborough, E. (1984) *Political Ideology and Voting: An Exploratory Study*, Oxford: Clarendon Press.
Schumpeter, J. (1943) *Capitalism, Socialism and Democracy*, Allen & Unwin.
Stewart, M. (1977) *The Jekyll and Hyde Years*, Dent.

Index

217

Index

218